KU-208-382

112597

THE UN AND THE PALESTINIAN REFUGEES

INDIANA UNIVERSITY

International Development Research Center

Studies in Development

NO. 1

WORLD POPULATION—THE VIEW AHEAD

(ed.) Richard N. Farmer, John D. Long, George J. Stolnitz

NO. 2

SOCIALIST MANAGEMENT AND PLANNING:
TOPICS IN COMPARATIVE SOCIALIST ECONOMICS

by Nicolas Spulber

NO. 3

THE UN AND THE PALESTINIAN REFUGEES:
A STUDY IN NONTERRITORIAL ADMINISTRATION

by Edward H. Buehrig

NO. 4

SOVIET AND EAST EUROPEAN FOREIGN TRADE:
A STATISTICAL COMPENDIUM

by Paul Marer

(forthcoming)

INTERNATIONAL DEVELOPMENT
RESEARCH CENTER

GEORGE J. STOLNITZ, DIRECTOR

Studies in Development: No. 3

The UN *and the*
PALESTINIAN
REFUGEES

A Study in Nonterritorial
Administration

EDWARD H. BUEHRIG

Indiana University Press

BLOOMINGTON

LONDON

Copyright © 1971 by Indiana University Press

ALL RIGHTS RESERVED

No part of this book may be reproduced or utilized in any form or by any means, electronic or mechanical, including photocopying and recording, or by any information storage and retrieval system, without permission in writing from the publisher. The Association of American University Presses Resolution on Permissions constitutes the only exception to this prohibition.

Published in Canada by Fitzhenry & Whiteside Limited, Don Mills, Ontario

Library of Congress catalog card number: 71-160124 | ISNB: 0-253-39603-4
Manufactured in the United States of America

TO
SONDRA, ANITA, KIRSTEN
AND ERIC

Contents

Preface

MY INTEREST in the United Nations Relief and Works Agency for Palestine Refugees was aroused in 1957–58 when I taught at the American University of Beirut as a visiting professor. In 1965–66 I returned to the Middle East to make a study of UNRWA, spending the greater part of seven months at Headquarters in Beirut as well as some time in the field. The second visit was made possible by sabbatical leave from Indiana University and a grant from the International Organization Committee of the Social Science Research Council.

The help of Laurence Michelmore, Commissioner-General of UNRWA, and his staff has been indispensible to unraveling the complexities of the Agency and to an appreciation of the problems with which it has grappled for twenty years. I want especially to acknowledge my indebtedness to D. Burnell H. Vickers, General Counsel of UNRWA during the period of my presence. He shared with me his professional knowledge, answered my many queries about UNRWA, and sustained and encouraged me through his friendship. Robert Fisher, who knows the many facets of UNRWA's operations since its beginning, was also of great assistance. I am much indebted to Professor Derek Bowett of Queens College, Cambridge, for his reading of the manuscript against the background of his experience of serving as General Counsel for two years. Also much appreciated is the help given by André Varchaver and Honour Haiart, both of Unesco.

I wish also to record my thanks respectively to Don Peretz, Di-

xiii

rector of Southwest Asia Affairs at Binghamton University, and Joseph E. Johnson, President of the Carnegie Endowment for International Peace, who shared with me their exceptional knowledge of and experience with the Arab refugee problem.

My colleagues at Indiana University, Robert Ferrell, Arghyrios A. Fatouros, and George J. Stolnitz have done me the great service of a careful reading of the manuscript, while the International Development Research Center, of which Professor Stolnitz is Director, has provided financial and secretarial help. Professor Stolnitz's ability to see both the trees and the woods has been of inestimable value and has placed me greatly in his debt. If the trees seem sometimes to predominate, the reason is the author's belief that a certain value attaches to the full exposure of the anatomy of a particular international organization, especially one as unique and highly operational as UNRWA.

In a matter as complex and controversial as the subject of this book, the author wishes to state with special emphasis that the findings and conclusions are his own.

EDWARD H. BUEHRIG
Indiana University, Bloomington

Summer, 1970

Foreword

THAT today's headlines are writ in yesterday's history is
obvious, but the nature of the linkages and their extent
are never-ending occasions for discovery. Moreover, the linkages
themselves may prove more enduring than the circumstances of the
headlines—a possibility significantly illustrated in this study. Although the vast social and humanitarian stakes represented by the
Palestinian refugee question have long been apparent, and their bearing on Middle East stability no less so, their emergence as an intimate
determinant of peace on a global scale could not have been anticipated when this work was begun. Yet, less explosive ingredients may
well outlast the fuels of crisis, as this scholarly, objective analysis
reveals in its treatment of a subject area rarely marked by detached
judgment. The more silent and longer-run forces which are the focus
of Professor Buehrig's research are sure to be major causal elements
in future—whether we think in terms of current events or much
longer periods of time, or from either regional or world-wide per-
spectives.

Written by a long-time, leading authority on international organization, the present case study reaches far beyond its specifics. Its key
themes are pervasive, continuing, and potentially crucial: international organization as an emerging prime force for change and development at world-wide, regional, and national levels; confrontation
between such organization and national sovereignty, an inevitable
and ever-evolving process; the problematic weight of economic development as an inducer of political stability; the many micro-arenas

of internal operation and tactics through which international organization's eventual larger place and strategies become fashioned. At the same time, the details of what follows are neither scrimped nor of small interest in their own right. Much of the carefully summarized evidence marshalled by Professor Buehrig covers subject or source materials which until now have been largely unexplored or remained almost wholly unanalyzed.

Both the generalist and the specialist, therefore, should find rewarding fare spanning a range of disciplines and sub-disciplines: international law and organization as process and outcome, the theory and practice of public administration, or recent development tendencies in the Middle East, to name a few.

The third volume in the *Studies in Development* series of the International Development Research Center at Indiana University, this book reflects the Center's ongoing special interest in international organization as a major part of its research program. Other such foci are development planning theory and practice, human resource development processes, rural modernization, and recent development transitions and systemic change in socialist-type economies. In each of these research clusters, major-scale research projects have been completed or launched by scholars from a number of behavioral disciplines.

Previous volumes in the *Studies* series were *World Population: The View Ahead* (1968) and *Socialist Management and Planning: Topics in Comparative Socialist Economics* (1971). In addition, Center papers are issued as soon as available for distribution to especially interested audiences.

Professor Buehrig's work, we are bold to believe, marks an auspicious beginning to the Center's ongoing efforts in the international organization field.

GEORGE J. STOLNITZ

July, 1971

THE UN AND THE PALESTINIAN REFUGEES

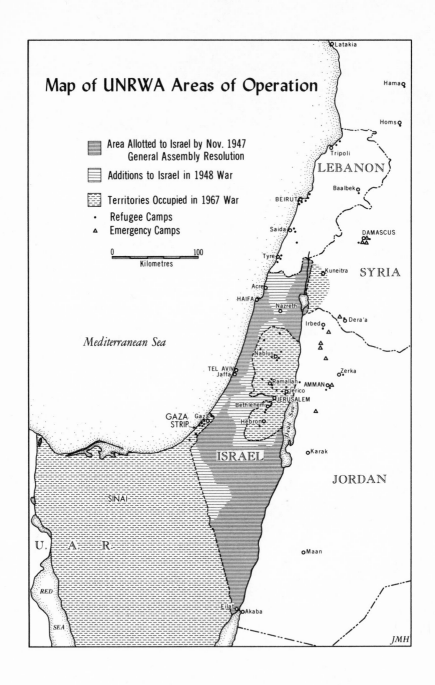

Map of UNRWA Areas of Operation

Area Allotted to Israel by Nov. 1947
General Assembly Resolution

Additions to Israel in 1948 War

Territories Occupied in 1967 War

• Refugee Camps
△ Emergency Camps

0   100
Kilometres

Latakia
Hama
Homs
Tripoli
LEBANON
Baalbek
BEIRUT
DAMASCUS
Saida
Tyre
Kuneitra
SYRIA
Acre
HAIFA
Nazreth
Irbed
Dera'a
Mediterranean Sea
Nablus
TEL AVIV
Jaffa
Zerka
Ramallah
AMMAN
Jerico
JERUSALEM
Bethlehem
GAZA Gaza
STRIP
Hebron
Karak
ISRAEL
JORDAN
SINAI
U. A. R.
Maan
RED
Eilat
Akaba
SEA
JMH

Introduction

POLITICAL REFUGEES, of whom there have been many millions since the end of the second World War, are the tragic product of an incompatible juxtaposition, whether of faction, class, religion, ideology, or nationality. Although typically refugees are victims of their native politics, some may have failed to withstand an influx from the outside. This last happened in Palestine. Strife with the immigrant Jew led to the 1948 flight of hundreds of thousands of Palestinian Arabs. For nearly twenty-five years the United Nations has struggled with the aftermath, mainly through an agency which is the subject of this book—the United Nations Relief and Works Agency for Palestine Refugees (UNRWA).

In 1947 Great Britain, hopelessly involved in a three-way struggle with Arabs and Jews over Palestine's future, announced abandonment of its League of Nations Mandate. The United Nations fell heir to a situation already out of control that has since grown progressively worse. At best only slowing a descending spiral, the United Nations has been a factor on the periphery of a grim struggle over living space. At the outset, however, it endeavored to be much more than that.

The United Nations first tried to legislate a settlement of the Palestine question. Seeking a sequel to the British Mandate, the General Assembly passed the partition resolution of 29 November 1947, the most ambitious attempt in the history of international organization to change the status quo by formal enactment. The resolution traced tortuous boundaries between a Jewish and an Arab state and provided machinery of dubious workability for their economic unity. Jerusalem and its environs, including Bethlehem, were to be separately constituted as an international enclave under United Nations control. These arrangements were to materialize under the authority of a United Nations Commission, with emergence of the two new states to be acknowledged in due course through admission to the United Nations.

This approach, even granting that the General Assembly had binding authority in the disposition of a former mandate, stood little chance of settling the matter, whatever the formula hit upon. At best, partition required military sanction, which the British were unwilling to attempt without prior acquiesence of both sides and which the Security Council neglected to provide, despite the resolution's invitation to invoke Chapter VII of the Charter if need be. Yet the resolution was not without consequence. It lent legitimacy to the Zionist demand for political independence; and the tactical advantage gained by the Jewish acceptance of the resolution, in contrast to the Arab governments' resort to force, further helped the Zionist cause.

Far from responding favorably to the November 1947 resolution, the situation grew more chaotic. Determined to leave, the British announced that their phased withdrawal would be completed on 15 May 1948. On May 14 the Jewish community in Palestine proclaimed its statehood. This ended the first round of the UN's bout with the Palestine question. Defeated in its attempt to impose orderly change, the United Nations shifted to mediation, a stance very different from that of the legislative approach embodied in the partition resolution. Moreover, whereas the latter was advantageous to the Zionist cause, the UN's subsequent interventions have in the main weighed on the side of the Arabs.

The commission that was to have implemented the partition plan —but that in fact never set foot in Palestine—was disbanded by a General Assembly resolution of 14 May 1948. Substituted was a mediator whose good offices were to keep essential public services in operation, assure protection of the Holy Places, and promote peaceful adjustment of Palestine's future. This difficult post was assigned to Count Folke Bernadotte. A vigorous man of strong personality, he was assassinated by Jewish terrorists in September 1948 and was succeeded by Ralph Bunche. In December 1948 the General Assembly established the Conciliation Commission. Its attempt to solve the refugee problem through repatriation, compensation, and resettlement is dealt with in Chapter I of the present study.

In April 1948 the United Nations had acted in still another way. Seeking to restrain and buffer the clashes between Arab and Jew, the Security Council established a Truce Commission. This agency underwent further evolution when, after war broke out in May, Count Bernadotte struggled to effect the two cease-fires successively proclaimed by the Security Council. The resolutions threatened enforcement action, but the threat never materialized, leaving to the Truce Commission the frustrating, largely futile, task of implementing the Council's pronouncements.

Between truce, on the one hand, and peace settlement on the other, was the middle ground of armistice. By August 1949, Ralph Bunche had achieved armistice agreements between Israel and each of its Arab neighbors: Egypt, Jordan, Lebanon, and Syria. The Truce Commission, now known as the Truce Supervisory Organization, was given the task of overseeing the agreements and reporting violations to the Security Council. Despite many vicissitudes, the Truce Supervisory Organization survives to this day.

Another buffer was established late in 1956, this time by the General Assembly. The United Nations Emergency Force (UNEF) helped to end the hostilities begun against Egypt by Israel, France, and Great Britain, and to secure the withdrawal of their forces from the Sinai peninsula. For more than ten years UNEF sealed the Israeli-Egyptian border. Its sudden withdrawal by the Secretary-General at Egypt's behest triggered the June war in 1967.

Finally, there remained the problem of aid to the Palestinian refugees. On Count Bernadotte's recommendation, the General Assembly in November 1948 invited governments to contribute to a Special Fund to be disbursed by the Director of United Nations Relief for Palestine Refugees (UNRPR). The Director was responsible for coordinating the efforts of local governments, international organizations, and voluntary agencies. UNRWA was UNRPR's successor. Founded in December 1949, it took over on 1 May 1950. Its mandate, successively renewed, was again extended by the General Assembly in December 1968. Currently it runs until 30 June 1972.

UNRWA had, in addition to relief, a major objective uncommon to international organization: that of creating employment, an objective designed to bring about permanent resettlement of the refugees. Having been frustrated in this, the Agency today is engaged in the direct administration of programs of relief, health, and education. It is less self-contained than most bureaucratic entities and therefore is more constrained in making decisions. Yet UNRWA requires that degree of control over personnel and policy essential to a body possessing its own identity. The outcome of the Agency's struggle for autonomy turns on a three-fold relationship: with the parent organization, the host countries, and the contributing governments.

Dependent on the United Nations for corporate status, UNRWA is capable of engaging in commercial transactions and establishing legally defined relations with governments, other international organizations, and employees. Chapter II of the present study relates how so versatile a body was founded merely by General Assembly resolution, and how, once incorporated, the Agency largely has been left to fend for itself, both in political direction and financial support.

While UNRWA has found the United Nations to be highly permissive, its relations with the host countries have been characterized by constraint. The Agency functions within the territorial jurisdiction of states, performing tasks which are normally the responsibility of government. The result is an unusual confrontation. Deriving its identity and mission from the General Assembly, UNRWA cannot countenance subordination to territorial authority. Nor can a state submit to an outside agency. UNRWA and the host governments are involved in a coordinate relationship requiring continuous redefinition, negotiation, and cooperation. A body so highly operational, employing some 13,000 persons, was hardly envisaged by the framers of the Charter, yet by reason of UNRWA's exceptional character, it serves to highlight the problem of legal status raised by the coexistence of states and international organizations. UNRWA's capabilities and limitations by virtue of such coexistence are encompassed in this book's subtitle: A Study in Nonterritorial Administration.

While UNRWA must adapt to local circumstances, it cannot ignore the hazard of becoming prisoner to the host countries. Corporate and staff immunity from territorial authority (Chapters III and IV) is, therefore, of particular interest. UNRWA's has been a painful but impressive struggle to keep clear of the fiscal regulations of individual governments and to maintain effective control over its personnel.

Whether or not UNRWA has, in spite of this exertion, lent itself unduly to the needs and purposes of the host countries can be determined only by an examination of the Agency's programs. Economic measures failed to solve the refugee problem (Chapter V) and gave way to increased emphasis on education as the preferred strategy (Chapter VII). Meanwhile, UNRWA's relief and health programs (Chapter VI) have continued and remain major activities even today.

Finally, UNRWA's solvency depends on its relations with the contributing governments. Because of that dependence, coupled with the General Assembly's reluctance to indicate its own preferences, the question arises as to the influence of the donors on UNRWA's choice of priorities. The answer involves UNRWA's budgetary procedures, which differ significantly from those of other parts of the United Nations. These matters, alluded to in Chapter II, are further examined in Chapter VIII.

UNRWA grew out of the unexpected turn of events resulting from strife between the Arab and Jewish communities over succession to the British Mandate. Reallocation of territory and authority in Palestine was in part effected by the partition resolution of 1947 and, for the rest, was determined by the violence and confusion of 1948. The convulsion of that year also produced the refugees. Their flight was new cause for contention, taking priority over the still disputed course of the succession.

While UNRWA was addressed to the immediate needs of hundreds of thousands of destitute people, relief was viewed as a stopgap pending the Agency's rehabilitation of the refugees through employment and resettlement. Events, however, did not respond to original intent. The refugee problem remains unresolved, and UNRWA is still engaged in relief. Yet the situation is not unchanged, nor has UNRWA been without consequence.

From the very outset, circumstances were unfavorable to the success of UNRWA's economic approach to the refugee problem. Though group identity among the refugees was at first amorphous, the simple longing to return to homes left in sudden flight, in itself, constituted a psychological obstacle to resettlement in the countries of refuge, and by 1960 UNRWA had abandoned its efforts at economic rehabilitation. Meanwhile, sentimental attachment to the homeland was evolving among the refugees into organized political expression, though only in 1964 was the Palestine Liberation Organization founded, and not until the profound shock of the 1967 war did the movement become a factor of major importance in the Arab-Israeli conflict. Throughout UNRWA's existence, politics has prevailed over economics, as was perhaps inevitable in a situation resulting from political rather than economic causes.

Despite the partition resolution's projection of an Arab state, the UN's subsequent approach to the refugee problem did not contemplate a Palestinian entity. UNRWA's purpose was to restore individual refugee families to economic viability in the belief that exile would then be acceptable to them. But UNRWA has had no such consequence, though certainly its programs contributed indirectly to the marked economic expansion that had occurred in the countries of refuge prior to the 1967 war, and this, in turn, redounded to the benefit of the refugees through the creation of employment opportunities.

However, the greater consequence has no doubt resulted from UNRWA's education program, even though its effect on the refugee population cannot be easily traced. Education, especially vocational, technical, and teacher training, has emancipated many individuals. Yet the point is not that education has eroded the essentially political nature of the refugee problem. More likely it has enhanced Palestinian consciousness while, at the same time, increasing the competence of the Palestinians to manage their own future.

The irony is evident. An agency designed to solve the Arab refugee problem through promotion of individual welfare was overtaken by the political character of the problem and now points to solution in terms of a Palestinian political entity.

I

The Refugees Become a UN Charge

THE 1948 flight of the Palestinian Arabs was an unanticipated by-product of the dissolution of the British Mandate. To be sure, the Arab and Jewish communities, recognizing the incompatibility of their aspirations, had long before ranged themselves in irreconcilable opposition to each other. Yet the outside world, indeed the protagonists themselves, were unprepared for the consequences. In retrospect it is apparent that the uprooting of hundreds of thousands of Arabs was the culmination of a struggle going back to the ambiguous promises of the British, who, desperately pressed in the first World War, led Jew and Arab alike to regard Palestine's future as his own.

In pursuit of coexistence, the General Assembly sought to accommodate the two communities in a partitioned Palestine. The Arab state was to consist of 725,000 Arabs and 10,000 Jews, the Jewish state of 497,000 Arabs (including some 90,000 Bedouins) and 498,000 Jews, while the Jerusalem enclave was to contain 105,000 Arabs and 100,000 Jews.[1] After the convulsion that followed in 1948, a Jewish state emerged a fourth larger in territory than that assigned to it in the abortive resolution of November 1947. In the Jewish-controlled area, where according to one estimate some 700,000 to 900,000 Arabs had lived, about 170,000 Arabs remained.[2] The rest had become refugees. An egalitarian community, rendered all the more closely knit by the traumatic events affecting it in Palestine and elsewhere during the Mandatory period, surpassed—both in diplomacy and in internal cohesion—the far more numerous Arabs, whose still traditional society was politically and socially fragmented.

BERNADOTTE AND PARAGRAPH 11

On 16 September 1948, the day before his assassination, Bernadotte sent a comprehensive report to the General Assembly. He proposed the establishment of a conciliation commission to consider among other problems that of the displaced Arabs. He estimated their number at 330,000. The figure was much too low; however, a more realistic estimate would hardly have altered Bernadotte's view that both in origin and disposition the refugee problem entailed a United Nations responsibility. He pointed out that Palestinians were without citizenship in the countries of refuge. As residents of a former mandated territory "for which the international community has a continuing responsibility until a final settlement is achieved," the refugees, he said, "understandably look to the United Nations for effective assistance." He was persuaded that the international community must "accept its share of responsibility for the refugees of Palestine" as a minimum condition for the success of UN efforts to bring about peace.[3] Bernadotte's emphasis on the United Nations as a third party—not just a forum—has continued to characterize subsequent United Nations actions in relation to the refugee problem.

Bernadotte commented only briefly on the immediate causes of the flight of the Palestinians. Remarking that the majority of the refugees came from territory assigned by the November resolution to the Jewish state, he said that the exodus "resulted from panic created by fighting in their communities, by rumors concerning real or alleged acts of terrorism, or expulsion." He added that it would be "an offense against the principles of elemental justice if these innocent victims of the conflict were denied the right to return to their homes while Jewish immigrants flow into Palestine, and, indeed, at least offer the threat of permanent replacement of the Arab refugees who have been rooted in the land for centuries."[4]

In a proposition of 26 July 1948 to Moshe Sharett, the Israeli

Foreign Minister, Bernadotte expressed his concern for the plight of the refugees and sought Israeli acceptance of the right of return:

For humanitarian reasons and because I consider the principle sound and the danger to Jewish security slight, I make the following proposals:

1. That, without prejudice to the question of the ultimate right of all Arab refugees to return to their homes in Jewish-controlled Palestine if they desire, the principle be accepted that from among those who may desire to do so a limited number, to be determined in consultation with the Mediator, and especially those formerly living in Jaffa and Haifa, be permitted to return to their homes as from 15 August.

2. That, among those who may wish to return, differentiation may be made between men of military age and all others in recognition of security considerations.

3. That the Mediator undertake to enlist the aid of appropriate international organizations and agencies in the resettlement and economic and social rehabilitation of the returning refugees.

This proposal followed the permanent truce ordered by the Security Council on July 15 and was made on the express assumption that no more fighting would be tolerated. However, with respect to the period of truce, Sharett in his reply of 30 July 1948 took the following position:

There is no doubt that the return during the truce of thousands of displaced Arabs to Israel, which is still beset by enemy armies, which forms a target of violent political attack and may yet again become an object of renewed military onslaught, would in fact gravely prejudice our rights and position, and would relieve the aggressor States of a large part of the pressure exerted on them by the refugee problem, while it would on the other hand most seriously handicap the war effort and war readiness of Israel, bringing into its territory a politically explosive and economically destitute element and saddling the Government with responsibility for all ensuing complications.

The Israeli note, while not explicitly precluding the future return of the refugees, further tied readmission to the prior requirements of both a viable Israel and a lasting peace. The Arab exodus, Sharett said,

was one of the cataclysmic phenomena which, according to the experience of other countries, change the course of history. . . . When the Arab

States are ready to conclude a peace treaty with Israel, the question will come up for a constructive solution as part of the general settlement, with due regard to our counterclaim in respect to the destruction of Jewish life and property. The long-term interests of the Jewish and Arab populations, the stability of the State of Israel, and the durability of the basis of the peace between it and its neighbors, the actual position and fate of the Jewish communities in Arab countries, the responsibility of the Arab Governments for their war of aggression and the liability for reparations will all be relevant to the question whether, to what extent and under what conditions, the former Arab residents of the territory of Israel will be allowed to return. For such a comprehensive and lasting peace settlement, the Provisional Government of Israel is ever ready, but holds that it cannot in fairness be required to carry through a unilateral and piecemeal measure of peace while the other side is bent on war.[5]

The return of former Arab inhabitants to the narrow confines of the emerging Jewish state was bound to be resisted. Coexistence was secondary to security. Yet Bernadotte was loath to concede the point. "I am convinced," he said in his report of September 1948, "that it is possible at this stage to formulate a proposal [with respect to the various questions at issue, including the refugees] which, if firmly approved and strongly backed by the General Assembly, would not be forcibly resisted by either side, confident as I am, of course, that the Security Council stands firm in its resolution of 15 July that military action shall not be employed by either party. . . . " On the refugee question, he recommended the following:

The right of the Arab refugees to return to their homes in Jewish-controlled territory at the earliest possible date should be affirmed by the United Nations, and their repatriation, resettlement and economic and social rehabilitation, and payment of adequate compensation for the property of those choosing not to return, should be supervised and assisted by the UN conciliation commission. . . .[6]

This and Bernadotte's other suggestions were incorporated in General Assembly resolution 194 (III) of 11 December 1948. With respect to the refugees, the Assembly resolved in paragraph 11 that those

wishing to return to their homes and live in peace with their neighbours should be permitted to do so at the earliest practicable date, and that compensation should be paid for the property of those choosing not to return and for loss of or damage to property which, under principles of international law or in equity, should be made good by the Governments or authorities responsible. . . .

In every subsequent year, the formula of repatriation or compensation has been reiterated by the General Assembly in its annual resolution dealing with UNRWA. An acknowledgment of the ancestral rights of the Palestinian Arab, the prescription is, in effect, an international pronouncement counterpart to the Balfour declaration,* which had been incorporated in the League of Nations Palestine Mandate. Ironically, the Balfour declaration precipitated its opposite, difficult though it is to reconcile paragraph 11 with the requirements of a viable Jewish state.

The crucial factor in the confrontation between Arab and Jew has been the power differential between them.† Fundamentally conflicting interests—their incompatibility unresolved by the General Assembly—have been opposed in an unequal power relationship. The situation has militated against a successful application of paragraph 11 to solution of the refugee problem. However, the Conciliation Commission—consisting of three members appointed by the French, Turkish, and United States governments—made the attempt. It sought to implement repatriation and compensation and to promote resettlement. Pursuit of the latter objective led to an economic survey of the countries involved, and we shall see that the survey resulted in the establishment of UNRWA.

*Incorporated in an official letter of 2 November 1917 from British Foreign Secretary Arthur Balfour to a private British subject, Lord Lionel Walter Rothschild, the declaration read: "H.M. Government view with favour the establishment in Palestine of a national home for the Jewish people, and will use their best endeavours to facilitate the achievement of this object, it being clearly understood that nothing shall be done which may prejudice the civil and religious rights of other non-Jewish communities in Palestine, or the rights and political status enjoyed by Jews in any other country."

† The extent to which the United Nations should, or indeed can, redress the balance is a moot question. The United Nations Emergency Force, though a frail instrument of little weight, performed just such a function, only to be jettisoned by the Egyptians. The Truce Supervisory Organization has been less of a makeweight. The utilization by the United Nations of a full-fledged military force would, judging by the British experience, invite fiasco.

REPATRIATION

The plight of the refugees was the Conciliation Commission's first concern and repatriation the foremost issue. Though unavailing,* the Commission's efforts to cope with the problem of return are an important part of the historical record.[7]

The Commission met with Arab governments in Beirut from 21 March to 5 April 1949 to discuss the refugee question in particular. The Arabs gave it "absolute priority," taking the position that all else was contingent on Israel's permitting every refugee to choose whether or not to return to his home. In Tel Aviv, however, the Commission was next told by Prime Minister Ben Gurion that the qualification contained in the General Assembly resolution, to the effect that returning Arabs must wish to "live in peace with their neighbours," made repatriation dependent "on the establishment of peace, because so long as the Arab States refused to make peace . . . Israel could not fully rely upon the declarations that Arab refugees might make concerning their intention to live in peace with their neighbours." The Prime Minister "made it clear that . . . Israel considered that a real solution of the major part of the refugee question lay in the resettlement of the refugees in the Arab States."

Both sides having agreed to meet with the Commission in Lausanne, negotiations were conducted there intermittently from late

---

* Except for some family reunions. During two prescribed periods, the second ending March 1953, the Israeli government, in accordance with procedures arranged through the Conciliation Commission, considered appeals made by Arabs still in Israel for admission of family members from the Arab side of the armistice lines. In accordance with the principle of reuniting a family in the place where the father was located, men could request the return of their wives and minor children (unmarried under fifteen). During the second phase of the reunion scheme, admission was granted also to fiancées of Arabs living in Israel, sons up to seventeen years old, and a limited number of Arab students over seventeen years old who had been studying abroad. Husbands were admitted in 150 hardship cases. Other instances included sons who, although over seventeen years old, were the only family member on the Arab side of the border.

Officially approved reunions totaled about 8,000 as of the beginning of 1957, by which time the greater part had occurred. In addition, it is estimated that from 20,000 to 30,000 infiltrators rejoined their families. Taken from Don Peretz, *Israel and the Palestine Arabs* (Washington: The Middle East Institute, 1958), pp. 50–56.

April 1949 to early fall. The Commission met separately with the various delegations, as well as with representatives of the refugees themselves. In the first round of talks, the Israeli delegation, wishing for security reasons to incorporate the Gaza Strip into Israel, declared a readiness to absorb as citizens the Arab population of the Strip, consisting of both the original inhabitants and the much more numerous refugees (totaling as of that time about 270,000 persons). For their part, the Arab delegations demanded the immediate return of the refugees coming from the areas controlled by Israel which, under the UN partition plan, had been allocated to the projected Arab state. However, neither side would entertain the other's proposal.

The delegations reassembled on July 15. Some small progress followed, more than at any time before or since—only to prove abortive in the end. The Israeli delegation was now prepared to accept the refugee question as the first item on the agenda and to readmit a limited number of refugees. However, repatriation was contingent on a final peace settlement covering all matters in dispute. Returnees, the Israeli representative said on August 3, were not to exceed 100,000. This number was to include both those who fled the territory which was initially allocated to Israel by the partition resolution and those who originated in the territory which was designated as Arab but had fallen subsequently to Israel in the 1948 war. Moreover, the returnees would be subject to resettlement "in areas where they would not come in contact with possible enemies of Israel" and "in specific places . . . that . . . would fit into the general plan of the economic development of Israel." Finally, both repatriation in Israel and resettlement elsewhere "would form part of a general plan . . . which would be established by a special organ to be created for the purpose by the United Nations."

The Commission, "considering the . . . proposal as unsatisfactory," transmitted it unofficially to the Arab delegations for their information. The latter pointed out the proposal's failure to conform with paragraph 11 of the General Assembly resolution of 11 December 1948. However, if the 100,000 refugees in question were to return exclusively to the territory originally allocated to the Jewish state, the Arab delegations "would not object" to adopting the proposal

ing progress in the Palestine Arab refugee problem." Johnson, President of the Carnegie Endowment for International Peace, was deeply engaged in the endeavor from August 1961 to February 1963. Though his proposals were never made public by the Conciliation Commission, Johnson indicated clearly the nature of his conclusions in an address to the American Assembly at Arden House in October 1963.

Returning to the original intent of paragraph 11, he spelled out its two somewhat contradictory requirements:

First, by adopting it [paragraph 11] and reaffirming it the United Nations has undertaken a commitment to and a responsibility for this particular group of refugees that places them in a unique category, different from all the other millions of unhappy persons displaced by the upheaveals of the last two decades. They are in a special sense wards of the UN, which must not accept any proposed solution that ignores their wishes. . . .

But the requirement that the wishes of the refugees be respected does not give them unconditional right of free choice. It is limited by the second requirement that the legitimate interests of states be safeguarded. Not only is this recognized by the phrase in the 1948 resolution conditioning the right of return upon a willingness to "live at peace with their neighbors . . . ," the United Nations and its members have a clear responsibility not to countenance any plan that would threaten the existence of Israel or of any other Member State.

The main feature of Johnson's proposal was the conduct of private interviews by UN officials, whereby refugees would be encouraged

to express their preferences freely, uninfluenced by external pressures, and in full knowledge of the real options open to them. The refugees need, for example, to be insulated from heavy political pressures by those who may claim to be their leaders and by politicians of the host countries. They need also to be informed what it would be like to live as an Arab in Israel today. They must be told what they may expect in the way of compensation, and what the opportunities are for resettlement in the Arab world and elsewhere. The refugees must also be told from the outset, first that their initial indication of preference need not be final, and second, that it may not be possible, in the end, to give them the option they most prefer.

Among other matters, UN officials would help a government to determine the acceptability of a particular refugee on security grounds, seeking to limit the possibility of arbitrary rejection.

Johnson conjectured that "fewer than one-tenth of the total of true refugees and their descendents" would choose to go home to alien rule. However, neither side was prepared to go along with the proposals. Israel considered them "unacceptable, and . . . the Arabs did not in the circumstances find in them a suitable basis for progress."[7a]

A half decade later, twenty years after the first appearance of paragraph 11, a State Department proposal which was designed to promote a settlement between Israel and Jordan continued to employ paragraph 11 as point of departure for the refugee question. As reported in December 1969, the proposal would give refugees from the 1948 Palestine war "the choice of repatriation to Israel or resettlement in Arab countries with compensation from Israel," subject to negotiation between Israel and Jordan as to "the number of refugees to be permitted repatriation annually. . . ." Further, it was anticipated that Ambassador Jarring, the UN Mediator, would "establish an international commission to determine the choice of each refugee. . . ."[8]

Thus paragraph 11 persists. Yet repatriation's feasibility is questionable owing not merely to Israel's demonstrated political capacity to resist it, but because resistance is dictated by the very character of the state itself. Jewishness is its essence, and the inescapable consequence of a viable Jewish state in Palestine is the Arab refugee.

One asks whether the General Assembly did the Arabs a disservice by encouraging expectations at odds with their power to oppose the Jewish presence. Of course, attachment of the refugee to his homeland is not a function of paragraph 11, which did not create but merely reflects that profound sentiment. Yet it holds out false hopes and may in some degree have contributed to the intransigence with which UNRWA has often had to contend. In the short run, at least, the uncompromising attitude of the refugee has been to his disadvantage, while even in the long run his prospect for returning home is unpromising.

Apart from paragraph 11's psychological effect on the refugees, there is the further question of whether or not undue reliance on the feasibility of repatriation has led Arab governments into untenable positions. One notes, however, that a principled and unyielding stance was as characteristic of Arab diplomacy before as it has been after 1948. Thus paragraph 11 cannot be charged with inducing—though it comported with—the inflexibility that has contributed to the Arab failure to cope realistically with Zionism. The record is ironical; Arab efforts to combat the Israeli state have abetted its expansion.

COMPENSATION

After repatriation failed to materialize, emphasis shifted to compensation, a charge also vested in the Conciliation Commission by paragraph 11.[9] The task was threefold, involving damages for wartime destruction, the release of blocked bank accounts, and compensation for abandoned property. Each was the subject of a proposition contained in the Commission's proposals submitted to the parties at Paris in September 1951.

With respect to claims for damages, the Commission proposed:

That an agreement be reached concerning war damages arising out of the hostilities of 1948, such agreement to include, in the Commission's opinion, mutual cancellation of such claims by the Governments of Egypt, Jordan, Lebanon, and Syria and the Government of Israel.

This would have entailed the abandonment of that portion of paragraph 11 calling for the indemnification of the Palestinian Arabs "for loss of or damage to property which, under principles of international law or in equity, should be made good by the Governments or authorities responsible. . . ."* On the other hand, Israel would be

---

* This provision should be read in light of the following comment in Bernadotte's report: "There have been numerous reports from reliable sources of large-scale looting, pillaging and plundering, and of instances of destruction of villages without apparent military necessity. The liability of the Provisional Government of Israel to restore private property to its Arab owners and to indemnify those owners for property wantonly destroyed is clear, irrespective of any indemnities which the Provisional Government may claim from the Arab States." *Progress Report of the UN Mediator*, 3rd Sess. (A/648), 16 September 1948, p. 14. In other words, compensation might be owing even in the case of a returning refugee or of an Arab who had not fled.

required to forego any claims against the Arab governments based on the allegation of aggression.

This proposal made no headway at all. The Arab delegations, charging that it went beyond the permissible limits of paragraph 11, declared that the responsibility of the Mandatory Power, of the Jewish terrorists, and even of the United Nations, itself, for the consequences of the Palestine conflict could not be glossed over. Nor was the Israeli delegation prepared to forego reparations, contending that the Arab states could not escape the moral and material responsibility for their aggression.

Another of the September 1951 proposals of the Conciliation Commission called for the mutual release of all blocked bank accounts, to be payed in pounds sterling. This matter had first been explored in the summer of 1949 through a mixed Committee of Experts—the only instance in which the Conciliation Commission was successful in bringing the parties face to face. Not until 1952 did the Commission and Israel reach an initial agreement, supplemented later by further arrangements. A first release was made in 1953. By 31 July 1965, 3,588,008 pounds sterling had been paid to owners of blocked accounts.* Of all the Commission's efforts at monetary restitution, this has been its only achievement.

Regarding other forms of property abandoned by the refugees, particularly landed property, the Commission included the following in its September 1951 proposals:

That the Government of Israel accept the obligation to pay, as compensation for property of those refugees not repatriated, a global sum based upon the evaluation arrived at by the Commission's Refugee Office; that a payment plan, taking into consideration the Government of Israel's ability to pay, be set up by a special committee of economic and financial experts to be established by a United Nations trustee through whom payment of individual claims for compensation would be made.

---

* Twenty-third Progress Report of the Conciliation Commission (A/6225, 28 December 1965). The contents of safety deposit boxes also presented a problem; they had not by 1965 been fully distributed.

There were about 6,000 Arab refugee accounts with a total value of approximately 4,000,000 Palestine pounds. About 450 Jewish accounts were frozen in Arab banks. Peretz, op. cit., pp. 222–223. Peretz recounts the technical and political obstacles met by the Commission in effecting the transfer.

The Commission had some reason to believe that Israel would regard this proposal as a suitable basis for discussion. To be sure, the Israeli delegation at Lausanne had linked compensation, no less than repatriation, with the consummation of a general peace settlement. However, this position had been modified in December 1950. In the course of the General Assembly debate on the Palestine question, the Israeli representative, reaffirming Israel's "willingness to pay fair compensation for abandoned lands" (this phraseology included appurtances to the land but not movable property), announced that his government waived its previous requirement that compensation be considered only in the context of a general peace settlement. The concession, urged upon Israel by the United States, was seen as inducement for Arab support of a resettlement scheme in the form of a "reintegration fund" to be administered by UNRWA.* Compensation on a collective basis was envisaged by the Israeli representative; it offered, he said, better prospect for a constructive solution than any attempt to resolve the problem on the basis of individual claims. A contribution of one million Israeli pounds to a Reintegration Fund was offered on condition that it be regarded as a first installment in compensation for abandoned property. The Conciliation Commission countered by urging Israel to make an offer without condition, contending that, as a demonstration of good will, such an offer would further a settlement of the refugee problem.

Without attempting once again to link compensation with the Reintegration Fund, which had been established in the fall of 1950, Israel was unresponsive to the Conciliation Commission's proposal of September 1951. Already in March 1951 the Israeli government, informing the Commission of expropriation by Iraq of the property of Jews emigrating to Israel, announced that it would have to curtail its support of the Fund in view of the need to rehabilitate some 100,000 Iraqi Jews. In the fall of 1951 Israel saw still further dif-

---

* Peretz, op. cit., p. 196. Israeli opinion was not generally averse to the principle of compensation. Foreign Minister Sharett told the Knesset that the emphasis on compensation and resettlement rather than upon repatriation would serve to remove from the UN's agenda "illusory solutions and . . . help concentrate on a practical solution." Ibid., p. 198.

ficulties. Its capacity to pay, Israel said, was affected by Egypt's closure to it of the Suez Canal and by the Arab economic boycott. Nor could compensation "be completely dissociated from the facts of the Palestine war and the responsibility of those who set it in motion." The final agreement on compensation would, Israel told the Commission, "have to put an end to the whole problem of the Arab refugees in all its aspects, both humanitarian and political. . . ."

The Arab delegations at Paris objected to any departure from paragraph 11, insisting that compensation "is an individual right of the refugee personally or of his beneficiaries. They should be able to exercise it without any limitation of time or space." Moreover, to relate payment to Israel's financial capacity would, the Arab governments charged, be equivalent to "pure and simple confiscation," tantamount, they said, to making a gift to Israel of refugee property.

Neither side has since shifted its position on compensation for abandoned property. Notable, however, is the Commission's global evaluation of refugee property, which was followed by the identification and evaluation of every piece of Arab property in those parts of Palestine passing to Israel's control in 1948. The task was performed by the Refugee Office, which was established by the Commission in accordance with General Assembly resolution. Charged with the assessment and payment of compensation in pursuance of paragraph 11, the Office consisted of director, legal expert, economist, and land specialist. It began work in Jerusalem in May 1951.

First it made an estimate of the value of Arab refugee property in Israel, which was the basis of the Conciliation Commission's urging of September 1951 that Israel pay a global sum as compensation for abandoned Arab property. Immovable property was valued at 100,000,000 Palestine pounds and movable at 20,000,000, fixed as of 29 November 1947, the date of the partition resolution. In dollar terms, based on the then existing exchange rate of $2.80 for the Palestinian pound, this comes to $336,000,000. The Commission held that this sum

constituted a debt by the Government of Israel to the refugees. Although the amount of compensation had been estimated on a global basis, the Commission considered that disbursement should in all cases be made to individual refugee property owners. It therefore believed that on the basis of abandoned Arab property as estimated by the Refugee Office, the Government of Israel should, as a first step, obligate itself to pay this sum of money as compensation for property abandoned by Arab refugees who were not repatriated.

The Commission, recognizing that Israel could pay only over a long period of years, said that the debt would have to be funded. But, as we saw, nothing came of the Commission's effort of September 1951. Nor was the matter successfully revived when in August 1955 Secretary of State Dulles offered American assistance in funding the cost of compensation.

Meanwhile, the Refugee Office, going beyond its global estimate of 1951, proceeded with the identification and evaluation of all landed property within the confines of Israel belonging to Arabs as of 29 November 1947—a necessary step in the payment of compensation on an individual basis. By the end of August 1957, the bulk of the identification was completed, though evaluation took much longer. Included was "each parcel of land owned by Arab individuals . . . partnerships, companies, and cooperative societies." Also included was land owned by religious bodies. In all, some 450,000 record forms of properties owned by Arabs were prepared—now on file at the United Nations in New York. What the cumulative value of these properties may be (including perforce that of Arabs who did not flee) and how it may differ from the 1951 global estimate has not been divulged by the Conciliation Commission.

How important a windfall the abandoned property was to the fledgling state of Israel, still to receive many new immigrants, is indicated by the fact that within the armistice lines cultivable land owned by Arabs was much more than half the total area then under cultivation.*

* Peretz, op. cit., pp. 143–144. Peretz treats in some detail Israeli legislation in regard to abandoned property. Commenting on its significance for the new state, he says in part: "abandoned property was one of the greatest contributions toward making Israel a viable state. The extent of its area and the fact that most of the regions along the border consisted of absentee property made it strategically significant. Of the 370 new Jewish settlements established between 1948 and the beginning of 1953, 350 were on absentee property. . . . Ten thousand shops, businesses and stores were left in Jewish hands. . . . Arab fruit sent abroad provided nearly 10 percent of the country's

RELIEF

By July 1948 the existence of an Arab refugee problem of major proportions had become evident. Twice that month the League of Arab States appealed to the Secretary-General for help. The latter, taking the view that the United Nations was not the appropriate body to meet the need, referred the matter to the International Refugee Organization in Geneva. But IRO was a temporary specialized agency designed specifically to deal with the aftermath of the European war. The limited scope of its mandate was pointed out in IRO's reply. There was no possibility of assistance from that source.[10]

International organization's response—arrived at through the United Nations and the Specialized Agencies, none of which was designed specifically to deal with refugee problems—was to a large extent influenced by Count Bernadotte. Though the General Assembly in creating the post of Mediator had not foreseen a refugee problem, its resolution of 14 May 1948 provided a point of departure for embarking on a program of relief. Bernadotte pointed out in his report of 16 September 1948 that the Mediator was authorized

to invite, as seems to him advisable, with a view to the promotion of the welfare of the inhabitants of Palestine, the assistance and co-operation of appropriate special agencies of the United Nations, such as the World Health Organization, of the International Red Cross, and of other governmental or non-governmental organizations of a humanitarian and non-political character. . . .

Moved by the desperate plight of the refugees, Bernadotte warned the Assembly that the "choice is between saving the lives of many thousands of people now or permitting them to die." He saw international responsibility limited to coordinating outside assistance and integrating that assistance with efforts of the Arab League and individual Arab governments. Disengagement would be

---

foreign currency earnings from exports in 1951. . . . The relative economic importance of Arab property was largest from 1948 until 1953, during the period of greatest immigration and need. After that, as the immigrants became more productive, national dependence upon abandoned Arab property declined relatively." Ibid., p. 143.

possible, he said, as the burden was increasingly taken up by the countries of refuge after the harvests of the following summer (1949) had been completed.[11]

Late in July 1948, at Bernadotte's request, a senior official of the Department of Social Affairs of the United Nations Secretariat made a rapid survey of the situation, adding information to that already secured by an officer of the League of Red Cross Societies. From every standpoint—food, water, sanitation, shelter, clothing, and bedding—the situation was critical. The Mediator undertook to deal with it in three phases.

The first was immediate relief of urgent needs. On 12 August 1948 he sought assistance from UNICEF, whose Executive Board promptly appropriated $411,000 plus shipping costs to provide food for children, pregnant women, and nursing mothers. Another step was rather extraordinary and might be described best in Bernadotte's own words:

I decided to appeal for cereals, which were most vitally needed, and for supplementary stores of other items, to those nations which had had important trade connections with Palestine and the surrounding Arab countries. I accordingly dispatched telegrams for certain specific items to twenty-four nations, asking them to divert to me at Beirut, if possible, any such stocks which were at the moment on vessels at sea or which were in ports adjacent to the Middle East for purposes of immediate relief. I also approached twenty-nine other nations by telegram, with the request that they provide any available general food requirements or funds, indicating the general needs.[12]

The second phase in the Mediator's program was designed to deal as systematically as possible with the period through December 1948, pending action by the General Assembly. Some sixteen officers were seconded from the United Nations and the Specialized Agencies, with a senior member of the former serving as Director of Disaster Relief, and headquarters were established in Beirut on September 11. Thus the technical resources of the international civil service were drawn upon at the very outset: FAO early surveyed the food situation and established caloric requirements; WHO provided specialists in medicine and sanitation; Unesco provided funds for thirty-nine schools attended by 21,000 pupils, but as yet had not become involved administratively. IRO, despite its limited mandate, made available specially qualified personnel to assist in procurement and transportation of supplies. In addition to paying the salaries of their seconded officers, the international agencies also contributed to general financial needs. Within the first year UNICEF, in addition to its initial allocation of $411,000, appropriated $6,831,000 for supplementary feeding, blankets, and medical supplies; Unesco used $15,000 from its Emergency Fund and $64,000 in contributions from governments and private sources; WHO contributed $50,000 to the medical and sanitation program; and IRO authorized an interest-free loan of $2,800,000.[13]

The period from December 1948 to September 1949 was the third phase. The Mediator's stop-gap role, he felt, should not continue beyond the year's end. Bernadotte, therefore, urged the General Assembly to take cognizance of the situation as it would exist from December 1948 on. Meanwhile, following Bernadotte's assasination, the Acting Mediator, Ralph Bunche, reported in October that the situation had further deteriorated.

Bernadotte had estimated the number of refugees at 330,000. Bunche's new estimate was 500,000. The increase, he explained to the Assembly, was owing to more complete registration, to the exhausted resources of those who temporarily had been able to support themselves, and "to an increase in the actual number of refugees as those previously in hiding in Israeli-held territory filter through the lines." The figure included, as had Bernadotte's, several thousand Jewish refugees evacuated from agricultural settlements on the Arab side of the lines. Not included were large numbers of persons "who have not left their districts but who are, nevertheless, totally destitute as a result of military operations."

The first shipments of food in response to Bernadotte's cabled appeals began arriving in Beirut the middle of September, and distribution began on October 1. Enough food was on the way, Bunche informed the Assembly, to take care of the situation until the end of November. The need for shelter and clothing, he said, was immediate: "every week's delay will mean a progressive death-roll from exposure." He warned that a new phase of the relief program should not be delayed beyond 1 December 1948.[14]

The General Assembly responded on 19 November 1948. It urged governments to contribute $29.5 million for relief to 31 August 1949 and an additional $2.5 million for administrative expenses. The Secretary-General was authorized to advance $5 million from the Working Capital Fund of the United Nations, to be repaid from later contributions. He was instructed to establish an administrative organization, the United Nations Relief for Palestine Refugees (UNRPR), and to appoint its Director, while the President of the General Assembly was to appoint an advisory committee to be convoked at the discretion of the Secretary-General.[15] Stanton Griffis, then the American Ambassador to Egypt, was appointed Director on December 1, and on New Year's Day 1949 the first shipment of supplies under UNRPR procurement arrived in Beirut—hardly more than six months after disaster had struck. When in November 1949 the Secretary-General submitted his first report on UNRPR's operations, its staff consisted of fifty persons. Headquarters, in charge of program and finance, were in Geneva, with the Office of Field Director in Beirut.

Improvised though it was, the response of international organization was remarkable in terms both of administrative adaptability and of the marshaling of material aid. It remains, however, to account for the conduct of operations in the field—the actual care of hundreds of thousands of destitute people.

Experience was to show the absence of an infrastructure in the countries of refuge equal to the situation. The Arab governments, newly independent, lacked not only material resources but also administrative organization and personnel to deal with the refugee problem, the more so because welfare in traditional Arab society is a family, not a public, responsibility.* There were, to be sure, Red Cross (Lebanon) and Red Crescent (Syria and Jordan) societies, but these were fledgling organizations. Gaza, the extreme case,

---

* In his report of 16 September 1948, Count Bernadotte suggested that outside aid "might indirectly be of permanent value in establishing social services in the countries concerned, or greatly improving existing services. This applies particularly to general social administrative organizations, maternal and child care services, the training of social workers, and the improvement of food economics." *Progress Report of the UN Mediator,* op. cit., p. 52.

was lacking almost completely in any indigenous structure which might lend support to an aid program, though there existed meager remnants of the health and educational services of the mandatory regime.

The vacuum was filled by the International Committee of the Red Cross, the League of Red Cross Societies, and by various Protestant and Catholic religious organizations, most notably the American Friends Service Committee. Responsibility was geographically divided among them by agreements concluded with UNRPR in December 1948. The Internationl Committee of the Red Cross operated in those areas of Palestine occupied by Jordan and Israel; the League of Red Cross Societies operated in Lebanon Syria, and Transjordan; and the American Friends Service Committee operated in Gaza. These organizations distributed food, administered health programs, and organized camps for shelter.*

Evident from the Mediator's and Acting Mediator's reports is uncertainty about the number of refugees. The question was still unanswered when the voluntary agencies took over. Enjoined by the Director of UNRPR to confine relief to bona fide refugees, their attention was directed in particular to the Bedouins, "who would naturally enough move on to places where food was being distributed."[16] However, this and other factors (noted below) were

---

* In Gaza the American Friends Service Committee found the original inhabitants increased three times over—some 270,000 in all—in an area 22 miles long, 6 miles wide, and one-third sand. The formidable situation there is described by the Quakers in one of their periodic reports to the UN. The refugees were found "huddled in what little remained of the old British army camps, in caves and holes in the sand, and in any doorway or corner of the few villages in the area." Of all the refugee areas "the Gaza strip was least able to furnish the basic requirements of fuel, building materials, cooking utensils and all other essentials of a mass feeding programme. It is almost impossible to imagine the difficulties of distributing foodstuffs, and particularly liquids, without adequate bulk containers or measuring utensils, or of receptacles into which the Arabs could receive their rations. A typical example was the problem faced in the UNICEF milk distribution of mixing many thousands of pounds of powdered milk daily under hygienic conditions in camps where there were no available buildings, no containers except rusty gasoline drums, and very little material in the area from which to make improvisations." *Report of the Secretary-General on Assistance to Palestine Refugees,* (A/1060), 4 November 1949, Annex II.

more than the voluntary agencies could manage. In March 1949, when their registration of refugees was believed to be reasonably complete, the voluntary agencies were ministering to 910,000 persons. Yielding to pressure of numbers, UNRPR increased the approved level of rations from 600,000 for January and February 1949, to 725,000 for March, and to 855,000 for April and May. The voluntary agencies had to make do by spreading the available supplies more thinly. When for June they requested more than a million rations, UNRPR allowed 940,000, which held through the fall.[17]

Acknowledging that the knottiest problem of all lay in determining the number of refugees, the International Committee of the Red Cross indicated the nature of the difficulties in its final report to the UN:

Several factors contribute to make a fairly accurate control in Arab Palestine almost impossible. First, it seems evident that it is more difficult to determine a refugee in his home-land, and to distinguish between him and a normal resident, who is a countryman of his, than to identify a refugee abroad, where he is a foreigner. Secondly, the public services in Arab Palestine are still somewhat disorganized; the poverty of the majority of the resident population is frightening and the local authorities have no means to alleviate it. Therefore, and seeing no other solution, they try to make everybody participate in the help brought into the country by international charity. . . . Finally, thousands of individuals, destitute persons and others, have tried to evade the controls by registering themselves in more than one region, or under several names, by increasing the number of family members, or by registering false births and hiding deaths.[18]

The question of the number of refugees was further confused because the educated among them and those possessing urban skills were not dependent on relief, at least not for long, and presumably many of them were never included on the relief rolls of either the voluntary agencies or of UNRWA. Educated and skilled refugees were later estimated by UNRWA to have constituted some twenty percent of the exodus.[19] This estimate is probably too high; even so, it is evident that the large majority of refugees seeking relief were farmers, difficult to employ in their accustomed pursuit and hard to adapt to new forms of livelihood.

The voluntary agencies often encountered among the refugees a lack of cooperative attitudes and effort.* This lack comports with a peasantry accustomed only to its narrow, traditional ways, vaguely conscious of a larger society, but unpracticed in community endeavor. This is an important point. Its relevance to an explanation of the exodus itself needs to be made explicit.

That the Palestinian Arabs should have fled in such large numbers in 1948 and again in 1967 cannot be explained alone in terms of the immediate pressures to which they were subject. The phenomenon was more complex. Admittedly the pressures were real; yet one asks why—granting that sacrifice would have been entailed —the pressures were not more resolutely resisted. One suspects that additional factors, not readily apparent, were involved in the exodus.

In their study of a sample of 1967 refugees, Dodd and Barakat found that, in addition to direct "situational" causes of flight such as airplane attacks and bulldozing of villages, there were causes "not directly mentioned by the refugees, but ones suggested by their accounts and by the accounts of others. These indirect causes are

* Added to the lack of organized social services in the Gaza Strip was "the absence among the refugees of trained clerical and supervisory staff." Continuing, the American Friends Service Committee said that slowly "a force of Palestinian assistants has been built up and every encouragement has been given to them to take as much responsibility as they can bear. Some outstanding men of proved loyalty and integrity have emerged in this process, but the numbers of those who are able to develop a sense of community responsibility is extremely limited." *Report of Secretary-General on Assistance to Palestine Refugees* (A/1060), op. cit., Annex II.

An attempt by the International Red Cross to place major responsibility in the hands of local authority had to be abandoned. The Committee reported that "conditions were too unstable, poverty too great, political and personal influence too prevalent. . . . After a few unpleasant experiences, all main control of funds, supplies and ration card distribution had to be taken back by the Swiss delegates in spite of the . . . repercussions. The reaction in various places was open hostility, attacks in the press, even false accusations in court and trials to stir up the refugees and create unrest in the camps. On the other hand, the refugees grew more and more friendly the longer the action lasted . . . and finally relations of mutual understanding and confidence between ICRC employees and themselves existed practically everywhere. . . . " *Report of the Secretary-General on UN Relief for Palestine Refugees* (A/1452), 24 October 1950.

connected with the social structure and values of the communities from which the refugees departed."[20]

Identifying one such factor as "lack of non-family loyalties," the authors point out that the family affords the main social bond in the typical Palestinian village. Decisional structures outside the family—whether political, economic, or religious—are weak, and in time of crisis, as in 1948 and 1967, the family decides.

Another point made in this perceptive study is the distrust with which the respondents regarded higher authority: "The refugee families felt that the only people who could be trusted were their kinfolk. Assurances coming from any other source, such as political leaders or the Jordanian government, were not to be relied upon." When the refugees were asked who was responsible for the defeat, the most common answer was "Arab traitors." After them, the refugees blamed the governments of the West, especially the United States. Seldom did they refer to the military capabilities of Israel. Yet so contradictory were the attitudes of the respondents and so lacking in realism that four-fifths had expected an Arab victory.

THE ECONOMIC SURVEY MISSION

As noted, the Conciliation Commission in August 1949 established an Economic Survey Mission in an effort to move the dispute away from political and on to economic terrain. Led by Gordon R. Clapp, Chairman of the Tennessee Valley Authority, and staffed by agricultural, engineering, and economic experts, the Mission began its work in Beirut on 12 September 1949. An interim report of 8 November led promptly to the establishment of the United Nations Relief and Works Agency for Palestine Refugees (UNRWA) to succeed UNRPR. The Mission's final report followed on 23 December 1949.[21]

Discrepancy between the origins of the Arab-Israeli conflict and the terms of reference of the Economic Survey Mission calls for comment. The struggle between two incompatible communities in Palestine was a political question for which the Survey Mission was instructed to find an economic answer. The Conciliation Commission—fully cognizant of the noneconomic character of what was at issue—deliberately shifted ground. For the moment Israel had agreed, as of August 1949, to take back a certain number of refugees and Jordan and Syria had agreed to resettle the nonrepatriated. Though the two sides were far apart as to which refugees and in what numbers, here at least was an opening, which the Commission tried to exploit through an economic approach. Glossed over was the choice between repatriation or compensation. While Israel was not precluded as a place where "reintegration" might occur, by implication the economic future of the refugees was bound up with the countries of refuge. Thus the terms of reference of the Survey Mission attempted to finesse the political question; but in the end economics was to show its limitations as a pacifier.

The Mission's report did not fail to remark that "economic development cannot of itself make peace . . . where the political will to peace is lacking." Indeed, contemplating the past, it saw politics as the scourge of the Middle East. Not natural causes but war destroyed a once flourishing civilization. Looking ahead, however, "the land remains, the rain still falls, the rivers flow. If the water be once more saved and spread upon the land, crops will grow again."[22]

Discussing the requirements for long-range economic development in the Middle East, the report concentrated on the countries bordering Israel. The latter was excluded from its prescriptions inasmuch as Israel

already has available technical men of all kinds and of the highest skill. . . . Moreover, the Israeli Government has already begun . . . with the relatively large funds placed at its disposal from abroad, to develop irrigation and to employ modern agricultural methods. . . . In addition, Israel possesses . . . research stations and laboratories . . . [that] compare favourably with similar institutions throughout the world.

Neither was Egypt prescribed for. "The knowledge and skill available in that country are already on a high level."[23]

As regards Jordan, Lebanon, and Syria, immediate possibility of large projects was rejected. Capital, skills, and research capability were lacking, as was governmental organization and administrative experience. Accordingly, the Mission outlined a "pilot demonstration project" each for Lebanon, Syria, Jordan, and Arab Palestine aimed at the conservation of water. The gradual multiplication of such projects would lead ultimately to large-scale, multipurpose undertakings, including the generation of hydroelectric power. To further this progression each government was urged to establish a National Development Board for planning over-all development and executing individual projects, with the help of international organizations and foreign governments.[24]

While the Clapp Mission's long-range objective was to solve the refugee problem through economic development, it also addressed itself to the immediate situation, inasmuch as need for relief was outrunning the existing arrangements under UNRPR. The voluntary agencies were unanimous in declaring their inability to carry on beyond spring 1950.

The Mission sought, as a short-run objective, to shift the emphasis from direct relief to public works. The aim was to halt the "demoralizing process of pauperization" and to reduce the need for relief to a level enabling the countries of refuge to assume the burden.[25] Reliance was on the emergency project with high-labor and low-cost inputs, such as afforestation, agricultural terracing, and road building. Work programs, it was believed, could be readied by 1 April 1950, to continue until 30 June 1951—subject to review at the intervening session of the General Assembly. Employment of 100,000 refugees was forecast by mid 1951, leading to removal of 400,000 persons (including dependents) from the relief rolls. Rations would no longer be supplied by the United Nations after 31 December 1950, "unless otherwise ordered by . . . the fifth session of the General Assembly, at which Near Eastern Governments concerned would have an opportunity to present appropriate proposals." Meanwhile, UNRPR's successor agency would "negotiate with Near Eastern Governments for the latter to take over as soon as possible, and at the latest by 31 December 1950, responsibility for the maintenance of such refugees as may remain within their territories."[26] Needless to say this timetable was never realized.*

* Indicative of the confusion and uncertainty as to the effect of the Mission's recommendations is Gordon Clapp's testimony of 16 February 1950 before the House Committee on Foreign Affairs on behalf of a United States contribution to UNRWA. He posed two questions: "One is, What happens to those

The new agency envisaged by the Survey Mission was to have "full autonomy and authority: to administer programs of relief and public works and to negotiate with governments." Emphasized also was the point that since "the programme of works relief must take precedence over that for direct relief, the latter decreasing as the former grows," both would have to be controlled by a single agency. It was "imperative," therefore, that "the two activities be under the same direction."[27]

Resolution 302 (IV), incorporating the recommendations of the Economic Survey Mission, was adopted by the General Assembly on 8 December 1949 without dissent. Sponsored by France, Turkey, the United Kingdom, and the United States, UNRWA was established by a vote of 48-0-6. Five communist governments and South Africa abstained. All of the Arab governments and Israel voted for the resolution. The resolution appears as Appendix II in this book.

When in the fall of 1950 the General Assembly had to decide on UNRWA's role beyond 30 June 1951, the choice was between

---

people who are still on relief in December 1950, assuming the United Nations relief program ends at that time? . . . Many . . . will fall back upon the assistance of the charitable agencies operating extensively in that area. . . . Many of the refugees will become charges upon the villages in which they are temporarily living. Some of them will drift away into other parts of the Arab lands. Some of them, if this new agency can work out appropriate plans for the Arab governments, would become recipients of relief programs of the Arab governments.

"I cannot assure this committee that those programs have the possibility of being taken over by the Arab governments after December 1950. However, one of the tasks of this new agency . . . will be to . . . negotiate with . . . them to assume more and more responsibility for the remaining load of direct relief. . . .

"The second question . . . is, What happens after June 1951? Another of the major tasks of this new agency . . . would be to negotiate . . . about plans the Arab governments can prepare for developments that could be initiated after this program is over in June 1951.

"Now what assurance is there that any such programs will be forthcoming? The only thing I can say to this committee is to express the hope that such programs will be developed by the Arab governments. . . ." U.S., Congress, House, Committee on Foreign Affairs, *Hearings on Palestine Refugees,* 81st Cong., 2nd sess., S.J. Res. 153, 16 February 1950 (Washington: USGPO, 1950), pp. 43–44.

devolving greater responsibility for relief and economic rehabilitation on the host governments or confirming UNRWA in the role of an autonomous body with direct responsibility for such programs. The latter course was taken. That public works would fail as a substitute for direct relief had not yet been demonstrated, nor was it yet realized how serious were the technical and administrative obstacles to large-scale development projects. As for political resistance to the latter, it was still hoped that the Conciliation Commission would soon settle the basic question of Palestine's future. Optimistically, the United Nations favored positive action and there was no dissent from the Clapp Mission's admonition that "if the Palestine refugees be left forgotten and desolate in their misery peace will recede yet further from these distracted lands."

Relevant to the choice of an activist policy was the attitude of the United States, whose contribution to UNRWA's budget has never been less than fifty percent, in some years has amounted to seventy percent, and through 1969 had accumulated to $456,000,000. Testifying before the House Committee on Foreign Affairs, 16 February 1950, on behalf of United States financial support for UNRWA, Assistant Secretary of State George McGhee saw the following connection between the Arab refugees and the future of American interests in the Middle East:

Let me speak very frankly on this question. The political loss of this area to the Soviet Union would be a major disaster comparable to its loss during war. Certainly the political strategic position of the Soviet Union would be immeasurably strengthened by the attainment of its objectives in the Near East, and the cold war materially prolonged. . . .

Against this background, our solicitude for the Palestine refugees, partly based on humanitarian considerations, has additional justification. As long as the refugee problem remains unresolved . . . attainment of a political settlement in Palestine is delayed . . . [and] the refugees . . . will continue to serve as a natural focal point for exploitation by Communist and disruptive elements which neither we nor the Near Eastern governments can afford to ignore. . . . The presence of three-quarters of a million idle, destitute people—a number greater than the combined strength of all the standing armies of the Near East—whose discontent increases with the passage of time, is the greatest threat to the security of the area which now exists.[28]

HOW MANY REFUGEES?

The number of Palestinian Arabs displaced in 1948 is not known with certainty and will always remain a controversial question. Bernadotte in September 1948 estimated the number at 330,000; Bunche's estimate a month later was 500,000. In the fall of 1949 the Economic Survey Mission put at 726,000* the number of persons "who . . . fled from Israel and are unable to return. . . ."[29] Its calculation was based on the estimated number of non-Jews living, as of 1947, in what subsequently became Israeli territory. From that estimate was subtracted the non-Jewish population remaining in 1949. Using the same starting point and method of calculation and allowing for natural increase at the rate of two percent per year, an Israeli representative in the Special Political Committee of the General Assembly said that as of 1956 "the number of refugees should be between 705,000 and 725,000."†

We saw that the number of rations supplied by UNRPR in the fall of 1949 was 940,000, which were stretched by the voluntary agencies to provide for 1,019,000 recipients. Recognizing gross inflation in these figures, the Economic Survey Mission recommended the reduction of rations to 652,000‡ by 1 January 1950. This figure

---

* Scattered as follows: Arab Palestine 280,000; Gaza 190,000; Lebanon 100,000; Syria 75,000; Jordan 70,000; Egypt 7,000; and Iraq 4,000. In April 1950 Jordan annexed the West Bank, embracing thereafter nearly fifty percent of the refugees. By this estimate there were about 125,000 families in all, each family averaging close to six persons.

† United Nations, General Assembly, 11th Sess., *Summary Record of Special Political Committee,* p. 129. An Israeli author, Walter Pinner, starting with an estimate lower than the Economic Survey Mission's of the number of Arabs originally in Israeli territory, asserts that the number of refugees as of 1948 was 539,000 and that by 1958 this number through natural increase had grown to 680,000. *How Many Arab Refugees?* (London: Macgibonn and Kee, 1959), 61. The book, a critique of UNRWA statistics, has a sequel by the same author, *The Legend of the Arab Refugees* (Tel Aviv: Economic and Social Research Institute, 1967).

‡ Omitted from the calculations of the Economic Survey Mission were 17,000 Jews who fled during the war from Arab to Jewish lines, and 31,000 Arabs displaced within Israel, who never left. Accordingly UNRPR allowed 48,000 rations for distribution in Israel. By 1952 the Israeli government had taken full responsibility for any remaining relief in its territory, after which UNRWA operations in Israel ceased.

included 25,000 persons "who still live at home, but are without means because they are separated from their lands by the armistice lines. . . . " These—the economic refugees—the Mission believed to be properly within its terms of reference. Not included were refugees deemed to be self-supporting: 15,000, the Mission estimated, were of independent means, while 20,000 were employed, and capable of supporting an additional 60,000. Another 4,000 had gone to Iraq. This left 652,000 "genuine refugees in need," including border-line cases.[30] But the reduction did not come to pass. When on 1 May 1950 UNRWA took over, it inherited from UNRPR and the voluntary agencies a ration roll of 957,000 persons.[31]

UNRWA has struggled ever since with the problem of rectification. By May 1967, just before the June War, the number of UNRWA registrants was 1,344,576.[32] This statistic, reflecting many additions and subtractions in the intervening seventeen years, is not easy to interpret. The largest increment was owing to natural increase in the refugee population, while subtractions included dead, emigrants, and false registrants. But not all ineligibles had been detected. Nonrefugees and multiple registrants were still benefiting from UNRWA's services. Though fairly well satisfied with its rolls in Lebanon, the Agency recognized that its May 1967 registration was seriously defective in Jordan and quite unsatisfactory in Gaza and Syria. Annually the Agency warns that its reported registration does "not necessarily reflect the actual refugee population owing to factors such as unreported deaths and undetected false registrations."

UNRWA's definition of a 1948 refugee entitled to registration is one "whose normal residence was Palestine for a minimum period of two years immediately preceding the outbreak of the conflict in 1948 and who, as a result of this conflict, has lost both his home and means of livelihood." Eligibility for registration also extends to the first and second generations. It should be noted that need is a criterion of eligibility for registration; however, a registrant who ceases to be in need is not deleted from the rolls—though some or all services may be withdrawn depending on the degree of his self-sufficiency.

Eligibility for registration as defined by UNRWA has a bearing on the discrepancy between UNRWA statistics and those resulting from an Israeli census of the occupied territories following the June War. Conducted in late August and early September 1967, the Israeli census[33] showed a count of 1948 refugees in Gaza and the West Bank far smaller than the number of UNRWA registrants in those areas. UNRWA had reported 317,000 registrants in the Gaza Strip as of May 1967. A few months later—before departures from the Gaza Strip for the West Bank and East Jordan had become numerous—the Israeli census counted 207,250 refugees of 1948. In the West Bank the Israeli census showed 106,000 refugees of 1948. By then, of course, some 150,000 "old" refugees had fled from the West to the East Bank. Notwithstanding, in 1968 UNRWA reported its remaining registrants in the West Bank to be 245,000. These large differences reflect, in part, false registrations that had gone undetected by UNRWA. However, other factors, as well, account for the discrepancy.

The Israeli government counted as refugees members of households whose heads had been born in what became Israeli Palestine, whereas UNRWA included household heads (and their families) who had resided in that portion of Palestine "for a minimum of two years immediately preceding the outbreak of the conflict in 1948," embracing thereby the Arab immigration into Palestine during the mandatory period. The other main factor that accounts for the difference is the treatment of the absentee in UNRWA statistics, involving some 100,000 Palestinians believed to be employed in the Arab oil-producing countries. These individuals were considered by UNRWA to be temporarily residing outside its area of operations. Though not eligible for rations, they were regarded as UNRWA registrants.

The 1967 June War produced a new wave of Arab refugees. UNRWA estimates that 175,000 of its registrants fled for a second time. Of these, 17,500 left the occupied area in Syria, while as of the summer of 1968 UNRWA was supporting in Egypt 3,000 of its registrants from the Gaza Strip, though the "total number of registered refugees . . . in the United Arab Republic is believed to be considerably larger." It is apparent that the bulk of those fleeing for a second time came from Jordan's West Bank. Not included among the 175,000 are between 40,000 to 45,000 registered refugees who by the summer of 1968 had left Gaza, some shifting to the West Bank, while the greater portion were admitted by Jordan to the East Bank.[34]

UNRWA has estimated the number of "new" refugees—those fleeing for the first time—at 350,000. Of these, 100,000 fled the occupied area in Syria.[35] Others left Sinai for Egypt. The remainder, by far the largest number, went from Jordan's West Bank to the East. Unlike those who fled in 1948, very few of the newly displaced persons crossed an international border; for the most part they were citizens who shifted from one area to another in their own country.

Again, as in 1948, the United Nations urged return of the refugees. By resolution 237 of 14 June 1967, the Security Council unanimously called upon the government of Israel "to facilitate the return of those inhabitants who have fled . . . " and on 4 June 1967 the General Assembly associated itself with this action. The results, however, have been meager.

The special representative of the Secretary-General in the summer of 1967 was unable to arrange anything on behalf of newly displaced persons in Syria and Egypt, though subsequently, under a family reunion scheme, 2,520 persons had by April 1969 returned to Gaza and 449 to the Golan Heights in Syria.[36]

Return of displaced persons from East Jordan to the West Bank was begun in 1967, but the scheme soon aborted. Not until August 12 was the distribution of application forms begun—after time-consuming negotiations between the International Red Cross and the governments of Israel and Jordan over the appropriate heading. Application was made by heads of families—adult sons and daughters applying separately. Amman reported submission of some 40,000 applications, covering approximately 170,000 persons, while Israel acknowledged receiving some 32,000 applications relating to about 100,000 persons. The number of returnees by 31 August 1967—the deadline set by the Israeli government—was reported by Jordan at only 14,150 and by Israel at 14,056. Though in response to a request by the Secretary-General Israel extended the deadline for those not yet returned whose applications had been approved, only a few of these succeeded in crossing. Israel also announced that West Bank residents could apply for the return of members of their families, and that requests based on special hardship would be entertained.[37]

Response to the Security Council resolution of 14 June 1967 was little better than fiasco and much recrimination ensued. Still present were the obstacles to coexistence that had frustrated repatriation after the 1948 war.

II

Constitutional Origins: A Comparative Treatment

UNRWA was founded under Article 22 of the United Nations Charter which authorizes the General Assembly to "establish such subsidiary organs as it deems necessary to the performance of its functions." It is one of several autonomous bodies that have been constituted under Article 22, among which the United Nations Children's Fund and the United Nations High Commissioner for Refugees afford interesting comparisons with UNRWA. The present chapter makes apparent the wide range of choices available to subsidiary United Nations enterprises in structure, policy determination, and mode of operation.

The traditional way of establishing an entity such as UNRWA would have been by treaty. Two recent welfare agencies constituted in this manner were the United Nations Relief and Rehabilitation Administration and the International Refugee Organization. To gain perspective on Article 22 as a constitutive device, we shall first examine briefly these two treaty-based agencies.

THE ALTERNATIVE OF TREATY

The United Nations Relief and Rehabilitation Administration (UNRRA), which, it must be emphasized, is wholly distinct from UNRWA, was founded by a treaty negotiated through a conference held in 1943. The International Refugee Organization (IRO) was also established by treaty, but in the context of Article 59 of the

43

Charter, under which the United Nations may "initiate negotiations among states concerned for the creation of any new specialized agencies. . . . " We are interested in how these two entities—differently arrived at while possessing in common the instrumentality of the treaty—compare with operational agencies* established under Article 22.

UNRRA was designed to meet urgent needs of relief and rehabilitation in allied countries freed from enemy occupation during the second World War. It centralized estimates of need, pooled resources for the purchase of supplies, provided for transportation of supplies, and supervised distribution. UNRRA promoted equitable access to goods in short supply. It also precluded an aftermath of debt between countries which would otherwise have burdened the postwar balance of payments.

The operational character of UNRRA's mission is evident from the size of its staff and budget. At the peak of its activities in June 1946, UNRRA employed more than 24,000 persons, of whom 13,000 were international staff, 10,000 were locally recruited, and 1,400 were the personnel of voluntary agencies, administratively responsible to but not paid by UNRRA.[1] Expenditure amounted to $3,900,000,000 in a period of about three and one-half years, between the start of operations early in 1944 and termination in mid 1947.

The budget differentiated between two kinds of expense: administrative and operational. Administrative costs totaling $45,000,000 were periodically assessed against all members—forty-four original plus four subsequent adherents. Operational costs were in a different category. Requirements too vast to estimate and in any event incapable of being fully met prompted the authors of the treaty to stipulate that contributions of a member government would "be determined from time to time by its appropriate constitutional bodies." Subsequently, it was decided that only those governments whose economies were relatively intact would be expected to contribute—at the rate of one percent of the National Gross Product, a percentage that was twice solicited by UNRRA. Thus governments

---

* For the meaning of "operational" see footnote below, p. 49.

most heavily reliant on its benefits, while contributing to UNRRA's "administration," contributed only nominally to its "operations"—the latter typically in kind. The United States accounted for nearly three-quarters of the total. Nongovernmental sources contributed $210,000,000, mainly from voluntary agencies in the United States and mostly in kind.[2]

One of UNRRA's responsibilities was the displaced person, for whom its task was conceived initially as merely relief and repatriation. It was soon apparent, however, that large numbers of persons from Russia and Eastern Europe were determined not to return home. More than a million rejected communist rule. Thus for the many displaced persons who became refugees, incapable of being absorbed in the countries where they were stranded, resettlement was the paramount need.

The issue of repatriation versus resettlement eventually burdened UNRRA beyond its capacity to continue and contributed to its liquidation earlier than would otherwise have occurred. UNRRA's decision-making rule of simple majority—both in its Council, consisting of all members, and in the Central Committee—was unable to withstand the clash of conflicting ideologies.[3] Yet a problem unmanageable in the context of UNRRA became soluble through IRO, a specialized agency.

The displaced person turned refugee had created a situation already demanding action when in 1946 the United Nations was inaugurated in London. Vigorous debate in the Third Committee (Social, Humanitarian, and Cultural) of the General Assembly further emphasized but did not resolve the political issue. The communist governments argued for repatriation; those refusing to return home were "undemocratic" elements undeserving of any assistance from the international community. The matter could be dealth with, they contended, through bilateral arrangements between the countries of origin and those in which the refugees were situated—though they would make an exception of the fugitives from Franco Spain. The Western governments, while agreeing that traitors and war criminals were unworthy of help, insisted that political expatriates were entitled to humanitarian consideration.

The General Assembly referred the matter to the Economic and

Social Council, which in turn established a Special Committee on Refugees and Displaced Persons. Membership consisted of the representatives of twenty countries which were concerned with the problem in different ways: as countries of origin, of temporary residence, and of potential resettlement. The Committee, meeting from 9 April to 1 June 1946, projected a specialized agency designed to accomplish resettlement. This proved to be a workable solution, though the founding treaty, accepted by the General Assembly on 15 December 1946, was voted against and never signed by the communist governments. The final vote was thirty to five with eighteen abstentions.

Establishment of a specialized agency was not the only course open under the Charter, but in view of the circumstances it was the preferable one, despite the long delay before ratifications were to give effect to the treaty. Alternatively, a subordinate organ could have been established under authority of the General Assembly in accordance with Article 22. Indeed, it was persuasive to argue, as the British and other delegations did, that responsibility for resettlement was the international community's as a whole and that the cost was properly a charge against all members of the United Nations. The contention of the Australian delegation, that the scattering of specialized agencies "all over the international landscape" was costly in personnel and money and took control away from the main organs of the United Nations, also carried weight. Nevertheless, a subsidiary organ under Article 22 would not have resulted in clear gain, since communist governments could then have obstructed policy as members of the United Nations, yet would have been none the readier to contribute money to the resettlement elsewhere of their dissident nationals.*

* Louise W. Holborn, *The International Refugee Organization* (London: Oxford University Press, 1956), pp. 35–36. Considerable confusion as to the upshot of proceeding through the device of a specialized agency was indicated by the communist delegations' favoring this course—though in the end they rejected the treaty. "The delegations representing the countries of origin agreed that, from a political point of view, an independent organization, specialized and not permanent, would be in a better position to deal with the wishes of the countries directly concerned; they attached particular importance to the temporary character of the organization. . . . The Soviet Union further

Finance was of central importance. The Soviet Union argued for putting all contributions on a voluntary basis. France favored the obligatory principle only as regards administrative costs with operational costs to be met through voluntary contributions. Canada urged that membership carry with it the obligation of full support, for the organization would "not be able to carry passengers. . . . [I]t would be most invidious if any state was able to be a party to the constitution with a reservation which would in effect allow it to avoid financial contribution." The United States took the same stand, favoring obligatory assessments in support of both administrative and operational costs. A matter of contention until the last, this latter view (including penalty of no vote for a member in arrears) prevailed in the Administrative and Budgetary Committee of the General Assembly, 12 to 6 with 14 obstentions, thus precluding the kind of situation alluded to by the Canadian delegate.[4]

It is doubtful whether IRO's legislative history influenced the manner in which the General Assembly dealt with the problem of the Palestinian refugees. However, if those responsible in the latter instance were aware of the earlier experience, they must have been struck by the long interval between adoption of the IRO constitution by the General Assembly in December 1946 and its coming into force in August 1948. Not until the latter date was the treaty ratified by enough states to assure seventy-five percent of the initial operational budget—the formula contained in the treaty for its effectuation.[5]

The delay of nineteen months before the constitution went into force was serious, for meanwhile, on 30 June 1947, care of the refugees and displaced persons by UNRRA came to an end with its scheduled liquidation. However, simultaneous with approval of IRO's constitution the General Assembly provided for a Commission to prepare the way for IRO. This Commission was based on an

suggested that the creation of a specialized agency would permit representation in its councils of the countries of origin in proportion to the numbers of their refugees and displaced persons. British feeling, however, was that if it were decided to establish a specialized agency, its members should consist of those countries that would bear the financial burden of the resettlement work rather than the countries of origin, with which the refugees would, in fact, have no further connection." Ibid.

agreement to come into force upon acceptance by only eight government signatories to the constitution of the International Refugee
Organization.[6] Ratification was not required, and on 11 February
1947 the Preparatory Commission for IRO (PCIRO) convened in
Geneva. It was expected at that time that IRO would be in existence
by 1 July 1947. Since this did not happen, owing to the slow ratification process, it was fortunate that the Preparatory Commission
had been authorized to take over any of the functions, assets, and
personnel of UNRRA deemed essential to an orderly assumption by
IRO of its responsibilities. Expenses of the Commission were to be
met through transfer of funds from UNRRA and advance contributions.

On the strength of these arrangements, PCIRO in May 1947 decided, with representatives of eight governments in attendance
(Belgium, Canada, China, France, the Netherlands, Norway, the
U.K., and U.S.), to become operational on 1 July 1947. For fourteen
months thereafter "PCIRO was actually engaged in work identical
with that of the . . . body for which it was originally instituted to
prepare. . . . "[7] In this way the hazard of dilatory ratifications was
overcome.

Two noteworthy features of IRO's constitution survived the committee and plenary deliberations of the General Assembly. One was
that "motions shall be carried by simple majority of the members
present and voting in the General Council and the Executive Committee," except that budgetary allocations required a two-third's
vote.[8] The other feature, already noted, was the obligatory character of financial support, even as regards operational expense.

No government hostile or indifferent to IRO's purposes would be
likely to commit itself to these propositions. Thus use of a treaty
resulted in a winnowing process. Whereas IRO had been envisaged
as comprising all fifty-four members of the United Nations, the
number of signatories was twenty-six, of which eight governments,
mainly Latin American, never ratified. In the end IRO's institutional arrangements were compatible with the purposes of eighteen
governments—including all of those important to the success of
the enterprise.

The operational character of IRO was reflected in the number of its employees and in the amount of expenditure. At peak strength, the international staff totaled 2,800 and locally recruited personnel, 3,200.[9] From July 1947 until liquidation in March 1952, expenditure was $429,000,000 of which $18,000,000 was for administration. The total required of the United States was $238,000,000.[10] IRO dealt with more than 1,500,000 refugees of whom 1,046,000 were resettled and 74,000 repatriated, the remainder presumably staying in the country of first refuge.[11]

IRO could never have functioned smoothly, if at all, as a subsidiary organ of the General Assembly, owing to the chagrin of the communist governments over refusal of many of their nationals to return home. Finance, too, was a consideration against constituting IRO under Article 22 of the Charter. While in principle there is no obstacle to charging expenditure of a subsidiary organ against the regular United Nations budget, in this instance there would have been strong resistance from the communist governments; and since the size of expenditures was large, other governments would have pleaded inability to pay.

ARTICLE 22 AS POINT OF DEPARTURE

Because of the urgency of the Palestine refugee problem, the treaty alternative was not feasible for UNRWA owing to the delay entailed by ratifications. Nevertheless, though political support and finance are problems with which UNRWA struggles constantly, these are hardly of a nature to be more tractable in a treaty than in an Article 22 context. The suitability of Article 22 to UNRWA's particular circumstances, in contrast to IRO, will become evident in what follows.

Scores of bodies have been established by the General Assembly under Article 22. They differ widely in purpose, structure, and mode of operation, each reflecting a variety of considerations, including political calculation. Among the various types, UNRWA falls in the category of an operational agency.*

* If one dare generalize about the variety of subsidiary organs established by the General Assembly under Article 22, there appear to be two broad categories of bodies. On the one hand are those relating to the internal

Also in this category are two other welfare agencies, the United Nations Children's Fund (UNICEF) and the United Nations High Commissioner for Refugees (UNHCR), though they are not operational in the same degree as UNRWA. Whereas the latter is in contact with the recipients of its services, UNICEF and UNHCR seek to avoid or minimize direct involvement of their own manpower. Typically they formulate and coordinate programs, preferring to leave execution to governments or private agencies. The contrast (as of 1968) is apparent in the numbers employed: UNRWA 12,000, UNICEF 840, and UNHCR 290. UNHCR's expenditure in that year was about $8,000,000. On the other hand, UNRWA's and UNICEF's budgets were not far apart, $44,000,000 as against $44,800,000—the size of the latter being accounted for by UNICEF's purchase of large quantities of supplies.

---

processes of the United Nations, such as the Advisory Committee on Adminisrative and Budgetary Questions or the UN Administrative Tribunal; or bodies engaged in study, such as the International Law Commission, designed to prepare the ground for General Assembly consideration of broad international problems.

On the other hand, there are subsidiary organs directly involved in the affairs of the international community, themselves participants in events along with governments. They are of two kinds—the political commission and the operational agency. The Conciliation Commission is illustrative of the former; it has grappled with governments at the diplomatic level in an endeavor to resolve the Palestine question.

The mark of the operational agency is performance of concrete tasks. These may comprise the whole range of governmental functions as in the case of the UN Temporary Executive Authority, an agency that governed West New Guinea for a period of months. Or the governmental functions performed may be selective, as exemplified by the health and educational programs of UNRWA. The welfare activities of the UN High Commissioner for Refugees are intertwined with those of governments and voluntary agencies, but the mix is such that the programs are unmistakably those of international organization. Technical assistance is the task performed by the UN Development Program, while the task of the UN Emergency Force was to serve as a buffer between hostile neighbors.

We would, then, define an operational agency as one interacting with governments through performance of concrete tasks and as having an administrative structure of its own. The characterization of an operational agency contained in *Repertory of Practice of UN Organs* (United Nations, 1955, Vol. I, p. 669) as one "entrusted with the task of executing programmes of relief, rehabilitation, and other forms of assistance by furnishing supplies and services to Governments or directly to the people concerned" seems too narrow.

All three agencies have a common origin in the simple device of a General Assembly resolution. The United Nations, a collective entity formed by states and possessing coordinate membership with them in the international community, served as an alternative point of departure to that of the treaty. UNRWA's founding resolution was a legislative act, but not the kind of enactment that defines legal rights and duties among a legislature's constituency, such as (leaving aside the question of whether or not with binding authority) the Assembly's partition resolution of November 1947, which endeavored to prescribe the future legal relations between the Arab and Jewish communities in Palestine. Normally such enactments can only be by treaty, not by General Assembly resolution.

UNRWA's founding resolution, on the other hand, pertained to the internal workings of the United Nations and was concerned with the posture of the Organization itself. It was a policy decision setting up a welfare agency, the counterpart of numerous enactments by national legislative bodies concerned with the bureaucratic structure of government. Such a resolution prevails over any government or any group of governments short of one-third of the votes cast and thus is an exercise of legislative power.*

Administrative Autonomy

Whereas subsidiary organs of the General Assembly are usually in the form of committees and commissions that meet intermittently, with staff responsible to the Secretary-General, the operational agency is intended to function continuously and possesses its own administrative apparatus. Accordingly, the General Assembly has provided each of the agencies here under consideration with an executive officer. The Executive-Director of UNICEF and the Commissioner-General (originally Director) of UNRWA are appointed by the Secretary-General in consultation with the governments con-

* Were the UN Assembly bound by unaimity, as was the League of Nations Assembly, the point as to its legislative power (in the sense indicated) would not be valid, for unanimity implies something less than legislative capacity. The shift to the two-third's rule makes an important difference in principle and also in practice, considering that conclusive actions of the UN Assembly which concern the workings of the Organization are often short of unanimity.

stituting, in the case of UNICEF, the Executive Board, and, in the case of UNRWA, the Advisory Commission. The High Commissioner for Refugees is elected by the General Assembly on nomination by the Secretary-General.

Having an executive officer—by whatever name—means that administratively each agency is self-contained; the staff is appointed through the executive officer, subject to his removal, and responsible to him.* Nevertheless, employment by UNHCR and UNICEF is subject, with minor exceptions, to the staff regulations and rules of the parent organization.†

Appointment and removal of staff by its executive officer is also a mark of UNRWA's administrative self-containment. In addition, however, the Commissioner-General promulgates his own Regulations and Rules—in agreement with the Secretary-General. This flexibility is needed by UNRWA as employer of thousands of locally recruited persons. On the other hand, conditions of employment pertaining to UNRWA's international staff compare unfavorably with those of the United Nations system generally—though retirement benefits are now provided—which poses problems of recruitment and retention.

---

* UNICEF is not an exception, though the text of its founding resolution makes it appear so. Resolution 57 (I) directs the Secretary-General to provide "staff and facilities required for the administration of the fund," for which no charge against UNICEF was to be made so long as assistance remained "within the limits of the United Nations budget." It was not practicable for the UN Secretariat to assume the burden; accordingly, UNICEF acquired its own staff, appointed in practice by its own executive officer. There is no ambiguity about the separateness of UNHCR's staff. Appointive power was conferred directly on the High Commissioner.

† The Staff Regulations are the legislative principles governing employment as laid down by the General Assembly. The Staff Rules, promulgated by the Secretary-General, spell out the terms of employment in detail. Their applicability to UNICEF and to UNHCR is qualified regarding promotion and termination for redundancy. In both instances, the only relevant manning table is the agency's own rather than that of the United Nations proper. A further qualification in the case of UNHCR is that appointments are never more than "indefinite" inasmuch as the General Assembly has yet to place the Agency on a permanent basis.

Budget

Budgetary problems are treated at length in Chapter VIII, but the financing of UNRWA requires brief mention at this point.

UNRWA, UNICEF, and UNHCR are financed by voluntary contributions, with the important exception of UNHCR's administrative costs, which are assumed by the UN budget. Of main interest here, however, is the contrast in budgetary procedures between UNRWA and the other two organizations. We shall see in Chapter VIII that the budgets of UNICEF and UNHCR are formally acted upon each year. In this way a stamp of approval is placed on policies reflected in the proposed expenditures. No contributing government can subsequently influence the intended program short of the extreme expedient of refusing to pay. UNRWA's expenditures, however, are not subject to formal approval, either by its Advisory Commission or by the Special Political Committee of the General Assembly. Although nothing precludes review by either body, there is no provision in UNRWA's founding resolution for formal consideration and approval of a budget. In the early years the Advisory Commission did review the budget, but more recently both of these bodies have, in fact, declined to do so. Consequently a contributor is well positioned to use the pledging conference—the final stage of UNRWA's annual appearance at the General Assembly—as an occasion for attaching conditions to its contribution. Short of an approved budget, the Commissioner-General is vulnerable to such intervention at the last moment, and orderly fiscal planning is more difficult.

Policy Determination

Several elements are involved in policy determination: the General Assembly's constituent resolution, the agency's annual report, the political organ attached to an agency consisting of representatives of selected governments, and the secretariat. These elements combine in different ways; UNRWA's pattern contrasts sharply with those of UNHCR and UNICEF, which also differ from each other.

UNHCR's founding resolution is more carefully drawn than either

UNICEF's or UNRWA's. Purpose and structure are spelled out in a statute comparable to a treaty in formality and detail.[12] Without unduly constricting the Office of High Commissioner, the statute has served as a firm point of reference in subsequent years. In sharp contrast, UNICEF's founding resolution is sketchy, though its failure to anticipate the Agency's future either as to function or structure has not hindered a satisfactory evolution. UNRWA's constituent resolution is loosely drawn, which may account for the unsatisfactory personnel and budgetary provisions already noted. Mainly, however, UNRWA lacks political guidance, though doubtless its tribulations in this regard are owing less to the defects of its Advisory Commission than to the intransigence of the situation to which it is addressed.

Having founded an agency, the General Assembly reviews the agency's annual reports, which affords further opportunity for the Assembly to consider policy questions. Reports of UNICEF and UNHCR go to the Economic and Social Council, which in turn transmits them, with recommendations if it so chooses, to the General Assembly. There they are subject to discussion in committee, prior to submission of a resolution in plenary session. Following a different procedure, the Commissioner-General of UNRWA reports directly to the Assembly through its President. The report is then considered by the Special Political Committee, with prior scrutiny only by UNRWA's Advisory Commission, which, however, has long refrained from any commentary of its own. Assembly review of the annual reports of its subsidiary organs does not normally result in resolutions containing precise directives. Here again, as is typical of the enabling resolutions, the language is far more general than that employed by a domestic legislative body. UNRWA's educational system, for example, came into being with little reference to it in General Assembly resolutions.

At most, the General Assembly is a sounding board for policy initiatives that have occurred elsewhere. One such source is the body of government representatives inserted by the General Assembly between an agency and itself, constituting an organ of executive counsel capable of more directly affecting policy than the Assembly.

UNICEF's founding resolution instructs the Executive Director to follow policies "established by an Executive Board in accordance with such principles as may be laid down by the Economic and Social Council and its Social Commission." Having in the initial resolution named twenty-six governments whose representatives were to constitute the Board, the General Assembly has subsequently twice altered the number and the method of selection, providing currently for a board of thirty states "to be designated by the Economic and Social Council for appropriate periods. . . ."[13] The composition of the board has been widely representative of UN membership, including the Soviet Union and East European countries. Reflecting the consensus engendered by UNICEF's humanitarian objectives, membership in the Executive Board has been unaffected by political considerations, except implicitly by the Assembly's desire for diversity.

The statute of the Office of High Commissioner states that the Commissioner "shall follow policy directives given him by the General Assembly or the Economic and Social Council." The statute also authorized ECOSOC to establish at its discretion a body advisory to the High Commissioner to consist of states selected "on the basis of their demonstrated interest in and devotion to the solution of the refugee problem." This ECOSOC promptly did, naming an Advisory Committee of fifteen states. Soon, in response to new directions in the Office of High Commissioner, the General Assembly requested ECOSOC to replace the Advisory with an Executive Committee "responsible for giving directives to the High Commissioner . . . and for exercising the necessary controls in the use of funds." An Executive Committee of twenty members was named by ECOSOC, which was enlarged to thirty in 1963 in response to the growing size of the United Nations and to the increasing numbers of non-European refugees.[14] It meets once a year or on call. Yugoslavia is the only communist member. General Assembly election by acclamation of Prince Sadruddin Aga Khan as High Commissioner in 1967 indicates that ideological conflicts present at the creation of the Office in 1950 have now subsided.

In the case of UNRWA, its Commissioner-General is provided with an Advisory Commission, consisting originally of France,

Britain, and the United States, with Turkey representing the Middle East. An unusual feature is accreditation of each of its members to each of the host governments—Egypt, Jordan, Lebanon, and Syria. The object was to facilitate negotiation of agreements for works and development projects between UNRWA and the host governments, the Agency being represented jointly by the Advisory Commission and the Commissioner-General. Agreements of this character were consummated in the first three or four years, after which the negotiating function of the Advisory Commission lapsed.

That "advisory" was in fact a misnomer is further suggested by the early practice of full-time appointments to the Commission, which, with a small staff of its own, was initially quartered in the premises of UNRWA. Moreover, each year through 1954, the Commission and the Commissioner-General presented jointly to the General Assembly a special report containing policy recommendations and budget estimates.[15] Though couched in general terms, their acceptance by the General Assembly was to be expected inasmuch as the chief contributors had already, through the Advisory Commission, put their imprimatur on the request.

The Advisory Commission was authorized by the founding resolution to add three more members from "contributing governments." The three added were Syria and Jordan in late 1952, and Egypt early in 1953. After the General Assembly had authorized two more members, Lebanon was added in December 1953 and Belgium in February 1954. That autumn was the last time that recommendations to the General Assembly were made jointly by the Advisory Commission and the Commissioner-General.

Adding the host governments to the Advisory Commission was favored by UNRWA as a way of easing relations with those governments* However, to bring them into formal association was to invite an adversary type of relation with the contributing governments and

* In his annual report (A/2470), 1953, para. 8, the Commissioner-General refers to their accession to the Commission as "an event of great importance, the effects of which have not yet been fully felt but which may be far-reaching. . . . Their [the representatives] familiarity with the points of view of those Governments and with the refugee problem has already assisted in overcoming administrative difficulties, and there is reason to hope that this assistance will increase as time goes on."

also with UNRWA. The interests reflected in the enlarged Commission became too disparate to permit that minimum of consensus
which the advisory function presupposes.

Even before the strains among its members imposed by the Suez
crisis in 1956, the Advisory Commission had ceased in 1955 to
associate itself with the Commissioner-General's annual report to
the General Assembly. Beginning in 1961 and for five years following, with virtually unchanged phraseology, the Commission acknowledged having "considered" the annual report, adding that
"individual members . . . have reserved the position of their respective Governments on a number of matters discussed in the report."
Because of the June War, the Commission did not meet to consider
the 1967 report, though the views of its members were solicited
individually by the Commissioner-General. Meetings of the Commission were resumed in 1968, but the political strains incident to
the June War and its aftermath have further reduced its utility as
an aid to UNRWA policy.

Needless to say, Israel is not a member of the Advisory Commission. Indeed, Israel is not a "host" but a government controlling
occupied territory, within which a major portion of UNRWA
registrants since June 1967 now reside. The bilateral relations
ensuing between UNRWA and Israel have included the latter's
perusal of the annual report in draft and the conveying to the Commissioner-General of its views and comments.

Paradoxically, because of the highly political context in which
UNRWA operates, the Commissioner-General receives little guidance from either the Advisory Commission or the General Assembly.
This leaves to him and his aides the major burden of policy determination. To be sure, the very nature of operational responsibility
enhances the influence of a secretariat. In such a context, power
accrues to the professionally skilled and otherwise competent
bureaucrat, whether international or domestic. Nevertheless, the
burden of decision falling on the Commissioner-General and his
staff exceeds what may reasonably be expected of a secretariat.

While a bureaucracy might normally welcome such freedom of
action as its parent body may be disposed to allow, UNRWA is in
special need of the kind of backing that only its Advisory Commis-

sion and the General Assembly can give. UNRWA is a welfare
agency dealing with the same kind of problems confronting such
agencies in domestic politics. Who are entitled to benefits? What
should be their variety and extent? What, if anything, should be
exacted in return for services rendered? UNRWA's answers to these
questions are subject to the extraordinary circumstance that its
programs are carried out within the territorial jurisdiction of governments. It requires political reinforcement in its perpetual encounter
with territorial authority.

Modes of Operation

UNHCR and UNRWA are both concerned with refugees;
through humanitarian endeavor, both seek to undo the damage
caused by the indifference to human considerations so typical of
international politics. Results, however, have not been the same.
UNHCR has been remarkably successful in healing political rupture,
while UNRWA has not. This difference prompts inquiry into their
respective approaches to the problem of the refugee.

We noted earlier that IRO through resettlement was expected to
reduce the postwar refugee problem—conceived as primarily
European—to the point where countries of residence could assume
responsibility for such refugees as remained in their respective
jurisdictions. As IRO's successor, the Office of High Commissioner
was seen as protagonist on behalf of the legal status of expatriate
and stateless persons, enabling the last of the unsettled refugees in
Europe to become accepted members of society in terms of their
legal capacity to own property, marry, and travel, and of their access
to education, employment, and social security. A conference at
Geneva in July 1951, acting on the basis of a draft prepared by
ECOSOC, adopted a Convention on the Status of Refugees. This
document serves as point of departure for the legal assistance and
protection that the High Commissioner seeks to provide. Though
written in a European context, the Convention counts among its
fifty-eight accessions (as of 1969) some twenty from Africa. In
effect the High Commissioner and his representatives in the field

are performing a consular function for the alien disowned by his government or lacking a national tie for other reasons.

However, even as regards the rapidly improving situation in Europe, the legal approach of the Convention was still not sufficient to deal with the situation. Refugees remaining in Europe required material assistance, while permanent solutions were for some still worth attempting. UNHCR granted annuities for care of the aged, subsidized low-rent housing, and provided vocational training. To facilitate such activities, the General Assembly in 1952 authorized the solicitation of voluntary contributions from governments and replaced the High Commissioner's Advisory Committee with an Executive Committee—though as regards legal protection the High Commissioner has remained directly responsible to the General Assembly.

Meanwhile, political explosions outside Europe shifted the main refugee problem to Asia and Africa. The General Assembly, having in 1957 specially authorized assistance to Chinese refugees in Hong Kong and in 1958 to Algerian refugees in Tunisia and Morocco, gave the High Commissioner in 1959 blanket authority "to use his good offices" anywhere[16]—still subject, however, to certain definitional limits as to eligibility.* In 1967 UNHCR sought support for programs relating to 800,000 refugees in Central, East, and West Africa.[17]

The High Commissioner, becoming increasingly involved in relief, repatriation, integration, and resettlement, has not operated on the pattern of UNRRA and IRO. These had financed and administered major aspects of their programs, while UNHCR sees itself rather as

* ". . . refugees considered as nationals by the countries which have granted them asylum (by and large refugees in 'divided countries') are not a UNHCR responsibility. Moreover, UNHCR is not concerned with refugees for whom another United Nations body has assumed full responsibility, such as the Arab refugees from Palestine under the mandate of UNRWA. Nor has UNHCR been called upon to assist in the situation created by the massive arrivals of Cubans in the United States of America during the past few years. (UNHCR is, however, concerned with Cubans who have arrived in a number of Latin American countries and in Spain.)" *Background Paper on UNHCR* (MHCR/48/66/Rev. 2), June 1966, p. 6.

"the planner and diplomatic go-between to enlist the help of all those governments, organizations and individuals likely to be in a position to assist in any given refugee situation."[18] This is a role of stimulation and coordination, one step removed from the task itself. At the outset restricted as to purpose and duration, UNHCR has evolved into a highly successful enterprise of broad scope with minimum utilization of manpower and money.*

UNRWA's manner of dealing with refugee problems has been quite different from UNHCR's, inasmuch as the Agency has directly financed and administered programs of public works, economic rehabilitation, relief, health, and education. Yet despite the depth and intimacy of UNRWA's involvement, the result has not been to dissipate the Arab refugee problem, whereas UNHCR has reached solutions in many situations.

UNRWA's different mode of operation, compared with UNCHR's, is to be accounted for in part by the history of the UN's relation to the Palestine question. Unlike any situation in which UNHCR has been involved, the United Nations was directly engaged as a third party, along with Jews and Arabs, in the disposition of the British Mandate. Only against this background can one account for international organization assuming direct responsibility for the welfare of the Arab refugees, a mode of operation that would be inappropriate in any other circumstance. Desperate need is so prevalent in the world that international organization could not afford on that basis alone to assume the full burden of welfare enterprises.

Another difference between the Arab refugee problem and comparable problems handled by UNHCR is the simple fact that the refugees in the former instance, unlike those typically dealt with by UNHCR, have not and do not welcome an alternative to repatria-

* At the end of 1968 the Office of High Commissioner had a staff of 102 professional and 184 clerical employees, about 40 percent at Headquarters in Geneva, the others in 33 branch and subbranch offices in various parts of the world. Its program budget was $4,600,000 and its administrative $3,500,000.

UNHCR in 1954 was awarded the Nobel Peace Prize, largely owing to the imagination and energy of G. G. van Heuven Goedhart, the first Commissioner.

tion. Though refugees falling to UNHCR's jurisdiction may long for home, ordinarily they have accepted defeat at the hands of domestic enemies and are amenable to an individual or group solution to their plight short of repatriation. The very size of the Palestinian exodus, the circumstances of the flight, and the disposition of the larger Arab community to identify with the refugee all militate against the successful application of methods of amelioration and rehabilitation such as those employed by UNHCR. We saw that UNRRA's attempted repatriation of displaced persons after the second World War was thwarted by political attitudes. UNRWA's is the opposite case, for in this instance political attitudes have defeated attempted resettlement.

CONCLUSION

Though the instrumentality of treaty was not feasible for UNRWA, it would have offered no important advantage even had the price of delay been paid. Article 22 has, in fact, largely outmoded the cumbersome and dilatory procedure of treaty-making —where the object is not to prescribe rules of international law (such as the Convention on the Status of Refugees), but to constitute machinery for implementing the purposes of the United Nations. The utility of Article 22 will become still more evident as we turn to a consideration of UNRWA's legal status. Though subordinate to the General Assembly, UNRWA lacks nothing in corporate capacity requisite to the performance of its localized and specialized functions.

A question remains whether the admitted advantages of Article 22 were fully exploited in UNRWA's founding resolution. Hindsight points to ways in which UNRWA, within the limits of Article 22, might have been more advantageously constituted. For example, members of UNRWA's international staff from the outset could have been employed under the Staff Regulations and Rules of the United Nations proper. True, UNRWA was designed to meet a temporary situation. Yet, whereas UNHCR, too, was so constituted, its staff was in all major respects assimilated to that of the parent organization. Budgetary procedure also could have been dealt with differently, making it conform to the standards generally employed in the United Nations system whereby budget and program are closely related and subject to formal enactment.

As for financing UNRWA by a more assured means than voluntary contributions, this was within reach of Article 22 as a constitutional but probably not as a political possibility. There would have been no obstacle in principle to charging UNRWA's costs against the UN's regular budget. Indeed an initial attempt to do so as regards administrative expense would probably have succeeded in UNRWA's case as it did subsequently in UNHCR's. However, similar treatment of UNRWA's operational costs would doubtless have been resisted, given the frugal habits of the General Assembly, lack of sufficient political involvement on the part of many of its members to sustain financial sacrifice, and, in the case of the communist countries, a political interest that could afford indifference. Only by treaty could UNRWA—like IRO—have escaped the uncertainties and importunities of voluntary contributions.

UNRWA's greatest dilemma has been the Commissioner-General's lack of a proper political underpinning for deciding the difficult and perplexing questions that confront him. Though he and his aides have shouldered the responsibility, it is more properly that of a political body than a secretariat. UNHCR, though controversial in origin, demonstrates that Article 22 can afford political guidance through a board consisting of government representatives. That UNRWA's Adivsory Commission has failed in this function is symptomatic of the deep fissures in the international community opened by the Palestine question. Nor has the General Assembly made up the deficiency. Through the generality and brevity of its annual resolutions, it has evaded consideration of issues that risk serious dissension.

The weakness of UNRWA's political foundation will become evident as we turn first to the Agency's struggle with governments over questions of legal status and second to the problems attending its programs of relief and education. A paradox will be brought out in the chapter on finance: the inability of the United States, despite its large contributions, to wield strong influence on UNRWA's behalf. We shall also note the passive attitude of governments not directly involved in the situation and their neglect to take an initiative aimed at strengthening the Commissioner-General's hand. The bargaining power vis-à-vis the host governments which is available to UNRWA by virtue of services rendered is largely unused in support of status and program.

III

Corporate Status and Immunities

JUNCTION between international organization and government occurs in a wide variety of contexts and is a significant focal point in contemporary international relations. Novel situations arise particularly between operational agencies* and governments, posing general questions of international law as well as policy problems at the program level.

UNRWA is performing functions normally the responsibility of government. Yet, unlike the United Nations Temporary Executive Authority that governed West New Guinea for a brief period, UNRWA is without territorial authority. Although the Agency asserts control over its own activities and personnel to the exclusion of government, it has no jurisdiction over the refugees to whom it ministers. The anomaly is that, without territorial authority, UNRWA is performing tasks that are normally the responsibility of such authority.

The question this raises is whether UNRWA can expect to have sufficient freedom of action to vindicate its international character. Before seeking an answer in terms of UNRWA's specific tasks, we must first inquire into a problem common to all international organizations—namely, their juridical capacity under international law. Of

* See footnote above, p. 49. There the term is applied to subsidiary organs of the General Assembly. More widely, however, it includes other international organizations: for example, the World Bank, the International Monetary Fund, and the European Communities.

initial concern, then, in this and the following chapter, is UNRWA's juridical standing in the presence of territorial authority.

A full treatment of this aspect of UNRWA's functioning over the past twenty years would not be feasible, since documentation in the confidential files of UNRWA, the United Nations, and the governments concerned is understandably not available. However, UNRWA's annual reports to the General Assembly contain enough on the subject to permit a review of the issues, even if questions about circumstances and outcome are often left unanswered.

DERIVATIONS OF UNRWA'S STATUS

The complexity of UNRWA's operations and the pressure for decision on questions, large and small, call for a sharp division of responsibility between New York and the field. The instrument of UNRWA's "incorporation," the resolution of 8 December 1949, devolved upon it a large measure of autonomy, without, however, divorcing the Agency from the United Nations—which only founding by treaty could have done. As a subsidiary organ of the General Assembly, UNRWA, in regard to both legal personality and program, is like an offspring whose familial ties, though attenuated, cannot be outgrown.

Even had legal status gone unmentioned in the founding resolution,* UNRWA would have shared those features of the parent organization set out in Articles 104 and 105 of the Charter. As an arm of the United Nations it is entitled to "such legal capacity as may be necessary for the exercise of its functions and the fulfilment of its purposes," and to "such privileges and immunities as are necessary for the fulfilment of its purposes," while members of UNRWA's staff are entitled to "such privileges and immunities as are necessary for the independent exercise of their functions. . . ."

The Convention on Privileges and Immunities of the United Nations (Appendix III, below), designed to spell out Articles 104 and 105, is also applicable to UNRWA. Approved by the General Assembly in 1946, it has been ratified by approximately one hundred states, including all those with which UNRWA has special rela-

* See Appendix II, para. 17.

tions. The Convention is concerned with juridical personality, immunity from suit, inviolability of premises, immunity from taxation and customs duties, freedom of communication, and privileges and immunities of officials. Hence it anticipates many issues that have arisen between UNRWA and governments, and the Agency has had frequent recourse to it, more often perhaps than any other part of the United Nations.

Yet the Convention, designed to cover representational arrangements between international organizations and governments, did not foresee an operational agency of UNRWA's characteristics. Many complications arise in applying the fiscal exemptions of the Convention to UNRWA's large-scale purchase and movement of supplies needed to shelter and feed hundreds of thousands of persons and to provide for their health and education. Nor did the Convention's provisions concerning privileges and immunities of United Nations personnel contemplate employment of thousands of locally recruited staff—ranging from highly trained professionals to day laborers—in the operation of a complex welfare enterprise.

Remarking in his 1956 report to the General Assembly that UNRWA's operations have "an importance in the life of the host countries that is unusual for an international organization," the Commissioner-General raised the question of where primary responsibility for the refugees lay between the United Nations and the host governments:

. . . it seems indispensable to ask the General Assembly to re-examine and make an appraisal of the Agency's terms of reference, and to determine how best the refugees are to be assisted. For example, does the Assembly consider that the Agency should continue to have direct operational responsibilities—and do the host governments desire this? Or does the Assembly wish the Agency's essential functions to be more limited, with operational control and responsibility entirely in the hands of the host governments? It is important that the nature and extent of the Agency's responsibilities and authority should be made clear, and agreed to by the host governments. It is also important for the Agency, no matter what its responsibilities, to have the open and full cooperation of host governments. It should be understood that, in the event that local conditions in any area unduly hamper the carrying out of those responsibilities, it may be necessary for the Agency to suspend or terminate its operations in such an area.*

The same issue was raised again by the Commissioner-General in 1959, at a time when the question of extending UNRWA's mandate beyond 30 July 1960 was before the Assembly:

It is incumbent upon the governments in whose territory the refugees are living to face the problems relating to UNRWA and decide on the type of assistance they desire. If they wish UNRWA to fulfill its responsibilities as an operating Agency they should accord it the treatment appropriate to its juridical position. If, on the other hand, they themselves wish to control and regulate the operations it would be logical for them to assume responsibility for the performance and administration of those functions.

The 1959 report continued by suggesting steps to improve future relations between the Agency and the host governments, including assured recognition of UNRWA's juridical status "by every unit of government dealing with the Agency," and settlement of outstanding claims and establishment of procedures to deal with future disputes. Also, a need was emphasized for standard basic agreements with the host governments supplementary to the Charter and the Convention on Privileges and Immunities.[1]

UNRWA has never achieved the full and formal resolution of problems of legal status that it sought in 1959, and the need for which it again stressed in 1967.[2] Especially difficult has been conduct of programs of relief and education without a basic understand-

* *Annual Report* (A/3212), 1956, paras. 76 and 84. In the ensuing resolution the General Assembly noted in a preambular response to the Commissioner-General's appeal "that the host governments have expressed the wish that the Agency continue to carry out its mandate in their respective countries or territories and have expressed their wish to cooperate fully with the Agency and to extend to it every appropriate assistance in carrying out its functions, in accordance with the provisions of Articles 104 and 105 of the Charter of the United Nations, the terms of the Convention on the Privileges and Immunities of the United Nations, the contents of paragraph 17 of resolution 302 (IV) and the terms of the agreements with the host governments. . . . " This was followed up by paragraph 2 of the operative portion: "*Requests* the host governments to cooperate fully with the Agency and with its personnel and to extend to the Agency every appropriate assistance in carrying out its functions. . . . " *Resolution 1018* (XI), 28 February 1957. The resolution of the following session employed identical language.

ing with territorial authority as to the prerogatives of international
organization.

Initiative for agreements dealing with problems of status peculiar
to UNRWA's circumstances is not dependent on New York—though
strong prodding of the host governments by the General Assembly
could be of assistance. Agreements, even if short of satisfactory, can
and have been made by UNRWA at the local level. In this connection, as in others involving Palestine, Count Bernadotte left his mark.
A 1948 agreement between him, as United Nations Mediator, and
the Prime Minister of Syria,[3] partly concerned Syria's contribution
of services and also exempted from taxes, from other official
charges, and from inspection all goods destined for refugees,
whether the goods were to be used in Syria or transported across
Syria to Jordan. The goods were to "remain the property of the
United Nations or the donating organization until . . . distributed to
the individuals." The Syrian government was also to accord "to the
representatives of the United Nations assigned for the service of
Palestine refugees, all privileges, exemptions, and facilities necessary
for the performance of their duties, both as regards their persons
and all articles used by them to this end."

The Commissioner-General reported in 1953 that negotiations
with Syria were in progress for revision of the Bernadotte Agreement. These talks continued fitfully for several years without result.
Much later an exchange of letters occurred in 1967 between the
Syrian Foreign Minister and the Secretary-General based on discussions held in Damascus in which the United Nations Under-
secretary for Legal Affairs participated. The exchange appears to
have dealt with importation and movement of supplies, definition
of "direct" taxes, and the status of both local and international
personnel.*

* Preceding the discussions in Damascus and unknown to UNRWA at the
time was a Syrian decree of 1 August 1967 contradicting in part the subsequent exchange of letters. The decree excluded all locally recruited United
Nations staff in Syria from the privileges and immunities of the 1946 Convention, other than exemption from taxation on salaries. The Agency asserted
that the "incompatibility . . . is clear . . . " between the decree and Syria's
unqualified adherence to the Convention. *Annual Report* (A/6713), 1967, para.
22 and Annex II, paras. 7, 8.

UNRWA concluded special agreements with Egypt and Jordan, in late 1950 and early 1951 respectively.[4] Both agreements are broad, neither going much beyond the Convention on Privileges and Immunities, with which Jordan, not yet a member of the United Nations, identified itself. Each government, at its own expense, undertook to provide UNRWA with certain services, including police protection. Brief mention was made of locally recruited staff: on the basis of names submitted by UNRWA and accepted by the government concerned, such personnel was to have the freedom of movement required for performance of its duties.

Seeking to revise the initial agreement with Jordan, UNRWA began negotiations in 1954. According to the Commissioner-General, the government sought increased control over the Agency's operations, "while the Agency considers that (a) it could do a more effective job in the interests of the refugees if there were less interference in its work; and (b) its status as a public international organization under international law should be fully recognized." Agreement was tentatively reached after three years, only to have a new government in Jordan decide on radical modification. No subsequent progress has been made.[5]

The agreement with Egypt failed to deal with a problem that subsequently never was resolved satisfactorily. The status of UNRWA in Egypt proper has not been in question, but there were difficulties in Gaza. A portion of the former Palestinian mandate which was not territorially a part of Egypt, Gaza had been placed under Egyptian jurisdiction by the armistice of February 1949, with a Governor-General appointed by Cairo, though the courts of the mandatory period continued to function and Gaza had its own legislative council. In the eyes of UNRWA and of its principal, the United Nations, Cairo was the responsible authority. The latter, on the other hand, insisted that Gaza was an entity with which UNRWA should deal directly. A confused situation resulted, with UNRWA suffering as regards the freedom of movement of its international staff.* However, the agreement of 1950 was never revised.

* The situation as described in the 1956 report seems, with fluctuations, to have held true at least for the following three years: "The position in Gaza

With Lebanon there was an exchange of notes in late 1954 concerning, for the most part, specific disputes, but also touching on broad principle. The government declared that it gave

full recognition . . . to the legal status of UNRWA and the privileges, immunities and facilities which the Agency and its officials should enjoy. In particular the Lebanese government is prepared to interpret the 13 February 1946 Convention on the Privileges and Immunities of the United Nations in accordance with . . . international practice.[6]

Despite subsequent difficulties, this point of departure has never been spelled out in further agreement.

Finally, UNRWA has on two occasions entered into agreements with Israel, by exchange of letters in late 1956 and again in mid 1967.[7] Each exchange followed military occupation by Israel of areas containing Palestinian refugees. Both times it was agreed that UNRWA would continue its services and that Israel would assume certain costs for handling and transporting supplies, provide security, and accord to UNRWA and its staff the privileges and immunities of the United Nations Convention.

Beyond problems unique to UNRWA's mission, there have been other sources of difficulty more usual to international organizations. Lack of awareness by many local judges and other lesser officials

---

became increasingly unsatisfactory throughout the year. . . . The Egyptian authorities refused permits for certain Agency officials to enter or re-enter the territory and withheld action on the applications of certain others. The effect was to prevent members of the staff from carrying out their assigned duties. . . . Although requested to inform the Agency of the reasons for their actions, the authorities in Gaza omitted to do so. The Egyptian authorities in Gaza also from time to time refused permission to certain staff to depart from the territory, in cases concerning both travel on official business and leave travel. This not only complicated the efficient execution of the Agency's operations in Gaza, but also severely impaired the morale of the staff stationed there." *Annual Report* (A/3212), 1956, Annex G, para. 13. Also *Annual Reports* (A/3686), 1957, Annex H, para. 11; (A/3931), 1958, Annex H. para 13; and (A/4213), 1959, Annex H., para. 14.

This last report records "progress with regard to procedures. . . . The period for which permits are valid was extended fom 3 to 6 months and all renewals take place on 1 January and 1 July thus reducing the administrative work involved. . . . Unfortunately . . . denials have continued to be made . . . and undue delays in other cases have not been eliminated."

of the status of UNRWA under international law poses for the Foreign Offices a problem of internal communication and discipline. In the ministries, too, successive officials must be acquainted with the nature of UNRWA's relations with government. Governments have tended inevitably to confuse traditional diplomatic status with the functional privileges and immunities appropriate to United Nations personnel, although the difference between them is especially important when applied to UNRWA's locally recruited staff. Finally, law in doctrinal outline is always deceptively simple and logic an often insufficient buffer between rival wills.

COMMERCIAL DISPUTES
AND JURISDICTIONAL IMMUNITY

Law applicable to UNRWA divides unevenly into two categories. The greater is public and the lesser private international law, also known as the conflict of laws. The latter pertains to UNRWA's numerous commercial transactions. In 1959, for example, the Agency was party to 5,000 contracts. Over 4,000 were for commodities, materials, and equipment, while others included an air charter agreement, hospital and insurance agreements, leases for land and buildings, construction contracts, and contracts for transport and services.[8]

Disputes arising from such transactions pose both substantive and jurisdictional questions in an area of law only now evolving in response to growing contact between international organizations and private parties. Private international law provides the criteria for selecting the applicable law in a situation where more than one jurisdiction is involved, a complicated problem for UNRWA because, like other international organizations, it is an "international body corporate" without territorial link to any system of law.*

* The quoted phrase follows a usage employed by C. Wilfred Jenks. He treats this subject, among others, in *The Proper Law of International Organizations* (London: Stevens and Sons Ltd., 1962), Part Three, "Legal Transactions of International Bodies Corporate with Third Parties in the Conflict of Laws," where he deals with such matters as international organization's ownership of property; its contracting for supplies, services, loans, etc.; its liability in tort; and its involvement in other aspects of private law.

The substantive side of commercial disputes is not germane to the present study. Relevant here is the question of the forum appropriate to their settlement. This matter, governed by public international law, is covered by Sections 1 and 2 of the Convention on Privileges and Immunities. Section 1 affirms the juridical personality of the United Nations, ascribing to it (and by the same token to UNRWA) "the capacity: (a) to contract; (b) to acquire and dispose of immovable and movable property; and (c) to institute legal proceedings." Thus, as plaintiff, UNRWA may bring suit in national courts. As defendant, however, it is immune from suit by virtue of Section 2 of the Convention, unless "in any particular case" immunity has been "expressly waived." Waiver—highly exceptional in United Nations practice—must be authorized by the Secretary-General on UNRWA's behalf.

The rigidity of the Convention on this point contrasts with the trend in domestic law away from government immunity from suit and with the same trend in international law in connection with trading activities of governments. Jenks, however, argues that "we are far from the stage at which developments in the law relating to the immunities of States . . . can wisely be applied to international organizations" inasmuch as "States have too much and international organizations too little authority." Not only is there danger of prejudice in some national courts but also likelihood of courts in different states interpreting in different senses the legal effects of acts performed by an international organization. Moreover, states by virtue of the reciprocal nature of their relations "enjoy a substantial measure of protection against . . . denial of justice or unreasonable interference by each other or each other's courts. . . ." International organizations are not in a comparable position. "In the absence of jurisdictional immunities they are completely at the mercy of their member States. . . ."*

* C. Wilfred Jenks, *International Immunities* (London: Stevens and Sons Ltd., 1961), Chapter XXXV and pp. 40–41. Speaking further to the rationale underlying international immunities, Jenks says that their "basic function is to bridle the sovereignty of States in their treatment of international organizations." The significance of these immunities, he suggests, "is comparable in varying ways to that of diplomatic immunities in the historical development of continuous peaceful intercourse among States during the formative periods of

Commercial disputes involving UNRWA, failing amicable settlement, are subject to arbitration in accordance with a standard provision contained in UNRWA contracts: an arbitrator to be chosen by the parties, or, if they cannot agree, appointed by the President of the Court of Arbitration of the International Chamber of Commerce. The standard provision asserts, moreover, that acceptance of an arbitral award does "not constitute waiver by UNRWA of its jurisdictional immunity from judicial process or execution whereso-ever derived."

IMPORTATION AND TRANSPORTATION OF GOODS

Measures adopted by governments for raising revenue and for regulating economic activities to their advantage confront UNRWA with a wide range of problems. The underlying principle is clear: an international body, representative of the larger community, cannot countenance the diverting of its assets to the financial support of a particular government.

Exemption from customs duties of supplies destined for the refugees has seldom been at issue between UNRWA and the host governments.* On the other hand, a variety of charges—lighterage, landing, warehousing, etc.—attach to the complex operations of a sea port. Paid by an intermediate agent, they are passed on to the consignee. Since UNRWA seeks reimbursement of any general tax not attributable to a specific service, it had, as of 1967, outstanding

---

the sixteenth and seventeenth centuries, to that of crown immunity in the supersession of feudalism by the national state, to that of ecclesiastical immunity in the survival of civilization during the dark ages, to that of the immunities of federal instrumentalities in the historical development of certain federal states, to that of parliamentary immunities in guaranteeing the freedom of the people's representatives in relation to the executive . . . , and to that of judicial immunities in contributing to the independence of the judiciary and the rule of law." Ibid., pp. 166–167.

* However, the toils of bureaucracy are evident in the following comment on Syrian practices: "Customs procedures are unduly complex and time-consuming, and customs committees, having quasi-judicial powers have sought to impose fines for delays in completing certain customs formalities on shipments from Lebanon to Jordan." *Annual Report* (A/4213), 1959, pp. 35–36. In 1967 "special problems regarding the importation and movement of supplies" were reported in Syria. *Annual Report* (A/6713), 1967, para. 21.

claims against the Lebanese government of $12,300 for "port dues on tonnage unloaded," and $14,300 for landing fees levied by the Beirut airport when in the early years the Agency used its own United Nations plane.[9] Simliar need to distinguish between a tax and a service charge did not arise at Port Said when it was used to supply Gaza. Except for stevedoring paid for by UNRWA, the costs of receiving and transporting goods to Gaza were assumed by the Egyptian government.

In 1954 Jordan sought to force purchase by UNRWA of domestic products on the ground that, though more expensive, local procurement would help relieve the depressed condition caused by the refugees. After much negotiation the embargo on importation by the Agency of soap and flour was rescinded. Instances have also been reported of host countries protesting importation of certain goods on the ground that the companies supplying them either maintain factories or carry on business in Israel.[10]

A continuously aggravating problem has been the existence of restrictions on the mode of transporting goods from Beirut through Syria to Jordan. Since 1923 the railroad connecting the three countries has benefited from an agreement among them favoring its use. Under new agreements in 1950, to which UNRWA was not a party, transportation by road of supplies destined for refugees was approved with the important exception of wheat, sugar, and their derivatives. Although a reduction in rail charges was to compensate in part for the lower cost of shipping these supplies by truck, UNRWA contends that the restriction greatly increases its costs. As of March 1967, when the governments were last approached on the matter, the resulting claims had accumulated to approximately $1,500,000. Meanwhile, use of the railway has not only entailed many delays but also has obliged UNRWA to assume greater risks, since the railway's responsibility for damages is limited under the regulations "and even more so in practice." In 1960 a reduction of rates decreased the gap between rail and road costs. In addition, the port of Aqaba was used from 1961 to the closure of the Suez Canal in June 1967 for importing bulk commodities into Jordan. However, with Beirut again Jordan's main port of entry since mid 1967, UNRWA's enforced subsidy of the railroad recommenced.

Apart from Lebanon's willingness to negotiate (conditional on a similar willingness on the part of the other two governments), no response as of the fall of 1968 had been elicited by UNRWA's reopening of the issue in March 1967.[11]

Though these issues involving importation and transportation of goods may seem gratuitous, it must be pointed out that the Convention on Privileges and Immunities is not well adapted to UNRWA's circumstances. The relevant provision reads as follows:

Section 7. The United Nations, its assets, income and other property shall be . . .

(b) exempt from customs duties and prohibitions and restrictions on imports and exports in respect of articles imported or exported by the United Nations for its official use. It is understood, however, that articles imported under such exemption will not be sold in the country into which they were imported except under conditions agreed with the government of that country.

Intended primarily to cover office furniture and the other accoutrements of bureaucracy, this language hardly anticipates the movement under United Nations aegis of huge quantities of goods necessary to the welfare of hundreds of thousands of people.* Though the property of the United Nations, the goods are not for its "official use." Yet UNRWA is not the only instance of international organization engaging in this kind of operation. The World Food Program and UNICEF are further examples, among others.

DIRECT TAXES AND EXCISES

Exemption from "all direct taxes" on United Nations "assets, income and other property" is prescribed in Section 7(a) of the Convention on Privileges and Immunities. Accordingly, UNRWA has refused to acquiesce in a government's determination of what is "direct" or "indirect," insisting that international, not domestic, law controls the matter. In this, as in all questions relating to privileges and immunities, the Agency has relied on the intent of Article 105 of the

* On one occasion, however, Syrian customs officials held that "certain kinds of office supplies imported by the Agency could not be admitted free of duty on the grounds that their use was not for the direct benefit of the refugees." Annual Report (A/2470), 1953, para. 240.

Charter as expressed at San Francisco: ". . . if there is one certain principle it is that no member State may hinder in any way the working of the Organization or take any measure the effect of which might be to increase its burdens, financial or other."*

Exemptions from tax on interest earned on UNRWA bank deposits was granted by Lebanon in 1953 and in 1954 by Syria, after the latter adhered to the Convention.[12] The issue seems not to have arisen elsewhere. UNRWA is now exempt from stamp taxes imposed on legal documents in Jordan and Syria, while in Egypt the annual sum resulting from such taxes does not present a substantial issue. In Lebanon a claim of $93,600 had accumulated by 1967 against the government on account of stamp taxes levied on UNRWA's insurance policies.[13] However, as of 1968 the insurance companies were no longer required to pay the tax, which was characterized by the Agency from the outset as "direct," inasmuch as it was added to the cost of a policy.

The Convention states "that the United Nations will not claim exemption from taxes which are, in fact, no more than charges for public utility services. . . ." Hence, while acknowledging obligation to pay for services rendered, UNRWA has protested municipal and other government surcharges attaching to electricity, telephone, and water bills. Accumulated claims in 1967 against Lebanon were $7,000 and against Syria $4,700.[14]

In regard to "excise duties" and "taxes on the sale of movable and immovable property which form part of the price to be paid," the Convention states that "the United Nations will not, as a general rule, claim exemption," with an important qualification:

nevertheless when the United Nations is making important purchases for official use of property on which such duties and taxes have been charged

* UNCIO Documents, Vol. 13, p. 781. The Commissioner-General points out that inasmuch as states are free to raise revenue through either direct or indirect taxation, "to leave the Agency liable to 'indirect taxation,' as defined by the legislation of the host State, could nullify its basic exemptions from taxation. Thus, the Agency has had to reiterate that it is not in this matter subject to the definitions or concepts of the particular system of municipal law of any host State. Similarly, it has had to reiterate that it is not subject, in presenting international claims, to periods of prescription prescribed by the local law." Annual Report (A/6713), 1967, Annex II, para. 5.

or are chargeable, Members will, whenever possible, make appropriate administrative arrangements for the remission or return of the amount of duty or tax.

The qualification is applicable to UNRWA's large-scale purchase of local supplies. In earlier years taxes attaching in the host countries to the sale of such commodities as petroleum products, alcohol, and cement—including customs dues incurred by the vendor—were passed on to UNRWA. Many of the Agency's claims for reimbursement have since been met, while others were still outstanding as of 1967: $24,000 against Lebanon for excise taxes and customs dues on purchases of cement and steel bars, and $58,300 against Syria for excise taxes and customs dues on petroleum products and cement.[15] In recent years such transactions normally have not been taxed, since the Agency was exempt at the time of purchase. Where such exemption is not practical, refunds are generally in order, though there may be a time lag while purchases accumulate and the requisite documentation is often burdensome.

Outstanding claims based on the Convention were recently consolidated and resubmitted by UNRWA to each of the host governments except Egypt, against whom there appears to be no accumulation. Considerable progress resulted in the case of Lebanon. Following presentation of a comprehensive *note verbale* in May 1967, a mixed commission consisting of Agency and government representatives was established, and in July 1968 the Foreign Ministry informed the Agency that the Lebanese government approved in principle UNRWA's claims and was prepared to pay them upon verification of the precise amounts owed—by UNRWA's estimate totaling some $165,000. Thus UNRWA assumes that its

interpretation of the concept of a "direct" tax . . . , its conception of charges for "public utility services" as being charges for specific services rendered which can be identified as such and justified as proportionate to those services . . . , and its view on the non-applicability to international claims of periods of prescription provided in local law were all, in principle, accepted by the Government.[16]

Syria was similarly approached when the Agency in October 1967 proposed the establishment of a mixed commission to examine some $75,000 in accumulated claims. The Foreign Ministry's reply in June 1968 was largely negative, though it proposed that a representative of the Agency explore certain claims with the Customs Administration and that the Agency present a more detailed breakdown of other claims. In 1968, concerned with the unresolved disputes with Syria over interpretation of the Convention on Privileges and Immunities, the Commissioner-General indicated—for the first time in these matters—his readiness to invoke Section 30 of the Convention:

If a difference arises between the United Nations on the one hand and a member on the other, a request shall be made for an advisory opinion on any legal question involved in accordance with Article 96 of the Charter and Article 65 of the Statute of the Court [the International Court of Justice]. The opinion given by the Court shall be accepted as decisive by the parties.

The submission of such legal questions would be at the instance of the General Assembly, which, however, has yet to act in this matter.*

As regards Jordan, consolidated claims from the past, comparatively small, were presented to the Foreign Ministry in April 1968, and in June the government indicated a willingness to discuss them in a mixed commission. A complicating factor, however, has been a counterclaim of some $155,000. Incident to Jordan's embargo in 1954 (noted above), UNRWA contracted to purchase local flour, which led to allegation by each side of breach of contract.

---

* *Annual Report* (A/7213), 1968, Annex II, paras. 16–18, where UNRWA formulates the issues as follows:

(a) Whether the Agency's claims are subject to periods of prescription provided for in Syrian law;

(b) Whether the Agency's claim to exemption from certain taxes on fuel for periods prior to 1 October 1953 is barred by the fact that the Government's accession to the 1946 Convention was, by Syrian law, effective only on that date;

(c) The question of what constitutes a "direct" tax for the purpose of section 7 of the 1946 Convention and whether the Agency is subject to "indirect" taxation;

(d) The meaning of the words "whenever possible" in section 8 of the 1946 Convention as applied to refund of taxes on cement purchased locally;

(e) Whether porterage fees are chargeable to the Agency on trucks carrying exclusively Agency supplies entering the Damascus Customs Zone.

While agreement in principle to arbitrate had been reached in 1959, there was disagreement on whether arbitration should be local or international. The Agency maintained "that in a dispute between a government and an organ of the United Nations, the arbitrator should be chosen on an international level." The Agency reported in 1969 its proposal of a lump-sum settlement whereby it would pay the government $3,400.[17]

INCOME TAX

UNRWA's cooperation in its capacity as employer has been sought by governments in two kinds of situations. One has been the garnishee of wages for the benefit of creditors. The Agency has refused to accept court orders in such cases on the ground that its assets are immune from legal process, and its position in this regard is now understood and accepted. UNRWA by its own administrative measures, including the ultimate sanction of dismissal, endeavors to preclude the possibility of the debtor taking advantage of this immunity, which exists not on his but the Agency's behalf.

The other instance is the governments' request that the Agency collect at the source income tax on compensation received from UNRWA by locally recruited employees. With the initial exception of Jordan, which was a special case, UNRWA refused, contending for one thing that it would be inappropriate for an international agency to incur on behalf of government the administrative expense involved. Additionally, however, the principle opposing diversion of international organization resources to government use applies quite specifically to salaried income.

Section 18(b) of the Convention on Privileges and Immunities states that "Officials of the United Nations shall . . . be exempt from taxation on the salaries and emoluments paid to them by the United Nations." Ample precedent exists for applying this provision to the internationally recruited official whose employment is within a territory other than that of his home country. The exemption of UNRWA's international staff from such taxation in such circumstances has never been questioned.

In drafting the Convention, it was the intent of the General

Assembly that governments make the same exemption for United Nations officials who perform their duties on home ground. This position was adopted after the question had been fully debated and only a few among the hundred states acceding to the Convention have placed a reservation on Section 18(b). Accordingly, exemption from income tax is claimed by UNRWA for its local employees. This position was accepted by Lebanon in 1953, and, in the same year, by Egypt. Negotiations with Syria had not by 1959 reached agreement in principle, though the report for that year stated that "the issue has remained in abeyance and no enforcement action has been attempted." Exemption has in recent years ceased to be disputed.[18]

The case of Jordan is different. There refugees (who constitute the great majority of UNRWA's locally recruited staff in all of the host countries) are citizens whereas in other host countries they are not. Moreover, Jordan did not adhere to the Convention on Privileges and Immunities until January 1958. Only then did the Agency cease to deduct income tax from the salaries of its locally recruited staff. When Jordan sought to collect the tax directly from the employees,[19] UNRWA elicited the intervention of the Secretary-General, after which the government desisted.

When in April 1970 the United States finally acceded to the United Nations Convention on Privileges and Immunities, it reserved the applicability of Section 18(b) to American citizens working for the United Nations within the confines of the United States. Therefore American employees continued after—as well as before—accession, to be subject to American income tax.* Thus Americans employed

---

* Earlier, Congress had enacted a statute on the privileges and immunities of international organizations and their officials (Public Law 291, 79th Congress, 29 December 1945), covering for the most part the same points as those contained in the Convention, but making no provision for the exemption from income tax of Americans who are officials of international organizations and assigned to duties within the United States. In the end, American ratification of the Convention was authorized by the advice and consent of two-thirds of the Senate, whereas previously authorization had been sought in the form of a joint resolution of both the Senate and House of Representatives. The Resolution was approved by a Senate majority, but just as the House was about to consider it, Gubitchev, a Russian member of the UN Secretariat, was arrested in New York (5 March 1949) for espionage. He was subsequently convicted. The House never returned

by UNRWA in the United States are subject to the tax, though few are affected—only such Americans as may be attached to UNRWA's liaison office in New York and those from the field for the duration of any visits to the United States on UNRWA business. Since its salary scale does not take account of any obligation to pay income tax, UNRWA reimburses American employees who have made such payments. Serious discrepancies would otherwise occur, resulting in unequal pay for equal work. The United Nations in New York is confronted with this problem on a large scale and endeavors to meet it through the elaborate device of the Staff Assessment Plan. UNRWA, affected in much less degree, absorbs the loss without instituting similar measures.

---

to a consideration of the Convention. John Kerry King, *International Administrative Jurisdiction* (Brussels: International Institute of Administrative Science, 1952) pp. 60, 193.

IV

Status and Immunities of Staff

THE PRECEDING chapter described UNRWA's struggles to keep clear of regulations adopted by governments for their financial support and economic advantage. Another of its concerns is control over staff, which in 1969 consisted of 110 internationally recruited and 13,000 locally recruited personnel. Freedom of the international civil servant from governmental pressures and enactments is a primary concern of international organization and for UNRWA is a particularly troublesome matter. A complex subject, it will be dealt with here under the headings of international staff, local staff, police power, and labor relations.

INTERNATIONAL STAFF

Distinction between the privileges and immunities of the diplomat and those of the international civil servant (comprising both internationally and locally recruited staff) is not clear-cut in theory and even more ambiguous in practice.

Underlying both the diplomatic and international systems of immunity from territorial authority is practical necessity; in a world of multiple authorities law must provide for coexistence. Starting from this common need, the privileges and immunities accorded the diplomat, which long were the preoccupation of international law, include immunity for him and his family from both civil and criminal jurisdiction, while the status of the international civil servant is more restricted.

Privileges and immunities of the latter are based not on customary international law but on Article 105 of the Charter which says in effect that a United Nations official is entitled to that minimum of freedom required for the independent exercise of his functions. These international privileges and immunities, which are called functional as opposed to diplomatic, are specified further in Section 18 of the United Nations Convention on Privileges and Immunities. The international civil servant, as opposed to the diplomat, does not have personal immunity, criminal or civil, except in respect to his official acts and statements. Thus his family is excluded. His car is not eligible for diplomatic license plates, he may not import goods free of duty except personal belongings at the time of first taking up his post, and he does not normally appear in the diplomatic list.

A qualification is immediately in order. Section 19 of the Convention accords the Secretary-General and Assistant Secretaries-General, as well as their families, "the privileges and immunities, exemptions and facilities accorded to diplomatic envoys, in accordance with international law." This is an acknowledgment of United Nations' membership in the international community, coordinate with that of states. In fact United Nations officials possessing full diplomatic status are more numerous than Section 19 would indicate. It extends, for example, to certain of UNRWA's officials by virtue of local practice or agreement.

The Commissioner-General* and his deputy, whom he appoints, possess diplomatic status in all of the host countries, while members of the Advisory Commission are representatives of governments accredited to each of the host governments. Beyond this point one cannot generalize. In Jordan, Lebanon, and Egypt the Agency's field representative, known as the Director of UNRWA Affairs, has diplomatic status. Prior to June 1967, the latter official doubled as Director of UNRWA Operations in Gaza, where his status was confused because of Cairo's insistence on Gaza's separate identity, though

* The change in name from "Director" occurred in 1962. The latter title is used in the United Nations Secretariat to designate heads of subdivisions within departments. Its application to the head of UNRWA led to confusion, sometimes making difficult the contacting of governments at a high enough level.

Gaza had neither foreign office nor diplomatic corps. In Syria diplomatic status is not accorded; there the Director of UNRWA Affairs possesses only the privileges and immunities of Section 18 of the Convention. In Jordan and Lebanon diplomatic status is granted to all officials of senior rank in the central administration, which means—in addition to the Commissioner-General and his Deputy—the Comptroller, the General Counsel, and the Directors of Administration and Relief, of Health, and of Education.*

The host governments do not accredit representatives to UNRWA. They do, of course, maintain accredited representation with the United Nations in New York, where UNRWA affairs are sometimes dealt with. In Beirut, contact by host governments with UNRWA occurs through their embassies by personnel accredited not to UNRWA but to the Lebanese government. As regards other governments, UNRWA deals with their Beirut embassies, particularly in the case of the non-Arab members of the Advisory Commission.

It would appear that about ten of UNRWA's staff—out of some 110 internationally recruited personnel—possess diplomatic status in one or more of the host countries. Such status facilitates negotiation with government and is undoubtedly justified as serving a "functional" need. At the same time, governments are tolerantly disposed toward the expansion of the privileges and immunities of the international civil servant into the area of those accorded the diplomat. In Syria the Director of UNRWA Affairs, though possessing only international status, appeared (as of 1966) in the diplomatic list, as did two colleagues also internationally recruited. Quite anomalous was inclusion at that time of the Field Operations Offi-

---

* UNRWA's special agreements with Jordan and Lebanon give particular attention to the question of diplomatic versus international status. Thus Jordan granted "the Director of the Agency, the members of his Advisory Commission and the senior officials of the Agency as may be agreed upon in writing . . . the privileges and immunities normally granted . . . to Diplomatic Envoys. . . ." *United Nations Treaty Series*, Vol. 120, No. 394, 14 March 1951.

Lebanon agreed that "a very limited number of senior officials . . . will be granted diplomatic status (four officials, plus the UNRWA Representative to Lebanon)." Ibid., Vol. 202, No. 2729, 26 November 1954. In subsequent practice Lebanon has gone beyond the limitation originally specified.

cer, a locally recruited Syrian national. There is also a tendency to relax the restriction whereby the international official may import goods duty-free only on first arriving at a post. Lebanon permits free importation for a year and admits motor cars duty-free throughout the entire period of an owner's employment with the Agency. Resale is permitted in accordance with the same arrangements applicable to members of diplomatic missions, though in practice procedural difficulties are often encountered.[1]

The United Nations considers the doctrine of *persona non grata* as inapplicable to its officials. They are not sent and accredited to a government in a way analogous to the bilateral exchange of representatives between governments, whereby the latter are subject to the restraint of reciprocity. Accordingly, the United Nations asks to be fully apprised of a government's allegation of a UN official's unsuitability and insists on judging the matter itself. Nevertheless, governments on occasion have interfered arbitrarily with the disposition by the Commissioner-General of his international staff.

In 1956, prior to Israeli occupation of the Gaza Strip, the complications over Gaza's legal status contributed to a particularly difficult period in UNRWA's relations with Egypt. Reporting "pressures to control our operations," the Commissioner-General, Henry Labouisse, continued in a statement before the Special Political Committee of the General Assembly:

But there were incidents concerning personnel of even more serious character. A total of four UNRWA international officials . . . were declared *personae non gratae* without apparent reason; seven other Agency officials were refused permission to enter the Gaza Strip on Agency business; some UNRWA officials . . . were prevented from leaving the Strip, whether on earned leave or on official business; by the end of October, the Egyptian Government had not yet answered "yes" or "no" to the Agency request of 14 May 1956 to bring to Gaza the official I had selected to be our head representative there.[2]

After return of the Egyptian administration to Gaza in March 1957, the Egyptian authorities objected to UNRWA's employing nationals of countries with which Egypt had severed relations.

However, the Agency rejected the complaint and insisted on its freedom of choice under Articles 100 and 101 of the Charter.*

The 1956 hostilities also precipitated a serious incident in Syria, reported by the Commissioner-General as follows:

On 5 November, military police officials made a sudden and unauthorized entry into the UNRWA premises in Damascus, took from their offices the Agency's representative in Syria and another senior officer [of French and British nationality, respectively], and placed them in cells, where they were detained, having first been deprived of their neckties, belts and shoes. They were released after about six hours on condition that they leave the country immediately. . . . In one case, it was charged that the official had lighted a match during an air raid alert; in the other case, the official was charged with having made derogatory remarks about a political leader. No evidence was produced to substantiate the charges, which were flatly denied by the two UNRWA officers.

The Secretary-General protested to the Syrian government, and to vindicate the principle of UNRWA's autonomy, the two officials briefly returned to their posts in Syria the beginning of May 1957.†

Concerning such incidents, the Commissioner-General said that "an important principle is at issue, the status of a United Nations agency and its personnel." If a particular host government is unwilling to permit the Agency "to decide freely upon its own staff requirements and to employ, utilize and terminate personnel according to its best judgement," then, he suggested, the General

* *Annual Report* (A/3686), 1957, Annex H, para. 12. In the following year, the Agency instructed its international officials in Gaza to disregard a questionnaire "amounting to a form of alien registration." The matter was settled by an understanding that Agency officials would fill in only the normal form used in applying for visas. *Annual Reports* (A/3931), 1958, Annex H, para. 17; and (A/4213), 1959, Annex H, para. 15.

† *Annual Reports* (A/3212/Add.1), 1956, para. 35; and (A/3686), 1957, Annex H, para. 21. In a statement to the Special Political Committee in February 1957 (A/SPC/9), the Commissioner-General reported another incident involving Syria: the expulsion of UNRWA's head field nursing officer "on the charge that she had entered the country illegally—this, in spite of the fact that she carried the documents normally accepted for entry into Syria of UNRWA staff on official duty. This latest incident has also been protested by the Secretary-General. . . . A reply has been received saying that this incident was the result of a misunderstanding."

Assembly should make some other arrangement, "one conceivable solution" being that a government could itself assume full operational responsibility, asking the United Nations only for technical and financial assistance as needed."[3]

Recently new difficulties have occurred in Syria over the freedom of movement of international staff. In 1968 an international official was "prevented from travel to headquarters . . . though provided with a United Nations *laissez-passer*. . . . " An initial protest was followed by another of February 1969—both unanswered as of that fall.[4]

Relation of its international staff to government is not UNRWA's sole concern regarding the status of such personnel. There is the further question of its conditions of employment. Whereas employment in UNICEF and UNHCR, as noted in Chapter II, is governed by the same Staff Regulations and Rules as obtain in the United Nations proper, UNRWA's conditions of employment, though they now approximate those of the parent organization, still diverge in one important respect. New York can offer career appointments with termination only for stated cause, whereas UNRWA's appointments of international staff (apart from officials seconded or on loan from other United Nations organizations) are, at most, "indefinite" in duration, and subject to termination on thirty days notice if, in the judgment of the Commissioner-General, "such action would be in the interest of the Agency."*

Formerly, the chief difference between UNRWA and the United Nations as regards employment was the Agency's nonparticipation

* UNRWA International Staff Regulations 9.1 and 9.3. In the fields of education and health UNRWA is heavily dependent on the interorganization agreement within the United Nations family governing loans of personnel, secondment, and transfers. The loan arrangement is most commonly used by UNRWA; the employee stays on the payroll of the parent organization in all respects, though in rare instances UNRWA may reimburse the lending organization. A seconded official, on leave from his parent organization, is placed on the pay roll of the receiving organization. In the case of transfers, the official is contractually separated from the releasing organization. All his past service falls under the Staff Regulations and Rules of the receiving organization. Thus transfers out of UNRWA are stimulated while transfers in are inhibited, inasmuch as UNRWA cannot offer permanent appointments or in case of redundancy assure absorption elsewhere in the United Nations system.

in the United Nations Joint Staff Pension Fund. However, arrangements were made in 1961 enabling the Agency's international staff to qualify for associate participation in the Fund, restricted to disability and survivor's benefits. Finally an agreement was reached with the Fund entitling UNRWA's international staff to full participation, retroactive to January 1961. The employee pays seven percent of his "pensionable remuneration," and his organization fourteen percent.

LOCAL STAFF

For reasons of economy and convenience, every establishment of international organization (and of diplomacy) recruits local personnel to assist it. To an extraordinary degree UNRWA is dependent on such personnel, which it employs in the thousands, drawn from the very group whose welfare is the object of its mission.

Precise determination of which United Nations personnel are entitled to the privileges and immunities of Section 18 of the Convention is contained in General Assembly resolution 76(I) of 7 December 1946 which states that "all members of the staff of the United Nations" are so entitled "with the exception of those who are recruited locally and are assigned to hourly rates." Few UNRWA employees are excluded by the formula, since virtually all of the Agency's locally recruited staff, including manual laborers, are paid by the month or in a few instances by the day. In keeping with the terminology of the Convention, all are "officials" of the United Nations.

Periodically the Secretary-General in accord with Section 17 of the Convention submits to member governments a list of United Nations officials, which in 1964, for example, contained 12,300 names. Listed in the Secretary-General's submission are locally recruited staff within the meaning of resolution 76(I), except for UNRWA. The latter's international staff is listed, but its local staff—solely for reasons of economy, the Secretary-General states—is excluded. Accordingly, UNRWA submits to the concerned governments its own list of locally recruited staff, which in 1964 came to 12,900 persons.

UNRWA's dependence on local personnel is indicated not only

by number but by level of employment. The 12,344 local staff employed as of February 1966 included 633 in the professional category, 2,038 in general administration, and 5,254 teachers. The remaining 4,419 were laborers. Customary international law offers little guidance concerning the status of local staff, while the conventional law of the United Nations does not go much beyond the broad principle of functional immunity contained in Article 105 of the Charter. Section 18 of the Convention is relevant, but the particularized privileges and immunities contained therein were designed primarily for internationally rather than locally recruited personnel. The general proposition on which UNRWA must rely is that such authorized actions of its local staff as may impinge on government's responsibility for law and order and the general welfare are without presumption of employee liability but are matters to be dealt with by the Agency at the official level.

Application of resolution 76(I) to its exceptional circumstances requires of UNRWA considerable expenditure of legal talent and effort, for the Agency is, in effect, creating its own precedents. Yet the exertion is warranted; many of the local staff exercise a high level of responsibility, while the laborer, too, performs tasks important to the Agency. Moreover, UNRWA is unequally matched; to submit to territorial authority in selected instances would invite encroachment in still others.*

The privileges and immunities of employees of international organization—whether of its international or local staff—touch territorial

---

* Status of local staff posed no problem for UNRWA's predecessor, UNRPR, which arranged for the International Red Cross Committee, the League of Red Cross Societies, and the American Friends Service Committee to work in the field. Although many Palestinian refugees were employed—paid for by UNRPR—their employers were private organizations, and international law was not involved. But this arrangement was temporary; the private agencies left when UNRWA took over. Designed for emergency tasks and paying the cost of their own administrative staff, they could not continue indefinitely.

Some tasks UNRWA farms out to entrepreneurs. Were it to use trucks of its own to haul supplies from Beirut to Syria and Jordan, the trucks would be obliged to return empty. It is more economical to go through a contractor, though his taxes may not always be a deductable part of UNRWA's cost. The arrangement is considered advantageous even though it is not feasible to specify the employment of refugees.

authority at two especially sensitive points. Police power is one and labor relations, the other. For UNRWA, because it employs local personnel in large numbers, delineation of these areas of immunity is particularly onerous.

UNRWA AND POLICE POWER

Whereas traffic violations are the main occasion for confrontation between other international organizations and the policeman, UNRWA's encounter with officials responsible for law and order are rather more varied, though UNRWA, too, has contributed its quota to the classic repertory of traffic episodes.* Carrying out their duties (as of 31 May 1967) in 54 camps sheltering 533,000 persons, bitter against fate, UNRWA's personnel, themselves refugees, easily become involved in situations affecting the peace and policy of the countries of refuge.

Lacking territorial authority, UNRWA cannot assume responsibility for security in the camps; it has machinery neither for police protection nor law enforcement. Nor could it in any event risk involvement in the complicated politics of the Palestine question. Hence, it is not only proper but imperative that the governments assume responsibility for security. UNRWA holds them liable in the matter, bringing claims where, in its judgment, the protection of property and persons falls short of what the international law of state responsibility requires.† However, negotiation in none of these

---

* In accord with an early action taken by the General Assembly applicable to drivers of official motor cars of the United Nations, UNRWA insures its drivers against third party risks. When incidents have resulted in the impounding of its vehicles, the Agency has protested vigorously on the ground of immunity from legal process. *Annual Reports* (A/2171), 1952, p. 44; (A/2470), 1953, para. 236; and (A/2171), 1952, p. 44. As for the drivers, UNRWA does not invoke immunity, though it protests if arbitrary detention results in hampering unduly UNRWA business. Fault and penalty are for court determination. In extenuating circumstances, the Agency may provide an accused driver with legal counsel.

† Riots in Jordan in 1956 resulted in loss and damage to property belonging to the Agency and its officials. The Agency submitted claims of nearly $50,000, directing the government's attention "to the well-established principle of international law which imposes a special duty of protection of the property of diplomatic missions, of public international organizations, and of their staffs."

instances has yet resulted in a settlement or in agreement on appropriate arbitral procedures.*

Annual Reports (A/3212), 1956, p. 40; and (A/4213), 1959, Annex H, para. 26.

A claim of $69,000 was submitted to Egypt "for damages suffered to Agency property during 1955 due to local riots following an incursion of Israel forces into the Gaza strip." Ibid., Annex H, para. 17. A second claim arising from similar causes was submitted for $1,970 in 1962. "Both claims have been rejected . . . on the grounds that the damage was not due to a lack of adequate precautions by the government. . . . The Agency has never accepted the rejection of its claims." Annual Report (A/7613), 1967, Annex II, para. 18.

In Lebanon, although "the authorities have shown goodwill and a desire to fulfill their obligations, the protection afforded has not always conformed with international law and practice. Some staff members have been attacked, Agency property has been damaged or looted, and there has been considerable interference . . . with the activities of the Agency. . . . " Annual Report (A/4213), 1959 Annex H, para. 29.

The Agency reported in 1956 that it "was the subject of virulent attacks in the Egyptian and Syrian press," and it also protested "a statement by a Minister of the Syrian government that the Agency's policy was to exterminate the refugees. This accusation, in addition to its defamatory nature, tends to encourage unrest and thus is clearly contrary to the Government's duty under international law to protect the Agency's property and the security of its officials." Annual Report (A/3212), 1956, Annex G, para. 25.

* Claims against Israel have been based on acts of government, itself, rather than on alleged lack of due diligence in controlling the acts of others: $3,400 for destruction of an Agency school caused by an incursion (declared by the Mixed Armistice Commission to constitute a breach of the Armistice Agreement) of Israeli forces into Jordan in September 1956; $310,000 in Gaza arising out of destruction of UNRWA property and the loss of eight lives among local staff members in the course of Israel's Sinai campaign in November 1956; and $62,500 arising from a collision in Gaza involving an Israeli military vehicle, killing one UNRWA staff member and injuring two others. These claims were partially settled in 1960 and the remainder in a lump-sum agreement in January 1968, including a counter-claim of $56,000 by Israel against UNRWA for services rendered. Annual Reports (A/3696), 1957, Annex H, paras. 4, 8, 10; (A/3931), 1958, Annex H, para. 5; (A/6713), 1967, Annex II, paras. 22, 23; and (A/7213), 1968, Annex II, para. 27.

New claims based on acts of government have arisen out of the June 1967 hostilities. Against Israel a claim of $709,000 for "damage to and loss of Agency property" was submitted 31 December 1968. Further claims against Israel are still to be made "in respect of damage or losses suffered by Agency staff which the Agency has obligations to meet, and for losses arising out of military incidents since the hostilities." Unclear, since the argument employed by UNRWA is not known, is the appropriateness of military necessity in rebuttal. The same question holds for "battle damage" to the Agency's Jerusalem Field

On the other hand, UNRWA refuses to recognize the validity of police intervention in two kinds of situations: (1) when it affects the inviolability of UNRWA's premises or communications, and (2) when it arbitrarily restrains the freedom of UNRWA's employees to perform their duties.

Inviolability

It should be emphasized that the refugee camps are not UNRWA premises. No more than refugees outside the camps do those inside bear a special legal relation to UNRWA. Whether in Jordan where they are citizens or in Lebanon where they are aliens, refugees are subject to territorial jurisdiction. However, they may rebel as they did in the fall of 1969, when fourteen of fifteen camps in Lebanon were taken over by commandos in the name of the Palestinian people.*

Palestinian claim to recognition as an entity is for the governments immediately concerned and for the General Assembly to consider. It would be inadmissible for the Commissioner-General to prejudge the question by withholding UNRWA's services in the Lebanese situation referred to, unless government were to enjoin otherwise or the General Assembly were to decide that withdrawal of services was warranted in order to preclude the possibility of an indirect subsidy to the guerrillas. While the Commissioner-General would have to defer to government in seeking to suppress insurrection, his own initiative to withhold services would require backing from the General Assembly, inasmuch as administrative decision in a matter of such moment can hardly substitute for legislative responsibility.†

Office for which $84,000 is claimed, half from Israel and half from Jordan. Similarly based is a claim of $12,000—halved between Israel and Egypt—for destruction of nine Agency schools in Gaza. *Annual Report* (A/7614), 1969, para. 159.

* New York *Times*, 13 November 1969. The correspondant visited a camp where a Palestinian flag was flying beside the Lebanese, the guard at the gate was a commando, and authority in the camp was entirely in the hands of the commandos. The police station at the edge of the camp was vacant and the furniture in the army post smashed. He reported that military training under the commandos was in progress in and around the camp.

† Referring to the events in Lebanon, the Commissioner-General, Laurence Michelmore, delineated the respective roles in the camps of the Agency and

Unlike the camps, buildings used by the Agency for administration are international premises and the principle of their inviolability has been asserted in a number of annual reports. During events in Lebanon in the fall of 1969, commandos occupied six of UNRWA's administrative buildings in the camps. Such acts move in the direction of the refugees assuming responsibility for their own affairs and are not compatible with an UNRWA presence. In vain, the Commissioner-General has asked the Lebanese government to arrange for the return of the buildings.[5]

Communications and records are also inviolable. In 1957 Egypt desisted after representations from having a censor present when the Agency was handling its mail pouch in Gaza. In Jordan in 1958, following arrest of a staff member for alleged complicity in the bombing of public buildings, the Agency's mailbags and premises were searched. Also a staff member was arrested when he refused to turn over Agency records. In these instances the Agency apparently arrived at a satisfactory understanding with government. Another kind of episode relates to inviolability in the context of exemption from labor law. Thus the Agency protested when Syrian

---

government. The latter, he pointed out to the Special Political Committee, is responsible for maintenance of law and order, the administration of justice, issuing permits for new building construction . . . and so on," while UNRWA is responsible for "roads and paths, water supply points, sanitation, health centres, schools, food distribution, supplementary feeding, distribution of kerosene, blankets and clothing to especially needy families, and, in some camps, youth activities centres and women's centres." UNRWA, he declared, "maintains control over the assistance it provides up to the point where the assistance is received by the intended beneficiaries. . . . In the case of two-thirds of UNRWA's program, it is quite obvious that the assistance is actually received and used by the persons for whom it is intended—children attending UNRWA schools, students in training centres, persons given medical assistance in the health centres, children drinking milk or eating hot meals. . . . The remaining third of the programme is the distribution of food rations. Here, too, rations which have been previously authorized for the eligible members of each family are placed in the hands of the head of family, who is required to identify himself as the authorized recipient. I am satisfied that the integrity of these UNRWA operations has been maintained, that UNRWA assistance goes, as it is intended, to needy refugees, and that it is not diverted to other purposes." A/SPC/PV.665, 17 November 1969.

A similar problem in different circumstances arose in Gaza prior to 1967. See below, p. 96.

officials were sent "to inspect its activities and working conditions in its premises." Subsequently in Egypt "there was . . . a new demand by the Labor Office in Port Said to inspect Agency staff records." It was dropped following UNRWA's appeal to Cairo.[6]

Restraint of Persons

Restraint by government authority of the personal liberty of members of UNRWA's local staff poses an interesting problem in international law. We noted that the privileges and immunities of the international civil servant particularized in Section 18 of the Conventon are considerably less extensive than those of the diplomat. Yet in an important respect they are greater. Whereas the diplomat has special status only in relation to alien authority, the functional privileges and immunities of the international civil servant apply against his own as against any other government. Relevant in this connection are immunity from income tax, national service, and legal process for official acts and statements.

Section 18(b) states that officials of the United Nations "shall . . . be exempt from taxation on the salaries and emoluments paid to them by the United Nations." We have dealt with this matter under the fiscal immunities of the Agency. It is not an immunity that turns on the freedom of the individual staff member from personal restraint.

Section 18(c) of the Convention provides without qualification for the immunity of international officials from national service obligations. The practicability of so absolute an exemption is questionable. Although the national civil servant in times of crisis is often exempted from military service and identical considerations may operate in the case of the international civil servant, in neither instance does unqualified immunity appear justified. More practicable than Section 18(c) of the United Nations Convention is the formula contained in the Convention on Privileges and Immunities of the Specialized Agencies which confines exemption to those officials who, by reason of their status, have been placed upon a list compiled by the executive head of the specialized agency and approved by the government concerned, while other officials are accorded only such temporary deferment as may be necessary to avoid interruption of essential work.*

Surprisingly few of the hundred states thus far party to the United Nations Convention have reserved the point on national service obligations, and none of the governments here in question is among them. Yet circumstances were such in the host countries that up to 1965 UNRWA was not much troubled with the problem, to which the annual reports make only fleeting reference.

Since the Lebanese armed services are volunteer rather than conscript, immunity from national service obligations claimed by UNRWA for its employees has never been at issue in Lebanon, where, in any event, their alien status makes the drafting of refugees unlikely. In Jordan, where they are citizens, compulsory service was not instituted until 1967. Previously, registration of its employees in the Jordanian national guard was protested by UNRWA.[7] Yet, unless an UNRWA staff member were to bear arms, it is difficult to see the basis for objection. So long as the working hours of the Agency are not encroached upon, lectures or other forms of civil-defense training would seem to be permissible. The political overtone of such exercises is another matter, though as a passive participant an UNRWA employee, not himself engaged in exhortation, would seem not to compromise his position as an international official.

In Syria the situation is different. There the refugee is deemed to hold Palestinian citizenship, but an Act of 10 July 1956 removes all legal obstacles to his entry into commerce, the professions, the civil service, or employment of any other kind. As counterpart of this high degree of assimilation, he has been made subject to military obligations. In 1959 the Agency reported that differences existed with the Syrian government over the national service ob-

---

* Section 20 of the Specialized Agencies Convention, *UN Treaty Series*, Vol. 33, no. 521. The disruptive effect of the Swiss militia system on the League of Nations Secretariat seems to have had a particular influence on the drafting of the United Nations Convention. King, op. cit., pp. 47–48. For further treatment of immunity from national service see Jenks, *International Immunities*, pp. 124–127; and Kulfit Ahluwalia, *The Legal Status, Privileges and Immunities of the Specialized Agencies* (The Hague: Martinus Nijhoff, 1964), pp. 122–127.

ligations of its employees but that the matter was abeyance.[8] The issue is still unresolved.

As for Gaza, the question of conscription into the Egyptian army never arose. The Strip was not annexed by Egypt, hence local rather than Egyptian law prevailed, and prior to 1965 Gaza residents were not subject to military service.

The founding in 1964 of the Palestine Liberation Organization, based on Palestinian Arabs outside Israel, introduced a new element in all the countries of refuge, foreshadowing the commando movement of the post 1967 period. Its object was "to regain the homeland" and its program was military as well as political, including recruitment and training of a Palestinian Liberation Army. In Lebanon this was without consequence for UNRWA, since the government refused to legislate military training for Palestinians. In Jordan the threat of a state within a state produced a crisis which in the summer of 1966 led to an acrimonious break between Amman and the governing body of the Palestine Liberation Organization. In Syria the advent of the Palestinian Liberation Army meant, merely, that Palestinians in the Syrian army were henceforth placed under their own command.

In Gaza, on the other hand, the situation changed radically. On 10 March 1965 a conscription law, voted by the local Legislative Council, was promulgated by the Governor-General with no exemption for UNRWA staff. The Agency has not indicated what negotiations may have ensued between it and the Gaza authorities. What is known is that, when conscription of its staff occurs in Gaza or elsewhere, UNRWA's practice is not to grant leave but to terminate the employee.

Actually UNRWA's chief problem arising out of Gaza's conscription law was of a different order, entailing a more difficult confrontation with territorial authority than one involving staff. Since the Gaza authorities refused to inform the Agency as to who the recruits were, the heads of refugee families from which they came continued to draw rations for individuals who, at least for the period of their military service, ceased to be in need. The strong objections to this situation voiced in the United States Congress were doubtless less concerned with the cost of some 10,000 to

14,000 rations than with the indirect subsidization by UNRWA of the Palestinian Liberation Army.* The United States government called attention to the situation in the Special Political Committee of the United Nations; it also protested directly to the Commissioner-General.[9] The latter arranged a compromise with the Arab governments, which was announced to the General Assembly in the fall of 1966. The Arab League agreed to pay $150,000 annually to meet the cost "of all rations consumed by the young men in question."[10] Implementation, however, was overtaken by the June War.

We come now to the most basic immunity that operates against the authority of an international official's own government. While exemption of salaries and emoluments from taxation is of great financial significance to international organization and simplifies for it the attainment of equity in the compensation of a multinational staff, and while exemption of its officials from national service obligations is in times of crisis a matter of consequence, more fundamental is Section 18(a) of the Convention whereby officials of the United Nations "shall be immune from legal process in respect of words spoken and written and all acts performed by them in their official capacity."

The vexed question at issue is who decides the official or private character of a particular act. For the international official of highest rank the problem is solved by the blanket immunity of diplomatic status. Less expedient and more satisfactory would be judicial scrutiny of official acts by an international court. This more sophisticated solution is available only in the European Communities, where there is no complete jurisdictional immunity for even the most senior officials, but where the Court of Justice of the European Communities may determine reparation for any unwarranted acts by an employee.[11]

* U.S., Congress, Senate, Subcommittee of the Senate Committee, *Hearings on the Judiciary to Investigate Problems connected with Refugees and Escapees,* 89th Cong., 2nd Sess. (Washington: U.S. Government Printing Office, 1966). For observations of Senators Edward Kennedy and Jacob Javits, see pp. 58 and 83 respectively, and for comments of Assistant Secretary Joseph Sisco, p. 75. The Subcommittee, prior to the beginning of these hearings in June 1966, had sent two members of its staff to look at UNRWA's operations on the ground. Senator Kennedy, too, had recently visited the Middle East.

Neither solution has ever been provided for the great body of international officials. For them ambiguity is unrelived as to whether territorial authority or that of international organization is to be conclusive. Though UNRWA has confronted the problem in scores of instances, reference to it is rare in the annual reports.*

An UNRWA employee no less than any other is subject to government's exercise of police power in suppression of crime. Indeed, lack of immunity from criminal jurisdiction is an important respect in which the international civil servant differs from the diplomat. Moreover, the Secretary-General has "the duty to waive the immunity of any official in any case where, in his opinion, the immunity would impede the course of justice and can be waived without prejudice to the interests of the United Nations."† It is

---

* Stating that the Jordanian Government failed on occasion "to accord full recognition to the legal status of the Agency and its officials," the 1956 report (A/3212, Annex G, para. 18) cited two cases in which proceedings were brought against Agency officials who "unwittingly trespassed on the property of third parties during the course of their official duties. . . . Fortunately, in both cases an amicable settlement was made whereby the plaintiffs withdrew their claims." The trespass in one instance seems to have been occasioned by the decision of a camp leader to move residents of his camp to higher ground because of a rain storm.

The following two episodes will further assist the reader to visualize the kind of situations that arise. In both instances one asks, Who determines at what point whether immunity is applicable?

In Jordan to curse another's religion is a punishable offense. Such a charge at the instance of a refugee was brought in court against a camp leader. If the charge was trumped up in animus, would the camp leader possess jurisdictional immunity by virtue of being an UNRWA official?

In Syria a charge of intended theft was brought (not by UNRWA) against two UNRWA employees who were observed moving barrels of powdered milk from a warehouse to a loading dock. If the movement was in connection with the normal process of distribution, not to be intrepreted as preparatory to misappropriation, would immunity apply?

† Section 20 of the United Nations Convention, which also declares that "Privileges and immunities are granted to officials in the interests of the United Nations and not for the personal benefit of the individuals themselves." Further, Section 21 obliges the United Nations to "co-operate at all times with the appropriate authorities of Members to facilitate the proper administration of justice, secure the observance of police regulations and prevent the occurrence of any abuse in connection with the privileges, immunities and facilities mentioned in this Article." Moreover, Section 29 states that the United Nations "shall make provision for appropriate modes of settlement of: . . . disputes

not, then, the employee's but the international organization's relation to territorial authority that is governed by international law. Yet, because UNRWA is not an ordinary employer, its employee may precipitate a triangular relationship involving himself, the Agency, and government, whereas an identical act of a privately employed person would entail only a bilateral relation between him and his government.

International organization cannot countenance an arrest within its premises.* Moreover, it will seek from government the information—indeed would wish to be informed before hand—concerning the arrest of an employee, wherever effected.† Further, interna-

---

involving any official of the United Nations who by reason of his official position enjoys immunity, if immunity has not been waived by the Secretary-General."

* For example, security police on 25 May 1949 entered the premises of the United Nations Information Center in Prague to take for interrogation Adolph Murdock, a Czech national employed by the Center. The police retired at the insistence of the Director of the Center, who protested to the Foreign Office and informed the Secretary-General. The latter instructed the Director to ask for the reasons prompting the attempted arrest and gave permission for Murdock to remain on the premises, which he did. The Foreign Office apologized for violation of the premises; and it explained that Murdock was wanted for questioning in connection with "suspicion of contacts with a group under trial for anti-state activities." On 21 June the Secretary-General further instructed that specific assurance be sought from the Foreign Office that any questioning of Murdock not refer to acts performed by him or words spoken or written in his official capacity. These assurances were given to the UN Information Center and Murdock left its premises 27 June. Carol McCormick Crosswell, *Protection of International Personnel Abroad* (New York: Oceana Publications, 1952), pp. 63-65.

† In the fall of 1949 the Korean Government arrested two of its nationals, a clerk and dispatcher employed by UNCOK. In a cable to the Foreign Minister, the Secretary-General stated that the head of mission should be informed beforehand of any impending arrest or interrogation; that assurance should be given that arrest pertain to actions not official in character; that questioning should not touch on United Nations matters; and that persons should be treated in accordance with universally recognized principles of justice. In its reply the Foreign Ministry said the evidence showed that United Nations employment was used by the men as a cover for conspiring with fellow Koreans engaged in terrorism, murder, sabotage, and espionage and informed the Secretary-General that the courts would determine guilt. The Ministry asserted that the circumstances did not permit advance notice of the arrests. The Secretary-General raised no further objections. Ibid., pp. 65-67.

tional organization insists on the right to visit a staff member held in custody.* Finally, international organization, like any other interested party, may provide a prosecutor with information that it deems relevant for determining whether a charge should be pursued or dropped. But it may do more. As a subject of international law coequal with the state, it has access to avenues which are inaccessible to ordinary employers. It may seek foreign office intervention. An agency like UNRWA may also choose in a particular case, through its annual report, to present its point of view in the forum of the United Nations.

In addition to allegations of ordinary crime as an occasion for government intervention against UNRWA employees, there also may be the charge of mixing in politics. The refugee community has on occasion been a major threat to the regimes in Jordan and Lebanon, and in Israel it is the object of strict surveillance. Needless to say, divorce from politics is prerequisite to immunity from territorial authority of the acts and statements of the international civil servant.

* A memorandum of 10 July 1963 internal to the United Nations Secretariat attached special importance to this right as a necessary concomitant of the Organization's right to diplomatic protection of its staff. This right was established by the International Court of Justice in its advisory opinion on Reparation for Injuries Suffered in the Service of the United Nations. It is clear, the memorandum states, "that the United Nations has the right to visit and converse with one of its staff members in custody or detention whenever there is any possibility that the United Nations or the staff member in the performance of his duties may have been injured through the violation by a State of any of its obligations either toward the United Nations or toward the person concerned.... The mere fact that there is no obvious connection between the reason given for the detention by the State and the staff member's duties is insufficient to nullify the right of the United Nations to visit. . . . Even if in fact there is no connection between the staff member's duties and the reason for the detention, the United Nations should nevertheless be allowed to visit... to ascertain... whether the person is being treated with humanity and with full observance of an international standard of human rights. This is particularly true when the presence of the staff member in what is to him a foreign country is due to his employment by the United Nations.... This broader scope of protection by the United Nations follows from the undesirability—stressed by the International Court of Justice in its advisory opinion on Reparation for Injuries—that staff members should have to rely on protection of their own States." *United Nations Juridical Yearbook,* 1963, pp. 191–192.

UNRWA must satisfy itself as to the abstention of its chosen agents from political activity. An oath to serve the interests of the Agency is required of the international staff members.* Local employees, although now they no longer are required to subscribe to an oath of loyalty, are subject to the Staff Regulations and Staff Rules which are applicable to locally recruited personnel and contain strict provisions on political activity.†

Often government's disapproval of political activity by members of UNRWA's staff is no less than the Agency's disapproval. Government's concern indeed extends beyond to the whole body of refugees within its jurisdiction. But this coincidence need not occur. Unlike their mutual condemnation of criminal acts, the Agency and government may have different attitudes toward political activity. Actions by local staff which are inadmissible from the Agency's standpoint may be viewed with approbation by government. Of course, political activities of refugees not on its staff are outside UNRWA's province.

Should policing of political activity by government point to the arrest of a member of UNRWA's staff, the Agency would, in accord with United Nations practice, wish to have prior notification with a view to ensuring that officials on duty were not interfered with except for reasons which UNRWA, itself, would want to take

* "I solemnly swear (undertake, affirm, promise) to exercise in all loyalty, discretion and conscience the functions entrusted to me as an official of the United Nations Relief and Works Agency for Palestinian Refugees, to discharge these functions and regulate my conduct with the interests of the Agency only in view, and not to seek or accept instructions in regard to the performance of my duties from any government or other authority external to the Agency."

† "1. Staff members shall not engage in any political activity which is inconsistent with their obligations under the Staff Regulations or with their status as staff members of the Agency. Accordingly, while retaining their right to vote and their own personal convictions, staff members shall not publicly support or publicly associate themselves with any political party, movement, group or candidate or with any political controversy, but shall so regulate their conduct as to maintain and protect at all times the impartiality and fundamentally apolitical character of the Agency.

"2. A staff member who engages in political activity contrary to the provisions of the Staff Regulations may on this ground alone be declared guilty of serious misconduct ... and be summarily dismissed. ... "

into account in order to determine whether the staff member was fit and suitable for United Nations employment.*

Detention of local staff for security reasons in the occupied territories has seriously interfered with UNRWA's work. The 1969 report states that in Gaza for the twelve-month period under review fifty-four staff members were arrested, forty of whom were detained for varying periods and then released, eight sentenced to imprisonment, and six still detained as of 30 June 1969. On the West Bank a headmistress and a doctor were deported, four other local staff were sentenced by military courts, eight detained and then released, while seven were still under detention.[12] Since the June War, detentions of UNRWA staff by fall 1969 totaled 128 in Gaza and forty-nine on the West Bank.†

---

* Syria, a government with which UNRWA has often had difficult relations, took a backward step, as earlier noted, when by decree of 1 August 1967 it excluded locally recruited personnel from all immunities except taxation on salaries. In January 1969 two senior members of UNRWA's local staff, under Syrian arrest for twenty-four hours, were interrogated in relation to their official duties. The Agency's protest was still unanswered as of fall 1969. *Annual Report* (A/7614), 1969, para. 14.

† *Letter* from Commissioner-General to Chairman of the Special Political Committee (A/SPC/136), 10 December 1969. Speaking generally of UNRWA's practice as regards detentions, the Commissioner-General informed the Special Political Committee that "the UNRWA field director takes up each case with the military government authorities as soon as the arrest is known, to ascertain the grounds for the arrest and to determine whether the alleged offense has any relation to the performance of official duties and consequently whether any question arises in connection with the Convention on Privileges and Immunities. . . .

"In . . . cases . . . which do not appear to raise questions under the Convention on Privileges and Immunities, the Agency has the concern of a good employer for its staff, and is interested in having cases brought to trial quickly so that staff members may return to their duties. The UNRWA field directors personally also endeavour to visit staff members in prison.

"The Agency must also inquire whether there is evidence of actions by a staff member that would affect his employment by a United Nations agency. This, of course, applies in the case of arrests not only in the occupied areas, but in all of the areas in which the Agency operates. The only criteria to be applied here are those set forth in the staff regulations and rules. . . .

"The Agency, with the collaboration of the officials of the United Nations

Deterioration in the stability of Arab governments bordering Israel, the guerrilla warfare of the Palestinians, and the strict security measures adopted by Israel in the occupied territories pose a serious question concerning UNRWA's future in a situation of growing menace and complexity. Reporting to the General Assembly in the fall of 1969, the Commissioner-General asserted that the "normal difficulties" inherent in the Agency's task had been "aggravated by the tensions, frustrations, suspicious and mounting violence" of the past year.[13]

UNRWA AND LABOR RELATIONS

A second area of special sensitivity in which international organization impinges on territorial authority is labor relations. Here again, as in the area of police power, UNRWA is a special case in point because of the large size of its local staff. UNRWA's autonomy extends to two matters relating to staff: recruitment and conditions of employment. Control over the latter has been attained, but government's recurring interest in UNRWA's choice of locally recruited personnel has never ceased to be a problem.*

Recruitment

Article 100 of the Charter obligates United Nations officials to carry out their functions without seeking or receiving instructions

---

Secretariat, attempts to resolve problems which arise and does not seek to publicize them while efforts for solutions are in progress. The Agency, in its annual reports, informs the General Assembly of difficulties which persist, and these reports become public." (A/SPC/135), 2 December 1969.

* Of general interest is an argument, reported by the Agency in 1954, that its "operational activities have deprived it of its wholly international character, making it a mixed international-national body, and rendering it subject to the control of government organs in matters such as recruitment and conditions of employment of Agency staff, their liability to taxation on their salaries and the amenability of the Agency to the jurisdiction of the local courts." *Annual Report* (A/2717), Annex G, para. 1. See also *Annual Report* (A/2978), 1955, Annex G, para. 1, where the term "commercial organization" is cited as the characterization of UNRWA encountered in some quarters.

from government, while Article 101 asserts that "the staff shall be appointed by the Secretary-General under regulations established by the General Assembly." Government, of course, cannot dictate choice of personnel, while these articles also preclude the United Nations from seeking a government's consent, or from acquiescing in its demand for concurrence, when appointing one of its nationals to an international post.*

Experience shows that governments have more than ordinary interest in the composition of a secretariat; the United Nations has weathered two major crises over the integrity of its staff—one instigated by the United States during the McCarthy era and the other by the Soviet Union during the Congo troubles. If the parent organization is thus affected, one need not be surprised at pressure on UNRWA as regards its local staff, whose political views are hardly a matter of indifference to the host governments, not to speak of the latter's reluctance to forego opportunities for patronage.

UNRWA's founding resolution designates the Commissioner-General as "the chief executive officer," authorized to "select and appoint his staff in accordance with general arrangements made in agreement with the Secretary-General, including such of the staff rules and regulations of the United Nations as the Director [Commissioner-General] and the Secretary-General shall agree are applicable. . . . " While the language reflects the presumed temporary nature of the Agency, implying the inappropriateness of permanent

---

* A proposal of Yugoslavia for government consent made in the Preparatory Commission—meeting in London prior to the inauguration of the United Nations—was defeated by a large majority "on the grounds that it impinged on the exclusive responsibility of the Secretary-General . . . for the appointment of his staff, that it would threaten the freedom, independence and truly international character of the Secretariat and that it would defeat the spirit as well as infringe the letter of Article 100 of the Charter."

The discussion was further reported to the effect that it is "common sense that the staff should, as far as possible, be acceptable to the Member Governments, and also that the Secretary-General would often require information regarding candidates from government or private bodies, but it would be extremely undesirable to write into the text anything which would give national governments particular rights in this respect, or permit political pressure on the Secretary-General. . . . " United Nations Preparatory Commission, *Summary Record of meetings of Administrative and Budgetary Committee* (PC/AB/66), pp. 50–51.

appointments with career benefits, it remains axiomatic that accountability requires exclusive authority for the Commissioner-General to appoint and terminate members of his staff.

A test of such authority came early when Jordan demanded a deciding voice in the appointment and termination of locally recruited staff. The Commissioner-General declared in his 1953 report that these matters were solely in his discretion "although the views of the Government would naturally receive serious consideration." The same question was a source of continuing friction with Jordan, according to the 1954 report, while in 1956 the Agency indicated that "two of the Governments have asserted, in effect, the right to veto the appointment of individual staff members. . . . "[14]

The procedure for some time in Jordan and Syria has been for the Agency to choose certain categories of personnel, such as teachers, with the assistance of selection boards on which a government representative sits in an advisory capacity, while a similar arrangement was agreed upon in Lebanon in 1969. In the case of Syria, however, long delays in filling vacancies were mentioned in the 1969 report.[15] The practice of consultation with government, it should be added, has some justification in territorial authority's ability to muster background information on a candidate not easily accessible to international organization.

Conditions of Employment

Here derogation from territorial authority has traditionally been very great indeed. Well-founded precedent* allows international

* To which the Agency referred thus in its 1954 report: "The question arises frequently as to the extent to which the Agency, as a public international organization, in matters arising out of its international administration, should take the national labour law into consideration. Whenever the relationship of the Agency to its employees is involved, it has, in accordance with the well-established principle of international law governing international organizations, refused to submit to the jurisdiction of local courts. It has, however, made available to the employees a number of international remedies, patterned upon the procedure and practice of other United Nations bodies. *Ad hoc* appeals boards have been created, whose duty it is to examine claims or disputes between the Agency and its employees and to make recommendations for settlement thereof to the Director. In the settlement of such claims and disputes, the Agency as a rule, whenever Agency and United Nations regulations are silent, refers to local legislation as persuasive authority." A/2717, Annex G. para. 9.

organization to control its relations with staff to the exclusion of both the legislative and judicial processes of government. By a diffuse process, which has been broadly dependent on judicial construction and administrative application of constitutional texts and general principles and is singularly unaided by supplementary treaties, a substantial body of law internal to international organization has evolved to govern its relations with employees. Such "international administrative law" does not come under the heading of privileges and immunities but is founded on exclusive jurisdiction to prescribe and enforce the legal principles and rules governing conditions of employment. Jurisdiction of local legislative and judicial authorities in such matters is precluded. As a matter of practicality assuring uniformity across different territorial jurisdictions, as well as a preclusion of unwarranted government interference, international administrative law is requisite to international organization's mastery in its own household.[16]

In its legislative aspect, the international administrative law of the United Nations consists of Regulations enacted by the General Assembly and of Rules, in elaboration thereof, issued by the Secretary-General. Together they comprise a complete body of civil service law, including social security. As noted in Chapter II, personnel of UNICEF and UNHCR are employed under terms applicable to the secretariat of the parent organization, while UNRWA's staff is in a category of its own, subject to conditions of employment prescribed by the Commissioner-General in agreement with the Secretary-General.

The Staff Regulations and Rules which have been promulgated by the Commissioner-General consist of two separate bodies of legislation. One, applicable to UNRWA's internationally recruited staff, has with time approximated the terms of employment of the United Nations proper, including as of recent date full participation in the United Nations Joint Staff Pension Fund. The second concerns locally recruited professional, technical, and secretarial employees—known as the General Service category. The manual laborer comprises a third, whose conditions of employment, however, have yet to be reduced to a corpus.

In 1968 UNRWA sought to place teachers in a category separate from General Services, subjecting teaching positions to a special classification, with academic qualifications for filling them specified, and with a salary scale designed to reward those with professional certification. However, the innovation met with widespread resistance among the teachers, who appealed to government for support. In Syria introduction of the new regulations was postponed, while in Lebanon the teachers struck for three weeks. High-level discussions in Amman in May 1969, over which the Prime Minister presided, failed to prevent a strike of UNRWA teachers in East Jordan and the regulations were suspended at government request, followed by suspension elsewhere in the UNRWA system pending further negotiations with teachers and governments.[17]

In principle the application of international administrative law to UNRWA's local employees accords with general United Nations practice and is not exceptional. Moreover, other United Nations operations, as in the Congo and West New Guinea, have employed local personnel on a large scale. None, however, has employed large numbers of such personnel over so prolonged a period as UNRWA has, whose conditions of employment pertaining to locally recruited professional, technical, and secretarial staff are a matter of particular interest.

Salary levels are adjusted to correspond with those prevailing in the respective governments, while other conditions of employment are uniform throughout the UNRWA system. Home leave is not relevant, but annual leave is provided. There are allowances for wife and children, but no educational allowance such as obtains in the case of international staff. UNRWA schools are available, provided there is space, and, in the case of vocational and teacher-training institutes, provided the employee pays half the cost. The health plan applicable to the international staff (on the basis of equal contributions from employee and Agency) has no counterpart in the case of local staff, though there is sick leave, as well as hospitalization in UNRWA-subsidized beds. Local staff do not participate in the United Nations Joint Staff Pension Fund. Instead, there is a Provident Fund, based on a contribution from the employee of two and one-half percent at the lower salary levels and five percent at the higher, and from the Agency there is a contribution of ten percent. On separation, the participant receives the sum in his Provident Fund account plus interest. There are, in addition, other social security benefits. Termination because of retirement, disability, or redundancy entitles the employee to a lump-sum payment (in addition to his accumulated assets in the Provident Fund); the maximum amount, applicable in the case of nine or more years of service, is eight months pay. In the event of death, dependents are beneficiary to a continuation of the deceased's monthly pay at the rate of one month for each year of service up to nine. Finally, in event of service-incurred death, illness, or injury, the Agency pays compensation in an amount "which would normally be payable in the circumstances of the case under . . . the labour law applicable to the coutry in which the death, injury or illness occurred. . . . "[18]

The manual laborer does not participate in the Provident Fund; on separation he is paid a "service benefit" amounting to one month's wages for each year of service. His level of compensation is now such that he does not draw rations, but his children, unlike those of other local staff, are admitted without charge to the vocational and teacher training institutes. The health services of UNRWA are fully at his disposal.

Turning from the legislative to the judicial aspect of international organization's staff relations, it is apparent that national courts are not the appropriate forum for trying cases based on legislation enacted not by government but international organization. Their lack of jurisdiction does not, then, depend on international organization's immunity from suit; jurisdiction would still be lacking even without such immunity. International organization would prefer that exclusive control over its staff be acknowledged on this broader ground. National courts, however, have generally been reluctant to do so, choosing to forego jurisdiction on the narrower and more conventional ground of immunity.

This, at any rate, has been UNRWA's experience with the courts of the states within whose territories it operates. These courts now generally concede the inapplicability of local legislation to UNRWA's legal relations with its employees, but have insisted that this is a consequence of the Agency's immunity from suit rather than of their own lack of competence on substantive grounds. In earlier years, when they often accepted cases brought by aggrieved employees, UNRWA's normal practice was to refuse the summonses, referring them to the Ministry of Foreign Affairs with the request that the court be advised of the Agency's legal status. The Agency has always strongly resisted any attempt to attach its assets (typically in the form of bank accounts), which in every circumstance are exempt categorically under Section 2 of the Convention on Privileges and Immunities from "any measure of execution."*

If national courts cannot adjudicate between international organization and its employees, international organization must provide its own administrative remedies. Initially UNRWA did this on an ad hoc basis, but since 1957 formal procedures have been available to its local staff, consisting in the first instance of a Joint Appeals Board advisory to the Commissioner-General. The Board can deal only with terminations, not with other kinds of grievances, including disciplinary action short of dismissal. Its three members are designated annually: a chairman appointed by the Commissioner-General, a staff member similarly appointed, and an elected staff member. In 1965, for example, the Board dealt with or was in process of considering five cases; and it has now handled some fifty in all. If a unanimous recommendation of the Board is accepted by the Commissioner-General, the plaintiff is barred from appeal. If the vote is not unanimous, and if the action then taken by the Commissioner-General is still unacceptable to the plaintiff, provision exists for a special panel of adjudicators, consisting of persons "of high profes-

---

* Thus payment of attachments occurring in Syria was avoided through the invoking by UNRWA of executive intervention. *Annual Reports* (A/2171), 1952, p. 44; (A/2470), 1953, para. 235; and (A/3212), 1956, Annex G, para. 27. In Jordan, however, payment was in one instance exacted: ". . . probably the first case in which assets of a public international organization have been attached and execution effected." *Annual Report* (A/2717), 1954, Annex G, para. 11. The Agency's demand for reparation seems not to have been met. For instances of local courts in Egypt and Gaza failing to acknowledge immunity in labor disputes, see *Annual Reports* (A/3212), 1956, Annex G, para. 14; (A/3686), 1957, Annex H, n. 34; and (A/3931), 1958, Annex H, para. 14.

sional and international standing," chosen by the Commissioner-General.[19]

Even though UNRWA now provides internal due process for dealing with objections by local staff to termination, the interesting question remains whether a grievance might ultimately be appealed to the United Nations Administrative Tribunal. Such recourse is unquestionably open to the international staff—to which the processes of the foregoing paragraph are, in any event, not applicable. Regarding local staff, one can only say that not even the lesser appeal to the special panel of adjudicators has been resorted to since it was first made available in 1957.

Prior to that time, when UNRWA as yet had no formal provision for dealing with grievances, the United Nations Administrative Tribunal* took jurisdiction over two cases brought to it by local employees, each of whom, resisting termination and charging breach of contract, had been frustrated in the local courts, whose competence UNRWA refused to acknowledge. In both cases, UNRWA's argument was the same. Surprisingly, in neither case would it admit to the competence of the Tribunal, contending that the autonomy granted to the Agency by the General Assembly—in recognition of its temporary duration and unique mission—carried with it the necessary implication of a staff distinct and apart from the United Nations Secretariat, whereas the Statute of the Tribunal limited its jurisdiction to the latter only. In the *Hilpern* case it was further argued that, "even if it could be claimed that those members of the Agency's staff who were recognized as internationally recruited . . . were staff members of the United Nations Secretariat, in no event would it be possible to assimilate locally recruited staff to staff members of the United Nations Secretariat."

Nonetheless the Tribunal held itself to be competent. In the *Radicopoulos* case the Tribunal, again asserting its jurisdiction, was

---

* In its judicial aspect, the system of international administrative law culminates in two tribunals: The United Nations Administrative Tribunal and the Administrative Tribunal of the International Labor Organization. The latter, descendant of the pioneer Tribunal established by the League Assembly in 1927, has jurisdiction over certain European-based specialized agencies in addition to the ILO. The purview of the United Nations Administrative Tribunal includes UNRWA, a subsidiary organ of the General Assembly.

quite emphatic as to the linkage between UNRWA and the United Nations:

The Tribunal notes that the United Nations Relief and Works Agency for Palestine Refugees in the Near East was established by General Assembly resolution 302 (IV) under Article 22 of the Charter authorizing the Assembly to establish subsidiary organs.

In that resolution, the Assembly laid down regulations relating to the staff of the Agency. In doing so, it exercised its power under Article 101, paragraph 1, of the Charter to establish regulations relating to the staff of the United Nations. By reason of the functions peculiar to the Agency, however, the Assembly confined itself to establishing the legal status of the Director and laying down the procedure to be followed in issuing regulations concerning the staff.

It follows from this resolution that the staff of the Agency is placed under the legislative authority of the Assembly, like the whole of the staff referred to in Chapter XV of the Charter, but no provision of that Chapter obliges the Assembly to establish uniform rules for all who serve the United Nations.[20]

The last paragraph affords within the context of the United Nations that flexibility which the Agency momentarily sought by asserting separateness from New York to the point of independence. The Tribunal was the more sagacious. As regards international personnel, the Agency has found, in fact, that advantage lay in seeking closer identification with the United Nations Secretariat. At the same time, the United Nations parentage duly emphasized by the Tribunal has not precluded sharp differentiation between international and locally recruited staff, nor, among the latter, appropriate distinctions between kinds and levels of employment.

CONCLUSION

International organizations are corporate entities capable of entering into relations with governments, other international organizations, employees, and commercial enterprises. Over and above mere corporate personality, however, they have been provided with important immunities from territorial jurisdiction enabling them to coexist with states as coordinate members of the international community. This and the preceding chapter have reviewed UNRWA's jurisdictional and fiscal exemptions from territorial authority, its exclusive legislative and judicial control over employment of personnel, and the status of its international and local staffs. These staffs are responsible to UNRWA for carrying out official tasks, while their private affairs remain subject to governmental control (except for the blanket diplomatic immunities possessed in one or more of the host countries by some of UNRWA's internationally recruited personnel).

In their relations with UNRWA, governments have conformed to diplomatic patterns which, based on acknowledged equality of the parties, entail negotiation as the method appropriate to mutual dealings. Inescapably, however, UNRWA is on the defensive toward territorial authority and often comes off second best, though its linkage—supplemented by its own initiative—with the United Nations provides footing for a tenacious struggle. Despite the pressures of a highly charged situation, UNRWA has not failed to insist on its own identity and point of departure as an agent of international authority.

V

Economic Rehabilitation

UNRWA, according to the Economic Survey Mission design, was to do three things in succession: first, sustain the relief program already begun; second, substitute public works for direct relief, and third, promote economic development as a basis of permanent resettlement. But the succession never occurred. Even at best, the practicability of a public works program was doubtful, and also questionable was UNRWA's ability to induce speedy economic development in the countries of refuge. However, the underlying obstacle to UNRWA's fulfillment of the Survey Mission's design was the unresponsiveness to an economic approach of a problem exclusively political in origin.

PUBLIC WORKS, REINTEGRATION, AND DEVELOPMENT

The Economic Survey Mission expected that direct relief would give way quickly to public works, with UNRWA overseeing the transition. By end of 1950 direct relief was to be down to a size manageable by the Arab governments, and by mid 1951, 100,000 employed refugees plus their dependents were to be off the rolls. This was the timetable, subject to review by the General Assembly.

However, progress toward a political settlement did not materialize, while other expectations also went awry. Work relief encountered psychological and administrative difficulties.* But even

---

* "Not only was it difficult to recruit sufficient workers, but demonstrations and threats to Agency personnel were made and . . . some of the workers dis-

at best public works were a wholly impracticable approach to the problem. At the program's peak, 12,000 refugees were employed at a cost five times that of direct relief, and upon completion of a project the refugees returned to tents and ration lines. The Commissioner-General reported that there was no enduring benefit for the refugees nor financial relief for the Agency, and public works were abandoned by mid 1951.[1]

Beyond public works but short of long-term development, the General Assembly late in 1950 invited contributions to a Reintegration Fund of $30,000,000 to help finance "projects requested by any government in the Near East and approved by the Agency."[2] Building on this approach a year later, the Commissioner-General and his Advisory Commission proposed and the General Assembly adopted "a comprehensive and conclusive" plan that envisaged an expenditure of $250,000,000 over a three-year period, $50,000,000 for relief and the remainder for reintegration. The object was to help 150,000 families become self-supporting. One-third, it was believed, could be settled in urban areas, helped by vocational training, grants-in-aid, and provision of housing. Another 50,000 families were to be settled on rain-fed land. Integration of the remaining third would be through agricultural projects dependent

---

played . . . an unwilling approach which greatly reduced output. However, in many places this attitude gradually changed; at some sites, requests for employment greatly exceeded the financial possibilities, and when work finally stopped, toward the middle of 1951, there was strong opposition to the closedown." *Annual Report* (A/1905), 1951, para. 44.

With reference to road building: "Government co-operation . . . varied considerably. In all cases, the roads were chosen in the first place by the government concerned, and approved or rejected by the Planning Board of UNRWA. The plant, such as stone-crushers and steam-rollers, was provided by governments, and the labour and material by UNRWA." Ibid., para. 49.

As regards afforestation: ". . . not all the governments . . . had as yet a clear idea of the importance of soil conservation and afforestation. . . . [E]stablishment of nurseries had to be cut to the minimum and . . . seeds had to be sown instead of seedlings. . . . [C]ertain governments had not initially adequate means and personnel for ensuring efficient technical control of work on such a large scale. . . . [T]he planting of fruit and nut trees rather than forest species would have been more advantageous to the local economy, particularly if . . . nearby villages . . . would agree not to keep goats. . . . However, . . . the Agency had no nurseries for fruit trees, and the governments had not the necessary legal powers." Ibid., paras. 50, 51.

mainly on irrigation. It was acknowledged that families were "mal-distributed as among the countries from the viewpoint of economic opportunity," but it was believed that the Arab Middle East possessed the absorptive capacity, and that the Reintegration Fund plus other outside aid would enable several Arab countries to admit immigrants concurrently with. a rising local standard of living. Moreover, the plan emphasized that the host governments would assume "maximum possible administrative responsibility at the earliest possible date."[3]

None of these expectations materialized. Two and one-half years later only $7 million of the Reintegration Fund had been spent—effecting 8,000 ration cuts.[4] Meanwhile, however, some progress was made toward long-term development.

Two large projects, the Yarmuk-Jordan and the Sinai, were in 1953 subjects of formal agreement between UNRWA and Jordan and Egypt respectively,[5] and by July 1955 feasibility studies had been completed and engineering specifications prepared. Development of the Yarmuk and Jordan rivers, it was estimated, would irrigate 126,000 acres and produce 167 million kilowatt hours of electric power, the former at a cost of $109,000,000 and the latter at $53,000,000. Construction would require 12,000 workers over a period of years. Ultimately the expansion of agricultural and ancillary employment would support 143,000 people—in family units averaging five to six members.[6] The Sinai project, purely agricultural, involved the diversion of waters of the Nile to be brought to and siphoned under the Suez Canal, permitting reclamation of a desert area sufficient to support from 50,000 to 60,000 refugees. Construction, at a cost of $30,000,000, was estimated to take three years. Moving the refugees into the area would require another five, while complete self-support would follow in three to six years after the last group had been installed.[7]

But neither of these projects came to pass. Intergovernment agreements necessary to the Yarmuk-Jordan project were not forthcoming.[8] As for Sinai, circumstances had so changed, the Egyptian government informed UNRWA, that it could no longer provide the water, stating "it could not undertake to make water available for a project for refugees when it was obliged to restrict the amount of water used by its own citizens." The Agency was told that not until completion of the High Dam at Aswan would there be sufficient water.*

With the Yarmuk-Jordan and Sinai projects shelved, it was evident by 1956 that development on a large scale under UNRWA tutelage had reached a dead end. Recognizing this, the Commissioner-General recommended an indirect approach, requesting the General Assembly to enlarge the Agency's mandate to permit loans or grants to governments for "general development programmes, with which the immediate employment . . . of refugees need not be directly connected, but which will eventually benefit the refugees through increasing . . . general economic activity. . . ."[9] The General Assembly complied, subject to agreement by a recipient government "that, within a fixed period of time, it will assume financial responsibility for an agreed number of refugees, such number to be commensurate with the cost of the project, without prejudice to paragraph 11 of resolution 194 (III)."[10]

Insofar as this differed from the former approach, it was less likely to attract capital, which in fact was not forthcoming. For that matter, very little of the Reintegration Fund was ever used. Established at $200 million in principle only—awaiting materialization of actual projects—the Fund had $28 million on hand as of 30 June 1953.[11] The greater part of this eventually gravitated to the Agency's operating reserve. That the Reintegration Fund should thus have run into the sands of relief (though not without advantage to UNRWA's educational program) symbolized the Agency's failure to fulfill its primary purpose of economic rehabilitation.

A contributory cause of UNRWA's frustration was serious lack in the fifties of administrative and technical personnel in the countries

---

* *Annual Report* (A/3212), 1956, Annex D, para. 39.

The Government explained that it had planned to conserve water for the Sinai project in three ways: "by drawing off storage water from the Aswan Dam; by a restricted system of cotton cultivation; and by the re-utilization of drainage water." However, "the development of the 'Liberation Province' (an Egyptian project for extending the area of cultivation along the Nile) had gone forward more quickly than expected and had, therefore, increased Egypt's own water requirements." Moreover, production of cotton had been increased to improve Egypt's balance of payments, and "the re-utilization of drainage water had not proceeded as rapidly as expected." Ibid., para. 38.

of refuge capable of planning and executing development projects. Commenting on shortage of such personnel, the Agency recalled in 1954 that its aim had been "to disassociate itself as much as possible from . . . operations in the field." It preferred "that projects should be developed and operated by governmental or quasi-governmental bodies, with the Agency providing technical and financial assistance and reserving the right of audit." UNRWA had given funds and made available foreign specialists to the Jordanian government to establish an Administrative and Technical Staff in its Ministry of Development, but conceded in its 1954 report that progress had been slow.[12] Meanwhile, in quest of results, UNRWA continued to exercise direct responsibility for rehabilitation endeavors to a degree exceeding the usual norms governing outside assistance to governments. Experience showed, however, that UNRWA's own processes were not a feasible substitute for those of territorial authority.

Yet the overriding obstacle—conclusive in itself—to UNRWA's achieving its goal of permanent employment for the refugees was their own attitude. Bitterly resentful of what they could understand only as eviction by alien intruders, they rejected any alternative to returning home—their adamancy reinforced by the General Assembly's resolution of 11 December 1948 whose key paragraph 11 proclaimed the right of repatriation. The implication of large-scale development under UNRWA auspices was plain; it meant permanent resettlement, and such negation of their Palestinian origin the refugees were unready to accept. This attitude was frequently referred to in UNRWA's reports in the fifties, a typical instance being the Commissioner-General's comment in 1955:

The outstanding factor which continues to condition refugee attitudes and to influence the policies of Near Eastern Governments . . . is the strong desire of the refugees to return to their homeland. This feeling has not diminished . . . , and its strength should not be underestimated. . . .

For the majority of the refugees, repatriation means a return to the conditions they knew in Palestine prior to 1948. It is not possible to know how many of them would in fact accept an opportunity to be repatriated if that repatriation would mean something different from returning to their old homes and to their former way of life. No prediction can be made until the refugees have been given the opportunity of choosing between distinguishable alternatives, namely, on the one hand, repatriation the true nature of which is clearly understood at the time of choice; and, on the other, the amount and form of the compensation that would be offered instead. It must be strongly emphasized that unless some opportunity is given to the refugees to make their choice, or unless some other political settlement can be reached, the unrequited demand for repatriation will continue to be an obstacle to the accomplishment of the objective of reintegration and self-support. . . . *

The governments, while inclined initially to cooperate with UNRWA, did not venture to resist the sentiments of the refugees and presently opposed tying economic development to solution of the refugee problem. Since UNRWA was identified with the refugees as such, economic development through its auspices was suspect. We shall note that in the sixties the countries of refuge made notable economic progress, but not owing to UNRWA which —focused exclusively on the refugees and burdened, therefore, with political overtone—was handicapped as an instrument through which to pursue economic growth.

Small-scale Rehabilitation

From the outset, UNRWA also sought opportunities for small-scale rehabilitation—whose beneficiaries were to surrender entitlement to the Agency's services. Included in these endeavors were a small number of agricultural settlements, utilizing such parcels of

---

* *Annual Report* (A/2978), 1955, paras. 35 and 36. Distinguishable from the longing to go home is a further aspect of refugee psychology: "Even where satisfactory projects are developed, it is often with great reluctance that the refugees are willing to participate and so give up their ration cards. For almost five years these cards have represented to their possessors tangible evidence of social security. With them they never really went hungry, they were able to obtain free treatment in Agency clinics and hospitals, their children were able to attend schools without any cost to the families, they were free of taxes, and they were often assured of a roof over their heads. The institutionalization of refugees has become a powerful factor in impeding the development of rehabilitation projects. The ration card has become, in fact, so much a part of the life and economy of the refugees that it is not at all unusual for it to be used as a tangible asset upon the strength of which substantial sums can be borrowed." *Annual Report* (A/2717), 1954, Annex C, para. 63.

land in Jordan and Syria as were made available by the governments or, in some instances, purchased by the Agency. They consisted typically of around fifty families. UNRWA provided each family with a house, tools, and animals, and constructed community facilities. Suitable land, however, was hard to get, the Agency pointing out in 1954 that "certain large areas of rain-fed or easily irrigated state land have not been made available." In Syria the Agency concluded that "rehabilitation of refugees by the development of small tracts of reclaimed sub-marginal desert lands is not only uneconomical, but impracticable."*

Through June 1958, little more than $2,000,000 had been spent on agricultural resettlement projects.[13] Subsequently, advantage was taken in 1959–60 of the availability of first-class land in northern Jordan in the area of the East Ghor Valley Authority. An irrigation project developed by the Jordanian government with assistance from the United States AID program, it constituted a portion of UNRWA's earlier projected Yarmuk-Jordan scheme. Three agricultural settlements were established, benefiting in all 137 families. The cost was around $450,000, including purchase of 4,260 dunums (1,065 acres) of land.

High cost per family and difficulty of finding land were not the only hindrances to the establishment of agricultural settlements. A

* *Annual Report* (A/2717), 1954, Annex C, paras. 61 and 38.

For example, a site made available late in 1952 by the Syrian Government consisted of "virtually uninhabited salt steppe . . . , 40 kilometres east of Damascus. . . . Although the Agency recognized that development costs . . . would be high, it undertook the project because it was the first concrete offer of land . . . in Syria and it was considered desirable from an experimental point of view." The Agency drilled thirty-two wells of which six produced sweet water in sufficient volume to justify the installation of pumps. Experiments in 1953 with maize, cotton, vetch, cucumbers, cabbage, etc. produced good results. Further experiments in 1954 were encouraging. In February 1955 some fifty families were settled, each receiving at Agency expense "twenty dunums [five acres] of irrigated land, a mud brick house, one mule, thirty ewes and some agricultural implements." Community facilities were also provided: school, mosque, administrative center, and market place. By 1956 another 14 families had been settled, though meanwhile a severe drought necessitated a new plan of irrigation. The accumulated cost was $450,000. Ibid., paras. 34–38. Also *Annual Reports* (/2978), 1955, Annex D, para. 29; and (A/3212), 1956, Annex D, para. 34.

degree of harmony within the settlement had to be assured, and among unsophisticated Arab peasants this meant paying due attention to blood relationships. Association based on impersonal ties outside the family does not come naturally to them.

At the outset in Jordan and Syria, the Agency made short-term unsecured loans for small enterprises, but repayment was so unsatisfactory that the program was abandoned and the Agency did not again directly involve itself in this form of rehabilitation. On the other hand, a bank would be capable of making professional judgments and acting on business principles. In 1951, at UNRWA's initiative, the Development Bank of Jordan was founded, which continued to function until 1967.

Capitalization, initially authorized at $1,400,000, was increased in 1960 to $2,800,000 of which $2,125,000 was paid up as of 30 June 1966, eighty-five percent provided by UNRWA, and the remainder by the Jordanian government and three commercial banks. Of the members on the Board of Directors, UNRWA appointed three (designating one as chairman), the government appointed one, and the three participating banks appointed one among them to serve in yearly rotation. From its profits, the Bank employed a general-manager, assisted by a staff of about eight persons. Though incorporated under Jordanian law, the Bank was exempt from taxes, and, unlike other banks, was not subject to inspection and control by the Ministry of Economy.

The total of all loans in the fifteen years of the Bank's operation was $3,942,000, including reinvested capital. There were 764 separate transactions, nearly all for agricultural purposes, with only sixty-eight accounted for by small industrial projects and construction of buildings. Refugees, lacking collateral, were seldom the borrowers, but it proved feasible to make loans to landowners and entrepreneurs on condition that refugees be employed. Beginning in 1962, the Bank also assisted in the founding of sixteen agricultural cooperatives, providing not only land but managerial and bookkeeping advice. Consisting of fifteen to thirty families each, these proved to be unstable and did not prosper—despite a low interest rate of three percent, a prolonged period for repayment, and an initial period of grace.

The Bank's contribution to the welfare of the refugees was indirect but significant. Thus, it was an important factor in the expansion of fruit and vegetable farming in the Jordan valley. While few refugees were permanently removed from the relief rolls, a large number found useful work in the valley. In 1966 the pay for unskilled laborers approximated two dollars per day and labor was sometimes in short supply.

By 1967 commercial and government loans had become available in Jordan on terms comparable with those offered by the Bank. Moreover, UNRWA badly needed funds for the construction in Jordan of new schools for the growing refugee population of school age. Accordingly, in May the Development Bank of Jordan was dissolved and its assets and liabilities transferred to the Government's Agricultural Credit Corporation. It was arranged for UNRWA to receive the par value ($1,813,000) of its shares in installments. The first of $497,000 was paid in May 1967, and the second, $182,000, in May 1968. Subsequent installments are to run for thirteen years.[14]

UNRWA found that nonreimbursable grants to selected families were largely successful in achieving self-support and separation from the relief rolls. Such grants, moreover, proved less costly and better assured of lasting results than group agricultural settlements. The device was used in Syria and Jordan. From November 1952 through February 1954, 226 grants were made in Syria at a cost of $110,000 against 1,229 ration cuts. In Jordan a more extensive program was in operation, extending from May 1955 through April 1957. Involving agricultural projects (262, such as poultry, dairy, vegetable, and dry farming), housing (225), industrial (175, such as tile and shirt factories, machine shops), and commercial (52), the program was more expensive than the Syrian—$2,127,000 for 714 projects in all, cancelling about 5,400 rations. Costing the most were the agricultural projects, which often entailed the purchase of land. Costing the least were the housing projects; the recipient surrendered his family's rations for a rent-free house at an average cost of $355 per family member. For budgetary reasons, no further use was made of grants after 1957.

From the beginning, continuing to the present, UNRWA has in a small way assisted individuals to capitalize on such skills as they might already possess, providing, for example, a sewing machine, a knitting machine, or a craftsman's tools. Such assistance does not require the recipient to relinquish entitlement to rations or UNRWA's other services. His eligibility for them continues until he is judged to be self-supporting—a matter for examination in the following chapter.

Finally, a means of rehabilitation was provision of ocean passage to emigrants. By the time this program ended in 1964 for lack of funds and because of political objections, such assistance had gone to 4,521 persons, most of whom went to the United States, 1,588 to Latin America, 157 to Australia, and 235 to Europe and Africa. All apparently came from Jordan and Lebanon.[15] Nowhere did UNRWA take the initiative in this highly sensitive matter.

By 1960 a marked decline had occurred in the Agency's activities aimed at economic rehabilitation. In that year, under impetus of the World Refugee Year, the Agency chose education as a preferred target for emphasis, thereby shifting its rehabilitation efforts from the aging to the new generation.

CONCLUSION

Direct results of UNRWA's attempts at economic rehabilitation were quite meager. The program of "reintegration" failed to materialize, while the attempt to generate employment through large-scale development projects was abandoned by 1956. Meanwhile, piecemeal rehabilitation, though of lasting benefit to some recipient families, made only a small dent on the relief rolls and contributed little to the economic development of the countries of refuge. Even these efforts virtually ceased in 1960, after which education was favored over economics as the chief means of promoting livelihood.

Yet by June 1967 remarkable economic improvements had occurred in the host countries, which provided employment opportunities for the refugees. Prior to the June War, Jordan's annual growth rate—approaching eleven percent—was astonishingly high and the chronic unemployment that had beset Jordan was disappearing. The Syrian and Lebanese economies had also maintained a high rate of growth with much activity in evidence. Even in Gaza, where un-skilled labor was in short supply in certain seasons of the year, improvement was discernible. Outside aid undoubtedly contributed to this result, including that of international organizations, except for UNRWA, whose schemes for large-scale employment of the refugees were frustrated, ironically, by the very fact of the Agency's identification with the refugees.

Policy, whether international or domestic, typically fails to fulfill original intent. Political, social, and economic variables are too numerous and subtle for the policy maker to be confident of pre-dicted results. We ought, therefore, to ask whether UNRWA has had economic consequences in any indirect, or unintended, ways.

Through 1970 UNRWA spent approximately $700,000,000. To this extent the economies of the countries of refuge have been spared the cost of caring for the 1948 refugees, and at the same time have gained valuable foreign exchange through UNRWA's local purchase of supplies and payment of salaries and wages. In some degree, then, UNRWA was a factor contributing to the economic growth of the sixties, and since the refugees shared the benefits of an expanding economy, the Agency in this indirect way redounded to their advantage. Yet in 1950 no one saw UNRWA as a device for channeling upwards of a billion dollars into the countries of refuge.

In addition to the perspective of national economy, UNRWA expenditure ought to be viewed as well from the point of view of individual refugee families. At the outset UNRWA's welfare services were important in the saving of lives. Destitution was so great among hundreds of thousands of uprooted people, cut off irrevoc-ably from their accustomed livelihood, that UNRWA, though its rations and health services were minimal, provided the margin for survival. It is a misapprehension, however, to suppose that this elemental function has remained unchanged in twenty years of UNRWA's existence—though, to be sure, a new wave of destitution followed in the wake of the June 1967 war.

Of course, destitute families remain even from the 1948 exodus. The Commissioner-General conjectured in 1964 that forty to fifty percent of UNRWA registrants were still destitute or nearly so. However, thirty to forty percent were partly self-supporting, while

ten to twenty percent, he believed, were securely re-established.[16]
Thus, for a sizeable portion of the registrants, UNRWA had ceased
to be indispensible and for them its services had taken the character
of a subsidy.

Such a concept was not in the minds of UNRWA's founders, and
need, in fact, remains today a criterion for retention on UNRWA's
rolls. Yet we shall see in the following chapter that determination of
need is administraively very difficult and that relatively few registrants have been placed in the category of "no-services." In effect,
then, UNRWA's small though regular injections into the economy
of a family—in the form of rations and health and education
services—has no doubt had an overall effect of greater consequence
than the sum of all specially designed small-scale rehabilitation
schemes applied to families on a selective basis.

Though shelter is provided by UNRWA for fewer than half its
registrants, the camps call for a special word. Admission to a camp
is based on need, but a family once admitted is not obliged to leave
on becoming partially or fully self-supporting. Thus, idleness is not
synonymous with residence in the camps, and they need not be
seen as merely transitional to some future solution of the refugee
problem. Many of them, rather, are new settlements that have become integrated with the surrounding community. Reviewing the
Agency's record in a special report of 18 August 1967 to United
Nations members, the Secretary-General said of the camps that

it is quite misleading to assume that because . . . [they] remained and,
in fact, grew in size and because the refugees continued to live in them,
no progress was being made towards the economic rehabilitation of the
camp inhabitants. This misconception seems to derive from experience in
dealing with the refugees in Europe, where great emphasis was placed
on clearing the camps as evidence of rehabilitation. Such ideas were not
applicable to the problem of the Palestine refugees. . . . In the circumstances existing and in the absence of a political solution, the best they
could hope for . . . was a gradual improvement of the living conditions
in the camps, and this is in fact what has been taking place—sometimes
to a marked degree, particularly where the camps were located in areas
in which good opportunities for employment existed. Some of the refugee
camps, indeed, had developed into thriving communities, even though

they were still at a fairly low social and economic level and still contained many families living on the edge of subsistence.*

Though a significant degree of rehabilitation had, prior to the 1967 war, occurred among the refugees by virtue of the general economic progress in the countries of refuge, UNRWA's contribution was indirect and peripheral. It remains only to comment once again on the putative connection between economic welfare and political consequence on which UNRWA was founded. Prosperity is no guarantee of acquiescence in otherwise adverse circumstances. President Nasser's provocative gestures of the spring of 1967 were not tempered by the rising standard of living in the Arab countries bordering Israel. Indeed the converse may have been true. Peace in the Middle East as elsewhere is dependent not merely on welfare but on a satisfied sense of justice and, beyond the subjectivity of human desire, may require as well a power equilibrium.

* *Special Report* (A/6787), para. 31. That fall, the Commissioner-General in his *Annual Report* (A/6713), 1967, para. 56, reiterated the Secretary-General's point that the camps were not transient settlements, and also defended the Arab governments against what he conceived to be unjust criticism: ". . . the widespread assumption that the refugees have been stagnating in idleness in . . . the camps all these years is untrue. Nor is there validity in the widespread belief that, because many of the refugees . . . were still living in camps so many years after their displacement from their homes, therefore no progress had been made towards their rehabilitation. These mistaken assumptions have given rise to the equally mistaken view that UNRWA was engaged in an endless operation of merely keeping the refugees alive to remain a charge on the charity of the international community. Finally, there is the widespread belief that the host Governments have been deliberately and inhumanely keeping the refugees in a state of destitution and dependence on international charity as a weapon in the prosecution of their political aims. This also needs correction. Although the host Governments have opposed mass schemes of direct resettlement, on the grounds that this would be contrary to the interests and expressed wishes of the refugees themselves, their record in promoting the rehabilitation of the refugees as individuals through education, training and employment has been notably humane and helpful. They have extended this aid to the refugees in spite of the grave difficulties which already confronted them in providing a livelihood for their own rapidly expanding populations."

VI

Welfare

UNRWA's relief and health programs, virtually constant in their services since the Agency's beginning, are complex operations administered with remarkable economy. The health program, in contrast to relief, poses no major problems in UNRWA's relations with governments. For the latter, however, the meeting of international and territorial authority is a critical juncture, bearing on two issues that UNRWA has never been able to deal with satisfactorily: Who is a bona fide refugee?, and Who among acknowledged refugees qualify for UNRWA's services?

RELIEF

Relief under UNRWA has been primarily a mass program concerned with food and shelter, though broken down to an extent into special categories for purposes of supplementary feeding and able in some small degree through social-service workers to take account of individual circumstances. We shall describe the program as it pertained in 1969 to "UNRWA registered" refugees.

Totaling 1,395,000 names as of June 1969, registration is by means of electronic tapes at UNRWA headquarters, an eligible person being one "whose normal residence was Palestine for a minimum period of two years immediately preceding the outbreak of the conflict in 1948 and who, as a result of this conflict, has lost both his home and means of livelihood." Also included as registrants are descendents of such persons, while the 350,000 "new" refugees resulting from the June War are not eligible.* Included in the present account are 175,000 "old" refugees who in 1967 fled a second time.

Rations are a main element in UNRWA's relief program, providing 1,500 calories a day per person, increased in winter to 1,600.† In 1969 UNRWA provided full rations for 806,000 registered refugees. The level, little changed since 1950, declined to a low of 772,000 in 1953 and reached a high of 866,000 in 1963. Such relative stability despite natural increase in the refugee population has been the result of a ceiling on ration recipients in each of the host countries, imposed in Jordan in 1951 and elsewhere in 1963. Prompted in part by the Agency's lack of financial means to absorb fully the second generation of 1948 refugees (and a third now already begun), the action was also designed, especially in the case of Jordan, to bring pressure on the government and the refugees to cooperate in rectification of the relief rolls. Any ineligible names

* Definition of eligibility was evolved by the Agency soon after taking over from its predecessor in May 1950. The General Assembly has never expressly endorsed this definition, but apparently has done so implicitly. As to the "new" refugees originating in 1967, General Assembly resolution 2252 (ES-V) of 4 July 1967 authorized the Agency "to provide humanitarian assistance, as far as practicable, on an emergency basis and as a temporary measure. . . ." In practice, separation of "old" and "new" refugees has often been hard to maintain and the two groups overlap as regards provision by UNRWA of both food and shelter. As of 30 June 1969 the Agency reported that it was administering the distribution of rations (242,000) "to all Government-registered displaced persons in East Jordan," subject to "reimbursement by the Government of most of the additional costs. . . . " Some categories of "new" refugees have benefited from UNRWA's supplementary feeding program, while the emergency camps established after 1967 by UNRWA, six in Jordan and four in Syria, included among their 100,000 inhabitants about forty percent "new" refugees, the remainder being UNRWA-registered refugees. *Annual Report* (A/7614), 1969, paras. 42, 53, 56, and Table 8. Despite complications, the Agency has succeeded in preserving the comparability of its post- and pre-1967 statistics.

† A monthly ration consists of 10,000 grams of flour, 600 grams of pulses (dried peas, beans, lentils, etc.), 600 grams of sugar, 500 grams of rice, 375 grams of oils and fats. In winter flour is increased by 400 and pulses by 300 grams. Kerosene is also distributed during the five winter months: one litre per person per month in Gaza, and one and one-half in the other areas. One piece of soap (150 grams) is given monthly to each ration recipient. Green vegetables, fruits, eggs, and meat are not provided; the refugees are left to seek these for themselves, except for those persons eligible for supplementary feeding.

purged from the rolls mean an equal number of rations available to children awaiting admission. As of 1969 the backlog of such children, mainly in Jordan, was 326,000—including babies not in any event eligible for rations until their first birthday. However, all are registered members of the refugee population, health and education services are available to them, and they participate in the program of supplementary feeding.

As of the same date, 13,500 persons were entitled to half-rations, these being inhabitants of villages cut off in 1948 from their lands by the cease-fire lines between Israel and Jordan. Many others among these villagers were still in 1967 receiving aid from UNICEF and voluntary agencies.

Finally, as of June 1969, 148,000 registered refugees who were once recipients of relief belonged to families (including those of professional and administrative staff employed by UNRWA) deemed to have incomes rendering them ineligible for further assistance of any kind. Another 27,000 were members of families (including those of manual laborers employed by UNRWA) with incomes high enough to disqualify them for rations but low enough to warrant the continuation of educational and medical services, while 74,000 without rations were from families not all of whose members were disqualified for receiving rations. In all, then, there were 1,395,000 registrants as of June 1969, 806,000 of whom received full rations, while 326,000 registered babies and children were not included on the ration rolls. Other registrants included 13,500 persons receiving half-rations, 148,000 who received neither rations nor services, 27,000 who received health and education services but no rations, and 74,000 individuals without rations from families not all of whose members were so disqualified.*

Shelter is another element in the relief program, though fewer registrants are provided with UNRWA shelter than with UNRWA rations. Apart from the ten emergency camps already mentioned,†

---

* *Annual Report* (A/7614), 1969, Table 1. In 1970 the number of registered refugees had increased to 1,425,000: in East Jordan 506,000; Gaza 311,800; West Bank 272,700; Lebanon 176,000; and Syria 159,000. UNRWA, *Registration Statistical Bulletin, Second Quarter 1970.*

† See footnote, p. 127.

the Agency in 1969 maintained fifty-three camps, housing 435,000 registered refugees. In Gaza sixty-two percent were so housed, in Lebanon forty-seven, East Jordan thirty-one, West Bank twenty-five, and Syria sixteen.*

We have already had occasion to mention that registrants who become ineligible for any or all of UNRWA's services are not required to leave UNRWA camps, which, accordingly, can be viewed as new settlements rather than merely as places of transient residence. Yet, in Jordan, for example, a typical family plot in a camp established prior to 1967 is only 105 square meters, with a concrete block or mud brick hut three and one-half by three meters and a second room being added in the case of the largest families. The refugee may add to this, often building a wall around his small compound. That such meager shelter should attract and hold the refugees is owing to even less desirable housing generally available to them outside the camps. The housing situation as described by the Commissioner-General in his 1964 report is still of interest:

Despite sustained efforts of UNRWA and of the host governments and other collaborating agencies, there are families who still live in dwellings which are unfit for human habitation: some in dark cellars, others in crumbling tenements, others in grossly overcrowded barracks and shacks. Efforts have been made and are continuing to be made to relieve some of the worst situations, but the living conditions of thousands of families will still be a matter of grave concern. Nearly all the UNRWA camps are extremely overcrowded with five or more persons living in one room. They lack adequate roads and pathways and many camps are deep in

* Also living during 1969 in the fifty-three camps antedating the June War were 56,000 persons "neither registered with UNRWA nor eligible for UNRWA assistance," consisting of newly displaced persons and refugee " 'squatters' who live in or on the fringes of the camps." *Annual Report* (A/7614), 1969, Table 7.

The percentage figure for Syria includes refugees in "UNRWA" camps only. In addition there are so-called "unofficial" camps in which an even larger number of 1948 refugees is housed. In both kinds, the refugees have built their own huts with financial assistance, in varying combination, from UNRWA and the Syrian government—whereas in other countries UNRWA had laid out, financed, and built the camps. In both "UNRWA" and "unofficial" camps in Syria, UNRWA provides relief, health, and educational services. The main differences are that (a) sanitation is the responsibility of UNRWA only in "official" camps, and (b) there is no UNRWA administrative unit, thus no UNRWA camp leader, in "unofficial" camps.

mud in winter and in dust in summer. There are rarely any sewers or storm-water drainage. The water supplies are communal and often inadequate, particularly during the hot summer months. Yet the refugees living in the camps (who constitute about two-fifths of the total number of refugees receiving relief) are, on the whole, probably better housed and better cared for than many of the remaining three-fifths living outside the camps in such dwellings as they have been able to provide for themselves. Understandably, UNRWA is under constant pressure from these less fortunate refugees to expand its camps and build more shelter.[1]

Supplementary feeding is another aspect of UNRWA's relief program. Since the basic ration lacks both fresh food and animal protein, certain groups in the refugee population (infants, children, pregnant women, nursing mothers, and tubercular outpatients) are singled out for special supplements of food. In the twelve-month period ending 30 June 1969, 108 feeding centers provided a daily average of 40,500 cooked meals, while 111 milk centers provided a daily average of 131,000 supplements of reconstituted milk.[2]

Formerly, UNRWA purchased and issued blankets, one every 3 years to each recipient of basic rations and to children over one year even though registered only for services. As of 1966 issue of blankets was restricted to cases of special need in Syria, Lebanon, and Jordan. At that time in Gaza the distribution was still general, but limited to only one blanket every six years. The Agency has never engaged in direct purchase of clothing, the exception at one period being cloth for children's garments; this practice, however, lapsed owing to financial stringency. Donated clothing—collected by voluntary agencies in North America and Europe—was formerly distributed to all refugees on a general basis. As of 1966 a general distribution was still deemed necessary in Gaza, but elsewhere only families in special need continued to receive this aid.[3]

UNRWA attempts in a small way to meet individual needs arising from chronic illness, old age, widowhood, and similar circumstances. In the twelve-month period ending 30 June 1969, 21,000 persons in these categories were helped with small cash grants, while others received special issues of clothing, blankets, and kerosene. In the same period, thirteen destitute aged people were placed in homes and 102 orphans in institutions, and case workers advised many thousands on personal problems.[4] The Agency employs a Field Welfare Officer in each country, and under these four officials in 1966 there were nine assistants, twelve area supervisors, and fifty-four social case workers.

The total cost of UNRWA's relief program in 1969, in round figures, was $19,200,000: for rations $12,900,000; shelter $274,000; supplementary feeding $2,000,000; special hardship assistance $555,000; and $3,400,000 representing the allocated share of administrative and other costs common to all programs.[5]

RECTIFICATION

The Economic Survey Mission estimated at 726,000 the number of Palestinians who fled in 1948 and were unable to return to Israeli controlled territory, and at 652,000—including an additional 25,000 "economic refugees"—the number who were in need and therefore entitled to United Nations assistance. The number of rations allowed by UNRWA's predecessor and distributed by the voluntary agencies, at the time the Agency took over in May 1950, was 957,000.* This comprised UNRWA's "registration" at the outset, which a year later had been reduced to 904,000 and which in 1969 had increased to 1,395,000.

While need is a criterion for an eligible registrant, the registration of a refugee who has become self-supporting is not cancelled. However, degree of self-sufficiency affects his eligibility for assistance and thus the laminated card issued by UNRWA to each head of family categorizes the family according to need. Category "R" means rations plus health and education services, category "S" means health and education services only, while category "N"— issued to families that have become wholly self-supporting—means no assistance of any kind. These cards, concerned with degree of need or lack thereof, constitute the only international documentation in the hands of the refugees testifying to their Palestinian origin. Moreover, because need is a necessary qualification for initial inscription on UNRWA rolls, the Agency's register has never comprised all of the 1948 refugees, since it was not intended to include

* See Chapter I, p. 39.

persons of independent means nor others who found immediate employment. As noted in Chapter I, the Commissioner-General once estimated that such persons constituted twenty percent of the 1948 exodus.[6]

On the other hand, UNRWA's criteria of registration excluded many Palestinians whose livelihoods were disastrously affected even though they did not lose their homes. Palestinians in this category have exercised considerable pressure, as also have the Arab governments on their behalf, to be included among relief recipients. In a special report on the matter in 1955 made at the direction of the General Assembly, the Commissioner-General referred to two groups in particular: frontier villagers in Jordan and the nonrefugee population of the Gaza Strip. The former constituted in 111 villages and towns an estimated population of 182,000, many of whom were cut off from their lands or other means of livelihood. In the Commissioner-General's judgment only eleven percent were fully self-supporting, while twenty-nine percent were almost fully in need.* He found that such relief of the frontier villagers as was afforded by UNICEF and certain voluntary agencies (Near East Christian Council, Lutheran World Federation, International Christian Committee, and the Pontifical Mission) fell short of UNRWA's standards as regards food, health, and education.

As for the Gaza Strip, the total population (as of 1955) was estimated by the Commissioner-General at 309,000. About 95,000 were described as nonrefugee residents, whose livelihood, except for the few owning land within the Strip itself, had been disrupted by the demarcation line. The report stated that 59,000 were receiving

---

* The Commissioner-General observed that there "is only a difference of degree" between the man who lost his home as well as his livelihood and "the man whose home was on the Jordan side of the demarcation line but whose land is now cut off in Israel, or who worked in what is now Israel Jerusalem, or who sold his produce in the coastal towns or exported it through Palestinian ports. . . ." He suggested that "the family which continues to reside in its former home, but whose nearby fields are no longer in its possession, may be in a more serious plight. The very proximity of its former possessions—the situation in which the original inhabitants must watch newcomers till their former fields and harvest crops from their former groves—increases the tensions and the psychological strains." *Special Report of the Director* (A/2978/Add. 1), 15 October 1955.

assistance from the Egyptian authorities, UNICEF, and CARE, at a level in food-stuffs of 1,050 calories per person per day.[7]

Responding to the special report, the General Assembly merely appealed "to private organizations to give . . . increased assistance to the extent that local governments cannot do so. . . ."[*] There the matter rested, except that the Agency continued to give half-rations to a limited number of frontier villagers in Jordan—a practice begun by its predecessor UNRPR. The maximum number of half-rations was 65,000 in 1953, down in 1969 to the 13,500 noted earlier.

While UNRWA registration presumably omits 1948 refugees who were never in need, and also excludes for the most part the "economic refugees" of Jordan and Gaza, a converse point to be emphasized is that unknown numbers of ineligible persons are included among UNRWA registrants, while among registrants otherwise eligible there is considerable margin of error in their assignment to the several categories of need. The rolls inherited by UNRWA included many thousands of families who by UNRWA's definition did not qualify as refugees or were duplicate registrants. Many deaths have been undetected (estimated cumulatively at 100,000 in 1961),[8] other persons have migrated, and still others are no longer in need. Though many deletions and changes of status have been made,[†] the integrity of UNRWA's rolls has never ceased to be

[*] United Nations, General Assembly, *Resolution 916* (X), para. 6, 3 December 1955. As late as 1965, the annual report stated that assistance from voluntary agencies to "other claimants for relief" was inadequate. "It is unhappily true that many of these 'other claimants' are in an even worse condition than many of the refugees eligible for assistance from UNRWA; particularly critical is the condition of the Azameh tribe of bedouin in Jordan, Gaza and the Sinai Peninsula. The Commissioner-General reiterates the opinion that the tragic plight of these unfortunate victims of the conflict in Palestine must surely weigh heavily on the conscience of mankind." *Annual Report* (A/6013), para. 22.

[†] Deletions in basic registration as of June 1969 included 140,850 deaths, 74,000 false and duplicate registrations, and 89,200 from miscellaneous causes. Additions, meanwhile, included 684,600 births, 46,200 new registrations (nearly all in the initial years), and 7,500 from miscellaneous causes. Thus up to June 1969 there was a total of 304,000 deletions from and 738,000 additions to basic registration. *Annual Report* (A/7614), 1969, Table 3. At the same time shifts were occurring among registrants as to category of need. As of June 1969, reduction or cessation of assistance had affected 229,000 individuals, offset by

a problem. This does not mean that greater accuracy would necessarily reduce UNRWA's expenditure, for we saw that a large
backlog of children awaits rations within the ceilings imposed by
UNRWA. This point is often stressed by the Commissioner-General,
who said, for example, in 1965 that the problem is "not exclusively,
nor even primarily, a matter of budgetary savings, but rather one of
equity among the refugees and of the integrity of the Agency in
discharging its mandate given it by the General Assembly."[9]

The well-known tendency of recipients of relief to be uncoopera-
tive with their benefactors is decidedly true of the Palestinian
refugees. A first and foremost reason is the feeling of outraged
justice. "From their standpoint," the Commissioner-General remarked in his 1965 report, "a nation has been obliterated and a
population arbitrarily deprived of its birthright." Continuing, the
Commissioner-General said:

This injustice still festers in their minds and they hold the United Nations responsible for their lot and for extending assistance to them until
a solution can be found to their problems. Their longing to return to
their homes, encouraged by the General Assembly's declaration on
repatriation and compensation in paragraph 11 of resolution 194 (III)
and referred to in many subsequent resolutions, remains unabated.*

Second, the refugee clings to the ration card as his entitlement to
repatriation or compensation, an attitude encouraged by the fact,
already noted, that his Palestinian identity has no other documen-
tary proof of international character.[10] Finally, there is deep-seated
suspicion, which the newspapers of the region do little to counter
and often stimulate, that UNRWA's motives for rectification are in

---

99,760 who subsequently lost self-support; while cessation of assistance in
135,000 absences was offset by 39,300 returns. Also, in case of 143,700 individuals
UNRWA assistance decreased or ceased for miscellaneous reasons, while in the
same period there were 34,300 increases in assistance for miscellaneous reasons.
Ibid., Table 2.

    * *Annual Report* (A/6013), para. 6. ". . . refugees are inclined to regard relief
in general, and rations in particular, not as something to which they must show
their entitlement, but rather as a right—as a partial payment by the world at
large for their involuntary expulsion from Palestine and continued exile from
their homeland." *Special Report of the Director* (A/2978/Add. 1), 1955, para.
73.

some way connected with an effort to liquidate the refugee problem in a manner that would deny the basic right of repatriation. Thus, any major effort to revise the rolls "tends to stimulate certain influential refugee elements to press UNRWA and the host governments to halt the process."[11]

UNRWA commands neither the information (demographic and economic) nor the police power to cope on its own with the problem of rectification. "It is an inescapable fact," the Commissioner-General pointed out in 1957, "that the Agency's system of control cannot be substantially improved without the full support and technical cooperation of the refugee leaders and of the host governments."[12] Identifying and counting people by whatever criteria, the keeping of vital statistics, the control of movements, and the gathering of economic data are functions which perforce only government can perform. To these perquisites of territorial authority UNRWA has adapted in different ways, but in none of the host countries has a satisfactory accommodation been achieved.

In Lebanon a census of Palestinian refugees was carried out by the government in 1962 with UNRWA's assistance. Of the 33,850 families then registered with UNRWA, 3,700 failed to come forward. Many among the latter were already in the "no services" category, while others represented false registrations. The net result, stemming from the families that did not appear and from rectifications among families that did present themselves, was 5,900 individuals newly transferred to the "no services" category, including 2,600 ration recipients. It is helpful to UNRWA that in Lebanon each refugee seventeen years of age and over holds an identity card issued by the government. On the other hand, death certificates, while available for UNRWA's inspection, do not identify Palestinians as such, and checking against them is further complicated by lack of a fixed family name among the Arabs. The government informs UNRWA of passports issued to Palestinians, thus apprising the Agency of departures. In Lebanon the Agency is not without serious problems as to the initial eligibility and the existence and presence of persons registered for its services, yet the integrity of its rolls in Lebanon are more nearly assured than in any other area of operation.

In Syria all refugees are registered with the Palestine Arab

Refugees Institute.* The PARI document is a family booklet, though anyone over 18 years of age is entitled to an individual identity document. The number so registered in 1966 was about 13,000 more than the number of rations issued by UNRWA on the basis of its own ration cards. PARI also maintains a register of births and deaths, though it is not consistently available for checking by UNRWA. Though Syrian statistics on the refugees are more systematic than any kept in other countries of refuge, lack of governmental cooperation leaves the Agency without assurance of the initial eligibility or of the existence and presence of those receiving rations.

In Gaza, under the Egyptians, there was neither census nor a government registry of refugees. Every male eighteen years or over held an identity card from the government, but without distinction as a refugee or as an original Palestinian resident of the Strip. False and multiple registrations, along with undetected dead and absentees, were still at the time of the June War major sources of inaccuracy in UNRWA's rolls in Gaza. By 1966, however, government records of births and deaths had been opened to UNRWA and passport information had also been made available.†

In Jordan, where the Palestinian (whether refugee or nonrefugee) is no different in legal status from any other Jordanian, such

---

* PARI is a public corporation with legal and financial autonomy. Through it, Syria, to a greater extent than any other host government, deals operationally with refugee problems, supplementing UNRWA's programs in such fields as housing and education and distributing commodities from UNRWA warehouses in its own or government-hired trucks.

† The backlog of inaccuracies was partly dealt with in 1965 through a systematic "line check" during distribution of rations (all males over 18 years of age were called in with the head of family, whereas the normal check was for the head of family to appear alone twice a year), to which "the government authorities gave support and effective help." This resulted in cancellation of some 4,300 rations. Among the total of 9,755 ration removals in Gaza at that time, others "resulted from checks against the . . . passport department records . . . , and against the . . . health department's records of death; the elimination of duplicate registrations; cancellations on grounds of income; checking the existence of aged refugees; checking family ration cards on which no changes had been recorded for several years, and other miscellaneous operations." *Annual Report* (A/6013), 1965, para. 40.

census data as exist contain no basis for identifying refugees. A cooperative attempt by the Agency and the Jordanian government in 1950–51 to carry out a census of refugees yielded unsatisfactory results, while subsequent investigations by the Agency were halted in 1953 by the government because of the intense hostility of the refugees. Indeed, "misunderstandings as to the true purposes of verification arose . . . and have not yet been completely overcome."[13] This observation by the Commissioner-General in 1955 has held for subsequent years. Between 1961 and 1964 there was some weeding out of false registrants, dead, and absentees, but, as we shall see, not until 1967 was it possible to do anything substantial. Death certificates in Jordan are available to the Agency but do not distinguish the refugee as such. An application from a refugee for a Jordanian passport sometimes necessitates the government's checking with UNRWA as to the legitimacy of the applicant's claim of origin. But the Agency knows nothing of the extent of the prospective absence, nor whether or not a passport is eventually issued. Throughout most of its existence, UNRWA's rolls in Jordan have remained grossly inaccurate and the cause of great frustration to the Agency.

In all of UNRWA's areas of operation, need (or lack thereof) is the factor determining the category of registration to which a family is assigned at any given time—whether, that is, a registered family fits in "R", "S", or "N" category. Given the elasticity of the concept of need, its application to the administration of a relief program is difficult at best, and even more difficult where, as in the Arab countries, governmental statistics on the economic circumstances of a population are limited both in scope and reliability. To these complications affecting UNRWA's use of the criterion of need must be added the problem of getting agreement with government on the cut-off points among categories. Only with Lebanon has there been a coincidence of views, and there only since 1965. Using the government's minimum wage legislation as a base, UNRWA withdraws rations from a family outside a camp when income reaches 175 Lebanese pounds a month (approximately $55) and from a family inside a camp at a 145 pound ($45) level. Though in principle the Agency is allowed to investigate a family's economic status at its own initiative, the Lebanese government for political reasons has at times restricted UNRWA in this regard. Nevertheless, 5,000 rations were cancelled in Lebanon during 1966 because of income, in contrast to 900 in Jordan and Gaza each and 300 in Syria during that year.

In general, reliable information about the economic status of UNRWA registrants is seriously lacking, while the Agency's use of such information as exists is largely frustrated by lack of government cooperation. It must be emphasized, however, that in bestowing a benefit, in contrast to imposing a deprivation, the Agency is in no way deterred from applying income scales of its own on the basis of whatever information it can muster concerning a family's economic circumstances, and it can in such instances make a decision without government concurrence. Thus families who previously were partly or wholly self-supporting undergo a full investigation when they apply for restitution of rations on grounds of reduced income. Also, employing a refugee on its staff, admitting a refugee family to a camp, and choosing among applicants for vocational training, teacher training, or university scholarships are all situations in which the Agency has freedom of action to decide on the basis of its own best information.

Confining registration to bona fide Palestinian refugees and limiting relief to needy cases are tasks that require full application of territorial authority. However, one must concede that these objectives would be difficult to attain even if undivided responsibility were to rest in the host governments. The wiles of the individual confronted by authority are well known in Arab society. Yet authority—whether territorial or international—is contending not merely with individual refugees but with a Palestinian collectivity concerned that its numbers not be minimized and that its solidarity be preserved. Through sympathy, the dilemma of the governments —whether to favor the welfare of the individual or the cause of the group—is all the greater. In Jordan, where there is little room for miscalculation of what police power can do, the dilemma is most severe.

There the problem of rectification has always been greater than in any of the jurisdictions within which UNRWA operates, and prior to 1967 it took an unusual and particularly troublesome form. Ration cards, possessing value because of the food-stuffs they command, were sold to so-called merchants who would collect the commodities at UNRWA's distribution points and profit from their sale on the open market. The New York *Times* of 21 March 1966 reported the holding of 1,100 ration cards by a single "merchant." In some instances a card was surrendered for a limited period in return for cash, thereby affording the refugee a choice in allocation of his limited resources. Illustrative of the preceding chapter's characterization of a ration as a subsidy rather than merely a life-saving expedient, the practice goes a step beyond the bartering of rations by a recipient refugee, which has never been frowned upon. Yet the practice was subject to serious abuse inasmuch as many of the cards held were those of dead and absentees. As we shall note presently, the political protection that the "merchants" built around their trafficking in ration cards was finally overcome in the exceptional circumstances following the June War.

Yet, however great the attending difficulties, government is where the essential authority lay for policing a relief program. This is borne out by UNRWA's experience and often has been acknowledged by the Agency. A major attempt by UNRWA in 1965 to cope with the problem of rectification started expressly with the premise that "the Governments possess records and have means of securing information . . . which place them in a far better position than UNRWA to determine need and eligibility."[14] Accordingly, the Commissioner-General was prepared to reconstitute the rolls on the basis of determination by the governments, themselves, of "eligibility for inscription on the lists, priority for the allocation of rations and the scale of rations which different categories of beneficiaries should receive. . . ." While retaining the criterion of need, he would be willing to accept a new and broad definition of eligibility: that relief recipients "be persons formerly resident in Palestine before 1948 . . . who have suffered loss or damage as a result of the conflict . . . , or the descendents of such persons. . . ." A minimum period of residence in Palestine would be dropped, the "economic refugees" no longer excluded, and the third generation of refugees unequivocally admitted to the rolls.*

The presumption was that the host governments would willingly police arrangements of their own choosing, under constraint, of course, of available funds, while verification of eligibility was to be jointly carried out by UNRWA and government. The hoped-for result of putting primary responsibility on the governments, as stated in UNRWA's 1965 report, was "a much higher degree of equity in distribution of rations within the refugee population than is reflected in the present UNRWA rolls."

Prior to the General Assembly being apprised of these proposals in the fall of 1965, they had already been the subject of negotiations between UNRWA and the host governments. The Commissioner-General reported that the latter

appreciate that, in view of the limited resources available to the Agency, it would not be practicable for UNRWA in present circumstances to extend assistance to large additional categories of beneficiaries. They have accordingly indicated that, without insisting, in the present circumstances, on the inclusion of the "other claimants" within the scope of the proposals, they would be prepared to implement those parts of the

* In his 1965 report to the General Assembly, the Commissioner-General remarked: "Recently a new problem of eligibility has arisen with the appearance of a third generation of refugees (i.e., the children of persons who were themselves born after 14 May 1948). On a literal interpretation of the definition of eligibility as it now stands, there may be some doubt whether these persons are eligible for UNRWA assistance. Under the proposals set out . . . , they would clearly be eligible . . . , subject to their being in need, and this would apply to subsequent generations also."

The Commissioner-General said further with respect to the third generation that "so long as international assistance is given the Arab refugee community, third generation children cannot humanely be denied health services at the time of birth (since their mothers receive medical care) nor use of UNRWA shelters. As these children' grow up, it would be harsh and uneconomic to deny them access to nearby UNRWA health services. . . . When they reach school age, it would similarly be difficult to insist that such children, especially those whose parents live in camps, be excluded from UNRWA schools and to demand that they travel to more distant government or private schools. As for including such children in the distribution of rations, [the] fact is that, if limitations such as the present ration ceilings have to be maintained in the future, third generation children would in any event have to join a waiting list." *Annual Report* (A/6013), paras. 21, 25.

proposals which require action on their part if the Commissioner-General on his part undertook to extend assistance to the third generation of refugees, when in need.

However, a subsequent development caused the host governments to back away from agreement. Pointing to announcement by the United States and Great Britain of intended reduction in their contributions to UNRWA, they said that they would have to be assured of continuation of the Agency's programs at existing levels.

The Commissioner-General could not, of course, guarantee the future, but meanwhile the deficit for the fiscal year 1966 was absorbed through a further reduction in the Agency's operating reserve, so that UNRWA continued to operate at its previous level. The Commissioner-General, who had already admitted the third generation to registration with the tacit consent of the General Assembly, again pressed upon the governments the need to confine relief to bona fide refugees requiring assistance.

In June 1966 success seemed finally at hand in Jordan. Agreement was reached June 15 between UNRWA and the government whereby all ration cards were to be exchanged for new ones. Heads of family were to appear in person with proof of identity. A family whose head failed to appear would be removed from the rolls. Where false or duplicate registration was suspected, cards were to be set aside for special investigation by a joint government/Agency committee. Also subject to joint investigation was any family, any member of which was suspected of being absent.[15]

At about the same time as the agreement, the New York *Times* (14 June 1966) reported from Washington that the staff director of the Senate Subcommittee on Refugees and Escapees, who had recently returned from an investigation of the condition of the Palestinian refugees, had disclosed the assurance given him by members of the Jordanian Cabinet that the chaotic state of the ration rolls in Jordan would be remedied. But if Jordan was attentive to the concern of the chief contributor to UNRWA's budget, it was subject as well to continuing internal pressures. Difficult relations between the Jordanian government and the Palestine Liberation Organization (seeking a degree of control over the refugees rivaling that of Amman's) culminated in an open breach at about this time, and on July 9 the government announced the "freezing" of its agreement with UNRWA.

A year later, in the aftermath of the June War, the Jordanian government had to cope with its own problems of false and duplicate registrations among newly displaced persons. Beginning in August 1967, the scheme which had been adumbrated in the previous year was partially effected in East Jordan, where "merchants" accustomed to trafficking in rations—after a last attempt at rallying opposition—were finally thwarted. In 1968 the Commissioner-General reported that "this long-standing abuse has now been largely eliminated and, given continuing vigilance by the authorities and UNRWA, should not recur."[16]

HEALTH

In 1968 UNRWA, jointly with the World Health Organization, ministered to 1,240,000 persons eligible for its health services at a cost of $5,300,000. The program employed only eight international staff, whereas 1,130 professional and technical personnel and 3,200 laborers were recruited locally.[17]

The size of the operation suggests a broader than curative purpose and the program includes, as well, a full range of preventive measures commonly undertaken by public authority. Such measures, dependent in important respects on government cooperation for their prosecution, are of a technical nature conducive to joint effort without the intervention of political considerations such as beset UNRWA's programs of relief and education. In general, the health program has been designed to provide services to the refugees approximately at the same levels as the host governments provide to members of their own populations who are in comparable economic circumstances.

Curative Services

As of 31 December 1968 outpatients were served in 116 clinics, ninety-five of which were manned and administered by UNRWA, ten by governments, and eleven by voluntary agencies (the latter two categories subsidized by UNRWA). Sixty-four of the UNRWA clinics were permanent installations, while the remainder consisted of nine mobile teams. In all, visits to the clinics during the year numbered 5,900,000.

UNRWA manned and administered two hospitals, but through subsidy it depended mainly on thirty government and thirty-eight private (mostly church-affiliated) hospitals. A total of 1,806 beds were available—some seventy-five percent for treatment of acute cases and the remaining twenty-five percent for chronic diseases. Hospital usage totaled 520,000 bed days. Diagnostic services were provided by university, government, and private laboratories, generally on a subsidy or cost basis, though occasionally free of charge. The Agency, meanwhile, maintained two small laboratories in Lebanon and one central laboratory in the Gaza Strip.

Preventive Measures

Even in periods of greatest vulnerability, such as 1948 and 1967, the refugee population has never suffered an epidemic. Virtually unknown are the most serious of the quarantinable diseases—cholera, plague, relapsing fever, smallpox, typhus, and yellow fever. Respiratory infections constitute a major group of communicable diseases, especially among infants and young children. Eye diseases, including trachoma, have continued a steady decline. The incidence of tuberculosis and malaria continue to respond favorably to routine cooperative measures undertaken by UNRWA and governments. Gastro-enteric infections have presented the greatest problem; often associated with malnutrition, the diarrhoeal and dysenteric diseases are the most frequent causes of illness and death in early life.

In 1968 health protection for mothers and children was provided in eighty maternity and seventy-seven infant clinics, while these groups also received special nutritional supplements through provision of hot meals and milk, inasmuch as the basic rations contain no fresh food or animal protein. Nutritional restoration of underweight infants was provided through eighteen rehydration/nutrition centers, with a total of 217 cots. School children were beneficiaries of a program of routine examination with follow-up care.

The Agency conducts a program of health education to enable the refugees to recognize health needs and to encourage their cooperation in meeting them. To this end health drives employ group discussions, lectures, and audio-visual aids. The UNRWA–Swedish Health Center, since its establishment in Gaza in 1966, has continued to give advice and assistance to married women interested in planned parenthood.[18] However, the extension of the program in Gaza has encountered opposition from the refugees, while elsewhere the host governments have not given assent to the establishment of similar programs.

In the schools, health is promoted through the curriculum and through health clubs. Of particular interest is a course on motherhood and child care introduced in 1966 in the Agency's preparatory schools for girls in Gaza, in which about 2,300 girls fifteen to sixteen years of age participate annually. The course's objective is to view the family in all its aspects, "with the implication of the need for spacing pregnancies to ensure better health of the child and of the mother."[19]

As of 1968 UNRWA was providing environmental sanitation for some 550,000 persons in its fifty-three established and ten emergency camps, involving supply of water, disposal of wastes, provision of latrines, and control of insect and rodent vectors. Evolution of the established camps into settled communities was evident in several public health respects. Of 80,000 families residing in such camps, 13,200 had secured private connections from local water authorities. Family latrines, construction of which is encouraged by the Agency through grants of cash and materials, numbered 40,000. In a few camps UNRWA had constructed sewage-drainage systems, while in a limited number of others such projects had been carried out by local authorities with the Agency's financial assistance.

Administration and Personnel

In December 1948 the World Health Organization, at the request of the Secretary-General of the United Nations, assumed technical responsibility for the health program then being administered by the United Nations Relief for Palestinian Refugees. Two medical officers were assigned to the task and $50,000 was granted to defray other expenses. WHO's role, reaffirmed when UNRWA took over in May 1950, has continued to the present, based on formal agreement between the two bodies. The Director of the Department of Health, provided by WHO, is responsible for planning and implementing the program within the budget set by the Commissioner-General. As of 1968, four other officials were provided by WHO, while three additional officials were internationally recruited. Increasingly, local personnel have been manning high posts of administrative responsibility.

In 1968 the Agency employed 120 doctors, five of whom were part-time. Full-time dentists numbered seven, while ten were employed on a part-time contractual basis—dental services being largely confined to extractions and simple fillings. Also employed were 116 graduate nurses, nurse-midwives, and public health nurses; over 100 midwives; and nearly 300 auxiliary nurses. Supply of such personnel is assured in part through scholarships at universities and technical and hospital-affiliated nursing schools. In addition, the Agency's own vocational schools provide two-year training programs for public health inspectors, laboratory technicians, and assistant pharmacists.

The field health officer in each of the host countries is responsible in technical matters to the Director of the Department of Health at headquarters in Beirut and in administrative questions to the UNRWA country representative. He must also maintain liaison with the government Ministry of Health and with local health officials. The complexity of the relationships is indicated by the following passage taken from an early annual report:

The burden of the health programme has fallen on the Agency with a varying pattern of government participation. Certain governments will admit refugee patients to government hospitals, either free of charge or at a minimal rate. In some cases, arrangements have been made so that refugees may attend government clinics, although it must be pointed out that in many instances, non-refugees attend Agency operated facilities. Joint anti-malaria campaigns have been conducted in many small communities which are made up of both refugees and nationals of the countries. Similarly cooperation has been attained in the control of typhus and relapsing fevers, since these two diseases, when they do occur among refugees, appear usually among those who live outside camps; i.e., in communities which consist largely of nationals of countries. In one country a diphtheria immunization programme was carried out jointly by the Agency and the government, with UNICEF providing the toxoid. Co-operation with governments is also apparent in the exchange of epidemiological information between the Agency and the governments. In Jordan, a well-developed public health diagnostic laboratory and vaccine production service originally established by the Agency has been turned over to the government, with the understanding that the service for UNRWA will continue to be rendered on the same scale as previously.[20]

Control of communicable diseases and provision of environmental sanitation often require cooperation with government. On the other hand, while dependence on government facilities and supplies is convenient and economical for UNRWA in carrying out the curative aspects of its health services, the clinical treatment of disease inherently does not require government cooperation. Moreover, the Agency's programs of health education, supplementary feeding, maternal health, and infant health are self-contained as regards facilities, supplies, and personnel.

The success of the health program has been the more notable for the program's economy. True, UNRWA's budget reflects neither the services and supplies donated by the local governments nor the donations of other governments and private agencies for specific projects. Yet the health of one and a quarter million refugees has been well looked after at a cost to the Agency of not much more than $5,000,000 annually, which is a signal achievement.

VII

Education

UNRWA's educational program at first supplemented and in 1960 supplanted economic measures as a means of rehabilitation. The attempt to integrate displaced Palestinians into the surrounding Arabic society through economic programs gave way to the cultivation of individual capabilities through basic education and vocational, technical, and professional training. This fundamental shift of emphasis meant abandonment of UNRWA's initial objective of rapid reintegration for a goal realizable only in terms of a new generation, and it carried the further consequence that the traditional, rural ways of the older generation would be replaced in the younger with a mobile, urban outlook.

Conducted in collaboration with Unesco, UNRWA's educational program has undergone marked evolution in contrast to the routine programs of relief and health. Expenditure grew from $300,000 in 1950 to $18,120,000 in 1969, when it accounted for forty percent of UNRWA's budget, and today the UNRWA-Unesco system affords educational opportunity the equal of, indeed in some respects superior to, that prevailing in the host countries. Yet its future is now threatened by intransigent attitudes over textbooks appropriate for its use, raising the extremely difficult question of educational content: a nation's conception of its own identity and interests versus international concern for reconciliation and nonaggression. Difficult enough to deal with in the abstract, the problem has proved to be virtually insoluble in the context of the Arab-Israeli conflict over Palestine.

PROGRAM'S EXTENT AND VARIETY

At the elementary level of instruction, which comprises the first six years, and at the preparatory level, comprising the next three years, UNRWA schools accommodate most of the refugee children, while government and private schools with financial assistance from UNRWA admit still others in these age groups. At the secondary level—the last three years of general education—UNRWA has no schools of its own. Reliance is entirely on government and private schools assisted by grants-in-aid from UNRWA.*

The Agency's goal of providing elementary and preparatory education for all refugee children is close to realization. During 1968–69, 161,000 were enrolled in UNRWA-Unesco schools at the elementary level, while 20,000 were in government and 7,500 in private schools. In all, this enrollment comprised eighty to ninety percent of the eligible age group, compared with eighty-eight percent of the elementary age group in Lebanese schools, eighty-one in Jordanian, and seventy-one in Syrian. At the preparatory level, Agency schools had an enrollment of 47,700 in 1968–69, with 8,900 in government and 3,200 in private schools. The Agency estimated that it was reaching sixty to seventy percent of the preparatory age group, whereas the comparable percentage for Lebanon was seventy-nine, for Jordan forty-nine, and Syria forty-seven. Finally, at the secondary level in 1968–1969, 17,200 refugee children attended government and 3,200 private schools.[1]

Of special note are the Agency's seven residential two-year vocational and technical training centers: two in the West Bank, two in Lebanon, and one each in East Jordan, Syria, and Gaza. Enrollment in 1968–69 was 2,098 men and 310 women. Total capacity recently has been increased to 3,100 places through grants

---

* UNRWA's subsidy of refugee children in government and private schools, totaling, for example, $1,040,000 in the 1966–67 school year (*Progress Report on School Year 1966–67*, pp. 44, 57, 70, and 83) covers only part of the actual cost. In 1966–67 governments incurred an additional expense of $3,447,000. *Annual Report* (A/6713), 1967, Table 22.

from private and government sources permitting expansion of certain of the existing facilities and the addition of an eighth center in East Jordan.

UNRWA points out the pioneering character of its vocational and technical centers, which have become some of the most important purveyors of this type of outside assistance in the Arab Middle East. Vocational training (some twenty different specialties in the metal, electrical, and building trades) begins at the end of the preparatory cycle, whereas technical training (in areas such as architectural and engineering draftsmanship, business, and paramedicine) entails post-secondary courses of study. An innovation for the region is the Women's Vocational Training Center in Ramallah (West Bank), inaugurated in 1962; offering a variety of courses (for example, dressmaking, clothing production, home and institutional management, and hairdressing), the Center prior to the June War was remarkably successful in finding employment for its graduates. Selected graduates in vocational training are afforded internships in industry abroad, some 1,000 by 1969 mainly in West Germany and Sweden.

To provide a source of professionally prepared recruits for its own educational system, which now exceeds 6,000 teachers, and by way of affording still another form of specialized training, UNRWA operates five pre-service teacher-training schools, mainly for elementary teachers: one in Lebanon, two in the West Bank, and two temporary centers in Amman, shortly to be amalgamated in a newly constructed center with money from a private source. Each provides a two-year post-secondary course of study leading to a certificate recognized as the equivalent of a government-issued teacher's license. Enrolled in 1968–69 were 1,186 students. A large majority of the graduates find employment outside the UNRWA school system, many with Arab governments other than those of the host countries.

While the teacher-training schools' purpose is to prepare new recruits, an in-service training program endeavors to improve teachers already in the UNRWA system. As an experimental program with possible application elsewhere, Unesco in 1964 initiated an Institute of Education, financed mainly by Switzerland, with Unesco supplying part of the staff and UNRWA providing logistical support. The Institute offers a two-year program employing two approaches in combination: instruction through correspondence courses; and direct help through some twenty field staff members who organize discussion groups, observe trainees in the classroom, and conduct intensive summer courses of two to three weeks. The Institute disseminates new educational techniques such as programmed instruction and audio-visual aids and has introduced radio and closed-circuit television as educational media. Enrollment has averaged about 1,500 trainees per year.

Whereas in 1964, when the Institute began, only 450 of the more than 5,000 teachers then employed in UNRWA schools were licensed, by April 1969 a total of 1,400 had earned certificates through the Institute. Unlike the certificate awarded a graduate of an UNRWA teacher-training school, an Institute certificate is not yet accepted by government as the equivalent of its own teacher's license, though UNRWA is pressing for such recognition. Meanwhile, the Institute certificate increases the opportunity of the recipient for employment elsewhere, while within the UNRWA system it carries a salary increase. Unesco looks upon the Institute as a highly successful undertaking.[2]

A total of 1,255 university scholarships were awarded by UNRWA in 1968–69 for use in the host countries, a large increase over previous years made possible by a donation from the West German government. Continuing scholarships numbered 533, while 722 were new. In addition a large number of university scholarships are awarded directly to refugees by the Egyptian and Syrian governments, and in small numbers by Algeria, Iraq, Libya, Pakistan, the Sudan, and Turkey. A few awards are made by European governments for study in their respective universities.

In the five-year period 1964–1968 there were in all 7,225 graduates of the vocational/technical and teacher-training centers, while university graduates subsidized by UNRWA in the same period numbered 638. Common to all of UNRWA's special educational benefits is permanent cancellation of a beneficiary's entitlement to Agency services after graduation.

COORDINATION WITH UNESCO AND GOVERNMENTS

Preceding UNRWA, Unesco in 1949 had solicited funds (and itself contributed $38,000) for the establishment of sixty-one schools and for subsidy of refugee children in government and private schools. In March 1951 formal collaboration between the agencies was provided in the first of several successive agreements whereby Unesco has assumed "technical responsibility" for the educational program, while UNRWA, in control of the budget, is "administratively responsible."[3] Division, however, is not clear-cut; and we shall see that confusion over policy has not been precluded.

Unesco is involved in both planning and execution. From the beginning it has filled the position of Director of UNRWA's Department of Education. At one time it provided as many as twenty-three educational specialists; a number reduced to eighteen in a 1965 agreement. Among the latter, five were assigned to the Institute of Education, while others were specialists in various academic and vocational subjects. Unesco officials are seconded personnel, paid by Unesco, with UNRWA's financial responsibility limited to office space and travel in its area of operation. The cost to Unesco is voted in its regular budget, an item amounting in 1968 to $345,000. Through 1968, Unesco's appropriations totaled $3,650,000. The vitality of UNRWA's educational system is largely owing to the professional competence that Unesco brings to it.

While coordination between UNRWA and the host governments in educational matters is indispensable, a joint-committee approach to its implementation has not proved successful.* Relations are

---

* The Joint Coordination Committee for Education, referred to in the annual report for 1965 (A/6013, para. 74) as having been newly established in Jordan, did not materialize as was expected.

The sometimes contentious character of relations with a government is suggested by this comment appearing in *Progress Report on School Year 1966–67*, para. 138: "Toward the end of the 1964–65 school year the Agency reluctantly decided that it could no longer operate its [teacher training] centre at Homs [Syria] . . . in the conditions then prevailing. Various proposals were made to the Government the last of which was an offer to it to take over the centre . . . and run it as a teacher training institution for refugees; but to date the centre remains closed. Discussions with the Government are still continuing."

formally channeled through UNRWA's country representative and the government's liaison office for refugees. Informal contact is maintained with a country's Ministry of Education, at which level UNRWA's Field Education Officer, typically a Palestinian, becomes involved. That he is Palestinian is convenient and desirable from a number of viewpoints, including the linguistic, though to strengthen the representative capacity of Field Education Officers it has been suggested that they be made members of Unesco's staff. However, such a step has been taken only at the Deputy Director level at headquarters through a Unesco-appointed Supervisor of Education Services in the occupied territories. The pattern of relations, then, is one of negotiation; the interests are sufficiently disparate not to presuppose consensus.

We have what appear to be parallel systems of education. But in fact the UNRWA system is much intertwined with the government establishments.* The weight of territorial authority is especially evident with respect to UNRWA's selection of teachers and determination of curriculum.

Appointment of teachers is within UNRWA's province and the Agency establishes standards and rates of remuneration on the basis of which vacancies are advertised. From among persons who respond, selection in a particular country is made by a committee consisting of UNRWA officials and, in an advisory capacity, a representative of government. The latter may strike names from the list of candidates for security reasons or because of a police record

---

* This was flagrantly the case at the outset, as is apparent from this comment in the *Annual Report* (A/1905), 1951, para. 209: "Close co-operation has been established between local education authorities and the UNRWA district educational officers. In the Gaza area, government school buildings are shared by local and refugee children, and nineteen teachers appointed by UNRWA are working in government schools, while one headmaster and two head mistresses appointed by the government are employed in UNRWA-Unesco schools. In Jordan, nineteen Palestinian teachers have been appointed in government schools by UNRWA, thus making it possible to absorb another 1,500 refugee pupils in these schools. . . . In Syria, the government passes on the qualifications of all UNRWA teachers and has supplied a headmaster and a teacher for the Naireb School in Aleppo. The government school at Mazzeh employs three teachers who are paid by the Agency."

derogatory on other grounds. Thus, while appointment rests with UNRWA, government interposes a screening process.

CURRICULUM AND THE TEXTBOOK CRISIS

Difficult curricular problems confront an educational system under international auspices such as UNRWA's. In the first place, the UNRWA system has the problem of relating structurally to the curricular patterns of the respective national systems, and second there is the substantive question of curricular content.

The UNRWA-Unesco system is not self-contained. Laterally it is supplemented by government and private schools, which take a portion of the refugee children at the elementary and preparatory levels. Thus any marked departure by UNRWA from the curriculum of the indigenous schools would make for invidious distinctions. A still greater constraint is that the UNRWA system, stopping at the preparatory level, is vertically incomplete. Admission to a government secondary school is determined by a uniform examination based on the syllabi and textbooks used in the government schools at lower levels. This progression dictates much of UNRWA's curriculum—and also puts a premium on rote learning.

Quite apart from these obstacles to autonomy is the more difficult matter of curricular substance and style. History, a cynic has said, is politics projected into the past. But even a striving for objectivity cannot neglect the function, legitimate to any national educational system, of imparting common identity and purpose. Indeed, the Universal Declaration of Human Rights proclaimed by the United Nations in 1948 concedes that "Parents have a prior right to choose the kind of education that shall be given to their children."* And

* Constituting the third paragraph of Article 26 of the Declaration, it is preceded thus: (1) Everyone has the right to education. Education shall be free, at least in the elementary and fundamental stages. Elementary education shall be compulsory. Technical and professional education shall be made generally available and higher education shall be equally accessible to all on the basis of merit. (2) Education shall be directed to the full development of the human personality and to the strengthening of respect for human rights and fundamental freedoms. It shall promote understanding, tolerance and friendship among all nations, racial or religious groups, and shall further the activities of the United Nations for the maintenance of peace.

an often-quoted excerpt of a resolution adopted by the General Conference of Unesco (1956) calls upon member states "To adopt the necessary measures to ensure that everywhere education shall respect the national, religious and linguistic traditions of the inhabitants, and that its nature shall not be altered for political reasons. . . ."[4] Governments are here admonished to respect minority rights. In the context of the UNRWA-Unesco educational system for Palestinian refugees, the admonition suggests that to seek an international point of view would itself be a political act.

Accommodation between UNRWA's educational system and the systems respectively of Egypt, Jordan, Lebanon, and Syria developed over the years from empirical adjustments of an ad hoc nature, which were bound to circumscribe UNRWA's freedom of action in the sensitive area of curriculum. While in Lebanon UNRWA has considerable freedom to choose its own textbooks, in all other host countries the practice prior to the June War had been to employ the same syllabi and textbooks used in the government schools. The resulting subordination of an international system to national curricula was suddenly thrown into relief by Israel's occupation of Gaza and the West Bank in June 1967. To be sure, military control has not brought the schools of these areas into the Israeli educational system—except in East Jerusalem, which in effect has been annexed. The Egyptian and Jordanian school administrations are still intact in Gaza and the West Bank respectively. Thus the structural links on which UNRWA depends for completeness of its own system are not necessarily in jeopardy, though at the level of higher education the absence of an Arab university in the occupied areas presents an awkward problem.*

* The Director-General of Unesco was informed by the Israeli Foreign Office in a note dated 1 February 1968 that "the Israel authorities have no objection to the principle of students continuing their education at a higher level within a system having the same socio-cultural characteristics. If in particular cases it is proposed that they should leave the military government areas for the purpose and return to them on completion of their studies, this will be sympathetically considered in each case with due regard to security requirements." Unesco, *Summary Record of Executive Board* (78 EX/16), 18 April 1968, p. 3.

Unesco's Executive Board was told by its Israeli member on 10 July 1968 that certifying examinations were held in the occupied areas in January 1968 in lieu of those that normally would have been held in June 1967. "Committees of

The crisis came over textbooks. These were impounded by military government in UNRWA-Unesco no less than in government schools. Thus a novel problem arose of relating the law of military occupation to operations of international organization; and textbooks used in UNRWA-Unesco schools were for international organization an unpropitious issue on which to have to take a stand.

Early in July 1967 the Israeli Foreign Office protested to UNRWA that textbooks used in Agency schools taught hatred of Israel and incited to violence.* Responding, the Commissioner-General conceded that a

bitterly hostile attitude to Israel has been a characteristic of the education given to children, both refugee and non-refugee alike, in the Arab host countries. . . . But to suggest that this has been a principal factor in maintaining Arab hostility to Israel and to imply that, without it, the Palestine refugees (and the Arab world in general) might have forgotten

---

Arab educators had organized the examinations (which were based on Jordanian and Egyptian syllabuses), corrected the examination papers and delivered diplomas which were recognized by the authorities of Israel. About 75 percent of the total of over 1,500 pupils who sat for them passed those examinations. It was expected that about twice that number would sit . . . during the current month. In addition, some 500 pupils from the West Bank had been authorized to sit . . . in Amman. They would, of course, be allowed to return to their homes . . . , and would be free to pursue their further studies wherever they wished." Unesco, *Summary Record of Executive Board* (78 EX/SR. 24) (prov.), 18 June 1968, p. 14.

* The Director-General of Unesco was so informed by letter from the Commissioner-General of UNRWA, 17 July 1967. Unesco, *Summary Record of Executive Board* (77 EX/34), 6 October 1967, Annex II. The New York *Times* of 8 July 1967 reported (without distinguishing between UNRWA and government schools) that "Israeli troops . . . in the Gaza Strip reported finding virulent anti-Israeli material in the textbooks and defamatory murals on the school walls. The Israelis also said they found a lesser amount of propaganda in Jordanian schools in the west-bank area. . . .

"An Israeli officer said one problem [in an arithmetic book used in Gaza] posed the following situation: 'If 10 Feydayeen . . . cross the border into Israel and kill 20 Zionists, what is the average number of Jews killed by each Feydayeen?' "

Regarding the latter assertion, the Commissioner-General informed the Israeli Foreign Office that the Agency on examining the relevant texts had found "no trace of the statement cited." Memorandum on Allegations of Political Indoctrination in UNRWA-Unesco Schools, UNRWA to Israeli Ministry of Foreign Affairs, 17 July 1967. Unesco, *Summary Record of Executive Board* (77 EX/34), 6 October 1967, Annex II.

their grudge against Israel is to ignore the deep roots which the hostility of the refugees and other Arabs towards Israel has in the established Arab view of the history of the past fifty years.

Stating that "the Agency's educational policy has been designed to integrate its schools and training centres closely into the pattern of the national systems of education" in the host countries, the Commissioner-General pointed out that the "refugee children are growing up in the environment of these countries" and that their "chances of employment depend on the education and training they receive and on their passing the state examinations and receiving government certificates." "In theory," he continued,

the Agency might have attempted to establish . . . a separate, internationally oriented and politically innocuous system of education. In practice such an attempt would have meant discarding the advantages of integrating the UNRWA-Unesco educational programme with those of the host countries. It would also have led the Agency into a direct collision with the host countries in matters of a highly political and controversial nature where not merely the interpretation of facts and events but even the very facts and events themselves are widely disputed. As a purely humanitarian organization, UNRWA has no competence in political matters and would have been treading on very dangerous ground if its officials had attempted to censor the texbooks prescribed by the host governments. This would have involved exercising a necessarily subjective judgement of their truth and objectivity. It seemed to the Agency, therefore, that in the very awkward dilemma in which it was placed, the best course for it to pursue was to comply with the wishes of the host governments regarding curricula and textbooks, while at the same time doing the best it could, through inspection and supervision, to restrain the teachers in its schools from exceeding the requirements of the officially prescribed curricula and texts.

This policy admittedly has left the Agency, as an international, subsidiary organ of the United Nations, open to criticism for permitting the use in its schools of certain textbooks in which are to be found elements of "national guidance," sometimes of highly political and controversial kind. However, the Agency felt that, provided it stood fast by its established policy of conforming to the practice of the education authorities in the host countries, it would be on defensible ground.

In accord with this policy, the memorandum had earlier referred to a meeting between the Deputy Commissioner-General and certain Israeli officials in which the former had

indicated that there would be no objection on the part of the Agency to producing the textbooks heretofore prescribed . . . on the West Bank and in Gaza for scrutiny by the education authorities in Israel. The question whether different textbooks should be prescribed could then be considered. . . . If the Ministry of Education in Israel now wished to prescribe different books . . . in the areas administered by Israel, he did not foresee that the Agency would raise objection.[5]

Replying 20 July 1967, the Israeli Foreign Office stated

that hatred and incitement should not be taught to young children in the schools of any country—least of all in schools conducted under the direct auspices of the United Nations and Unesco. . . . While UNRWA has admittedly had difficulties in the Arab host countries, the principle involved is so fundamental that . . . [the Israeli] government cannot acquiesce in its violation.

Discussions between UNRWA's Director of Education and the Israeli Ministry of Education, the Israeli note concluded, "will no doubt deal with such matters as the screening of teachers and the replacement of textbooks."[6]

The Director-General of Unesco, troubled by the textbook issue (a question "relating to the content of education, for which Unesco is competent not only within the framework of the UNRWA-Unesco agreement, but also according to its very Constitution"), felt that he could not associate Unesco with the Commissioner-General's memorandum of July 17. Accordingly, UNRWA informed the Israeli Foreign Office, 29 September 1967, that the document in question did not reflect "in any way Unesco's views, except for matters which it is expressly stated were the subject of prior discussion and agreement" between UNRWA and Unesco. Meanwhile, the Director-General sought guidance from his Executive Board, and on 3 November 1967 the Board resolved that Unesco should deal with the textbook issue on the basis of the principles contained in Article 26 of the Declaration of Human Rights and in the resolution of the

General Conference concerning the education of minorities[7]—both of which have been quoted above.*

From among the impounded textbooks, Israeli authorities had meanwhile released those deemed unobjectionable. The others were banned, which in Gaza included virtually all, and in the West Bank one-third, of the books formerly used. To replace the proscribed texts, UNRWA's Department of Education mimeographed in the early months of the 1967–68 school year 46 sets of "teaching-notes"—in all, 104,750 copies, totaling 8,238,000 pages.[8] In effect the banned texts were reproduced with challenged portions omitted.

This response to immediate need was accompanied in January 1968 by a policy—jointly adopted by the Commissioner-General and Director-General—of refusing to use in the occupied territories or elsewhere in the UNRWA-Unesco system any *"new* or *revised* textbooks that appeared *prima facie* to contain material incompatible with the principles set out in the Executive Board resolution [of 3 November 1967]."[9] The policy gave notice of the unacceptability in the occupied territories of Israeli substitutions for the banned textbooks, while in East Jordan, Syria, and Lebanon the formula applied to new or revised textbooks that the governments might henceforth introduce—texts which prior practice would have automatically admitted into the UNRWA-Unesco curriculum. Inasmuch as the UNRWA teaching notes were unexceptionable to Israel, the new policy seemed to assure the continued availability in the occupied territories of textual materials in the sensitive areas of instruction. Elsewhere, however, there was no such assurance; in fact, it was predictable that the Arab governments would prohibit teaching notes in substitution for such of their newly published textbooks as might be rejected for use in UNRWA-Unesco schools. The immediate effect of the joint UNRWA-Unesco policy entailing qualitative judgment on textual materials was to eliminate seven texts as against seventy-six in continued use in East Jordan, and in Syria, thirteen against sixty-one. To be sure UNRWA could make do with obsolete texts until they wore out, while in Lebanon any

---

* See pp. 153–154.

consequences of the policy would be minor because of relative free-dom there to choose among alternative texts.

Syria reacted with vigor to the new UNRWA-Unesco policy. In a note of 1 May 1968 to the Director-General of Unesco, the Minister of Education expressed surprise at UNRWA's refusal "to purchase certain school textbooks prescribed in Syria, giving instruction in 'civics, history, reading and religion,'" UNRWA having insisted, the letter said, "that these books . . . should be examined in order to ensure . . . conformity with the ethical ideals laid down in the Unesco Constitution and in Article 26 of the Universal Declaration of Human Rights. . . ." The Minister appealed to the Director-General to consider the problem "in a spirit of justice and equity which will serve the cause of true culture throughout the world, a cause that is bound up with that of freedom, moral values and world peace." Is there, he asked, "any clause in the United Nations Charter, the Declaration of Human Rights or the Unesco Constitu-tion that forbids us to say to our children: 'This is your land, your country, these are your holy places. Learn to love them, guard them and defend them?'" Referring to the preparation by UNRWA of teaching notes to replace the textbooks banned by Israel in the occupied territories, the Minister said that "it amounts to an act of collusion . . . against Arab sovereign rights in the occupied territory." Moreover, their content, he said, could only be "superficial" and "would lead to the distortion and disfigurement of Arab culture and the isolation of students attending these schools from any true culture or serious education."

Approving UNRWA's long-standing policy of using the textbooks prescribed by a host government, the Syrian Minister said that it accorded with the "principles of sovereignty" and with the right of the host governments "to lay down the curricula which are con-sistent with their conditions and national principles. . . ." He asserted that "UNRWA schools are but private schools,* bound, like other

---

* The same assertion as to the applicability to UNRWA-Unesco schools of laws governing private schools was made collectively by the Arab host govern-ments in June 1970. The occasion was their meeting with UNRWA and Unesco officials in the fourth annual conference on educational problems of the UNRWA-Unesco system. *Annual Report* (A/8013), 1970, para. 93.

private schools, to follow the national curricula of the host states, and have no right, whatever the reason may be, to deviate from this principle, which is supported by general international law and the agreements concluded in this respect."[10]

Having been apprised by the Director-General of the Syrian communication, the Commissioner-General disclaimed any knowledge of agreements concluded between UNRWA and Syria in the matter at issue. Asserting the "paramount importance" of the principle "that any United Nations activity must remain under the control of the United Nations as such," the Commissioner-General declared that

the Agency is subject to the directives of the General Assembly, representing the membership as a whole. . . . No United Nations organ ever falls under the 'sovereignty' or jurisdiction of a Member State in the sense of being literally bound to regulate its activities in conformity with the laws, regulations or instructions of the host State. The relationship is properly one of coordination and co-operation, not of subordination. Insofar as the Agency is a subsidiary organ of the General Assembly, the host State retains the right, in the exercise of its sovereignty, to require it to cease its activities. But so long as it continues to operate, the Agency must do so as a United Nations organ, under the control of the United Nations and not of the host State.

Reacting to the allegation that the teaching notes were a distortion and disfigurement of Arab culture, the Commissioner-General sent a complete set to Unesco. UNRWA, he said, would be content to accept Unesco's judgment in the matter.*

Having in November 1967 specified the principles† governing the content of instruction, Unesco now took a further step. The Executive Board in June 1968, acting on recommendation of the Director-General, authorized him to appoint a "commission of outside experts . . . with the agreement of the member states concerned,

---

* *Letter*, Commissioner-General to Director-General, 24 May 1968 (78 EX/16, Add., 31 May 1968, pp. 7–10).

The Commissioner-General reported that Syrian newspapers published the note of the Ministry of Education under such headings as "UNRWA carries out the will of Israel in isolating Palestinians from their cause and nationality."

† Again, the reader is referred to pp. 153–154.

with a view to (1) examining the textbooks used in UNRWA-Unesco schools . . . and (2) making recommendations thereon which the Director-General would submit to the member states concerned, for their assent and cooperation."[11] The resolution (as was the one of 3 November 1967) was adopted unanimously, including the votes of the Egyptian, Israeli, and Lebanese members of the Board.

The Commission of Outside Experts—consisting of three Arabic scholars, an American, a Frenchman and a Turk—reported to the Director-General 24 February 1969. Syria having refused to co-operate, no Syrian textbooks were included among the 127 examined. The Commission recommended use of forty-eight in existing form, modification of sixty-five, and withdrawal of fourteen.

The Commission construed the criteria set out in the resolution of 3 November 1967 as permitting an "historic or juridic" account of events in Palestine since the Balfour Declaration; such a presentation would not "constitute fanaticism or systematic hostility toward Judaism. . . ." As regards the "struggle against colonialism," the Commission felt that it would "be very difficult to refuse the authors . . . the right to recall to the young generation that . . . liberation of their respective countries, or more generally of the 'Arab Nation,' was not accomplished without difficulty. . . . The attachment of a people to its national values and the recalling of the example of those who contributed to forming them, can very well be reconciled . . . with the ideals of the United Nations." Moreover, "to overlook the special psychological situation in which the texts were written," would deny the right of the refugees "to express their confusion or their desperation," even if in terms "that an outside observer may sometimes find excessive. . . ." The manner of treating the concept of the *jihad* was gratifying to the Commission. "It is dealt with so prudently and moderately that there is an obvious determination not to transform the Israeli-Arab conflict . . . into a new war of religion. . . ."

On the other hand, there was much to which the Commission took exception. It objected to grammers setting exercises and giving examples "obviously meant to maintain nostalgia for the 'unsurped homeland' and to strengthen the desire to reconquer it. . . ." The recurrent theme in Arabic readers of liberation from colonialism, with special reference to Palestine, is likely, the Commission said, to "create or strengthen frustration or the idea of revenge in the minds of children;" properly the texts "should be stimulating their curiosity about the world outside," and conveying "the riches of the culture to which they belong. . . ." Certain of the history books, the Commission said, endeavored "to show that the Arabs, after having been the victims of the Crusaders, the Mongols and the Ottoman despotism, are now the victims of international imperialism and Zionism." The Commission granted that such a view of Arab history "is frequently backed by undeniable factual data" and "is in no way incompatible with international ethics," but it questioned whether "from a strictly educational point of view it would not be better to avoid bringing up a whole generation in so acute an atmosphere of despair, frustration and antagonism."

Finding that maps of Palestine never showed the Israeli state, the Commission commented that "refusal to recognize de facto a situation which is also rejected de jure is understandable, but in a school geography whose inspiration should be scientific and educational, why forget that geography is a descriptive science . . . ?" Textbooks on religion were characterized as "well written" and for the most part "educationally excellent." Regarding the delicate matter of the relations between the Prophet Mohammad and the Jewish tribes of the Hedjaz, "some of the textbooks, particularly those for beginners, handle this . . . subject very tactfully or even pass over it in silence." Others, however, "are much less discreet, not hesitating to demonstrate . . . that, since the time of the Prophet, the Jews as a whole have worked hand in glove with the enemies of Islam." Some of the civics books failed "to observe the distinctions which . . . should separate civics from political propaganda." An international organization, the Commission said, should regard "systematic political indoctrination" as incompatible with "the proper intellectual and moral education of the children entrusted to its charge."

The Commission emphatically ruled out "the slightest incitement to violence," objecting to "equivocal" terms such as "liberation," "the usurper," and "the return," which it regarded as invoking violence by implication. The Commission also rejected "all terms contemptuous of a community taken as a whole." Hence, "liar, cheat, usurer, idiot—terms applied to Jews in certain passages, and part of the deplorable language of international anti-semitism—cannot be tolerated." Permissibility required simply "that each book is true to its own kind; that a grammer remains a grammer, a history a history, a geography book a geography book—without their authors trying to transform them into manifestoes for political choices which may be perfectly legitimate in their own way but have absolutely no place in school textbooks."

On the basic question of Arab-Israeli relations the Commission declared its neutrality. Yet if objectivity—not to speak of neutrality —is to characterize texts used in the UNRWA-Unesco system, one must recognize that authorship by any of the interested parties would necessarily be ruled out. Cognizant of the dilemma, the Commission in a final paragraph suggested the possibility of Unesco preparing model textbooks of its own. Based on "the enormous heritage of the Arab world, these could give pupils in the UNRWA-Unesco schools a broader view of the world around them, and, with a more objective and more optimistic view of life, generate in them greater confidence in themselves."[12]

Such a solution, needless to say, could hardly prevail against government, on whose sufferance UNRWA-Unesco schools exist. Yet in return for benefits rendered, international organization can insist on a *quid pro quo*. What it cannot claim as legal prerogative it may, as an international actor coordinate with states, seek to gain by negotiation. Failing an appropriate arrangement, it may choose finally to withdraw its benefits as the only course compatible with its international character.

The Director-General of Unesco promptly accepted the Commission of Experts' recommendations and entered into negotiations with the concerned governments. But as of spring 1970 new complications had arisen. In Gaza, where the most difficult situation existed, Egypt had virtually closed the door to acceptance of any of the modifications suggested by the Commission,[13] while importation of Commission-approved texts was conditioned by Israel on Egyptian compliance with the recommendations as a whole.[14] The teaching notes, too, were caught in the deadlock. Seventeen sets for students and seven for teachers had been withdrawn by UNRWA on Egypt's demand,[15] based on the availability of approved texts if Israel would permit their importation. *

The Jordanian government informed the Director-General in January 1970 that it accepted modifications in certain of its textbooks as recommended by the Commission of Experts,[16] while in February Israel withdrew its former objection to importation into the West Bank of Commission-approved texts containing Jordanian national emblems.[17] However, the latter concession was conditioned on the texts used in the UNRWA-Unesco schools in East Jordan conforming fully with the Commission's recommendations. UNRWA reported in January 1970 that of the full complement of 220,000 texts needed by UNRWA-Unesco schools in the West Bank, only 143,000 copies of largely obsolete texts, together with some teaching notes, were available. As for the latter, the same rule is followed in the West Bank as in Gaza. An approved textbook results in withdrawal of the corresponding teaching notes even though Israeli consent to its importation has been refused. Thus teaching notes on social studies used in the West Bank have been withdrawn and destroyed at the request of the Jordanian government.[18]

In Syria, out of eighty-eight textbooks prescribed by the government for the 1969/1970 school year, twenty-eight post–1967 books were judged by the Secretariats of UNRWA and Unesco to be

---

* In a communication from UNRWA to Unesco in January 1970, the situation in Gaza was described as follows: "Out of the 75 textbooks prescribed for use in the elementary and preparatory cycles, only the Koran is generally available. After the Director-General had indicated that he had no objection to the use of certain additional textbooks, the Commissioner-General was asked by the Government of the United Arab Republic to withdraw the corresponding teaching notes. The 11 sets of notes still in use, together with small quantities of obsolete texts, represent only 18% of the total quantities needed by the schools. No books or teaching notes are available in any of the nine grades for the teaching of social studies. No books or notes are available in the three preparatory grades for the teaching of English. In round figures, the 60,000 students enrolled in the Gaza schools in 1969–1970 need 500,000 school texts; they have only 90,000 teaching notes and obsolete textbooks, the latter for the most part falling to pieces." Unesco (84 EX/5), 29 April 1970, p. 8.

unacceptable for use in the UNRWA-Unesco schools.[19] Only in Lebanon were the UNRWA-Unesco schools relatively unaffected by the mounting textbook crisis.

CONCLUSION

The worth of the UNRWA-Unesco educational program to the refugee children cannot be questioned. It has assisted thousands to overcome the handicaps of exile. The program's authorship in the Secretariats of UNRWA and Unesco has received the approbation of the General Assembly—though more tacit than express, inasmuch as Assembly resolutions have referred to the subject only twice in a policy context.* Moreover, the contributing governments, notably the United States and the United Kingdom, have always looked with favor on UNRWA's educational effort.

On the other hand, inasmuch as UNRWA lacks territorial jurisdiction over the refugees, the system's autonomy as a projection of the United Nations cannot escape jeopardy. Dependence on the respective national systems for structural completeness presents a problem but not the main one; more difficult is knowing what to teach about the identity and aspirations of the national community to which the system ministers. Strictly in the area of methodology, a country might willingly license international organization to establish a model system of education, but it can hardly be expected to do so for the substance of its national history, which indeed may include an important religious component.† Here international organization

* In 1958 the Agency was requested "to plan and carry out projects capable of supporting substantial numbers of refugees and, in particular, programmes relating to education and vocational training;" while in 1959 the Agency was directed "insofar as is financially possible, [to] expand its programme of self-support and vocational training. . . . " It should be added that UNRWA's founding resolution commends Unesco, among other specialized agencies, for assistance rendered to the refugees and urges its continuation. *Resolutions 1315* (XII), 12 December 1958, para. 4; *1456* (XIV), 9 December 1959, para. 6; and *302* (IV), 8 December 1949, paras. 3 and 19.

† The Koran is inseparable from the teaching of Arab history. The Bible, of course, is similarly related to Christendom—particularly in the Middle East, where the Western concept of separation of church and state is alien. This poses less of a problem for UNRWA's schools than might be supposed. Only in

is stubbornly confronted by the particularism of the nation concerned. The complexities become truly formidable in Gaza and the West Bank where the authority of an occupying power renders tripartite a bilateral relationship already confused as to the respective prerogatives of international organization and the indigenous society.

From time to time specific educational problems have been dealt with by written agreement between UNRWA and the host governments, but UNRWA's relation to government in this area is undefined in any fundamental document. Indeed, the relationship is so complex—far removed from the modalities of technical assistance—that one doubts whether a program of education such as UNRWA's could ever have come about by prior agreement between international organization and territorial authority. The implications for both parties are too exceptional to have permitted it.

Lebanon is there a substantial number of Christians among the refugees, and there settlement in the camps tends to follow religious lines, which in turn is reflected in the composition of the schools. In UNRWA-Unesco Christian schools some religious instruction is provided by the Pontifical Mission.

VIII

Finance

Since the Arab refugees constitute but one among many urgent needs around the world, choice of obligatory assessment against United Nations members as the method of meeting UNRWA's costs would have set a questionable precedent. Moreover, the habitual penury of the General Assembly—reflecting the inability of some members to meet large assessments and the indifference of others toward particular situations—might well have resulted in UNRWA's receiving less support on an obligatory than on a voluntary basis. On the other hand, dependence on the latter method has put a disproportionate burden on the United States; and this, combined with UNRWA's unorthodox budgetary procedures, would seem to invite preponderant American influence in UNRWA affairs. Yet the greater constraint may well run in the opposite direction and the better conclusion may be that the United States is captive to its own largess.

SOURCES OF INCOME

UNRWA's total income from 1950 through 1969 was $696,000,000.[1] Government contributions totaled $667,000,000, of which the United States accounted for $456,000,000 and the United Kingdom $110,000,000.* In all, some eighty governments have contributed to

---

* Other governments outside the area whose contributions cumulate to more than $2,000,000 have been Canada $24,000,000, France $16,000,000, Sweden $11,000,000, West Germany $8,250,000, Australia $4,150,000, Saudi Arabia $3,400,000, Denmark $2,750,000, Switzerland $2,580,000, and New Zealand $2,500,000.

the Agency, while in 1969 about fifty did so. Many governments ceased contributing after the early years, and many contributions have been nominal. Originally eight Latin American countries made small contributions, but in 1969 only two. Contributions from Asian and African countries have been negligible, except for India and Indonesia at the outset. The only communist country to contribute is Yugoslavia.

Contributions from the host countries are typically in kind—port services, water, vaccines, rents, and transport—evaluated by UNRWA as the equivalent in fiscal 1969 of $164,000 for Jordan, $88,000 for Syria, and $50,000 for Lebanon. After 1967 Israel resumed its practice of earlier years and is now again contributing to UNRWA's budget, $905,000 in 1969; this was mostly in kind, with about $350,000 in cash.

Direct services to the refugees by the host governments and Israel are not reflected in UNRWA's budget. By estimate of the governments, such expenses totaled $13,000,000 in fiscal 1969 for education, shelter, health, security, and social welfare in that order, ranging from $5,700,000 for education to $1,050,000 for social welfare.[2]

Cumulative income from nongovernment sources totaled $28,-500,000 through 1969. Of this amount, UNRWA realized $11,500,000 from its own operations,* while contributions of Unesco and WHO to cover salaries and emoluments of their seconded personnel had accumulated to $3,650,000 and $840,000 respectively.

A total of $12,400,000 through 1969 was received from private sources—individuals, religious and other voluntary associations, and business firms—numbering well over 150 in 1969. Exceptional among the voluntary associations is the American Middle East Rehabilitation Inc., which was designed in the early years specifically for the needs of Palestinian refugees. Another such organiza-

---

* In 1966, for example, the sale of empty containers (flour sacks, oil drums, etc.) netted $230,000, interest on bank deposits came to $185,000, while $17,000 was from sale of unserviceable equipment and scrap. (UNRWA, *Accounts for the Year Ended 31 December 1966*, Schedule E.) An unusual source of income in 1967 was payment to the Agency of $497,000 by the Jordan Agricultural Credit Corporation as a first installment in liquidation of the Development Bank of Jordan in which UNRWA was chief shareholder. (See above, p. 121.)

tion was formed in the United States after the June War and through 30 July 1968 contributed nearly $6,000,000 for a variety of UNRWA projects mainly in East Jordan. Known as The Near East Emergency Donations Inc. (NEED), it is an association of business corporations, foundations, and private citizens, headed initially by Dwight D. Eisenhower as Honorary Chairman.

Solicitation of funds—requiring of the General Assembly neither instruction nor concurrence but only acquiescence—has been an important factor in the expansion of UNRWA's training programs. The objective is attractive to both private donors and governments, eliciting contributions from the later over and above support of the "regular" budget. UNRWA's strategy in this regard is an instance of the initiative available to a Secretariat.

World Refugee year was conceived in England on the model of the World Geophysical Year and, on the urging of the High Commissioner for Refugees, was proclaimed by the General Assembly to begin in June 1959. Commissioner-General John H. Davis made World Refugee Year the occasion for launching a fund-raising campaign to expand UNRWA's vocational, technical, and teacher-training programs. The Agency prepared films and informational literature for distribution by national refugee-year committees formed at United Nations prompting. The response over the next two years came to $4,473,000, slightly more than half from private sources in some fifteen countries, the rest from governments, with the United States further increasing the total through contributions of $1,700,000 earmarked for UNRWA's training programs for each of two years.[3]

An unusual feature of World Refugee Year was the Stamp Plan, undertaken by UNHCR with UNRWA's cooperation. Postal authorities were invited to bring out commemorative issues and place a portion of each at the disposal of UNHCR for sale through established dealers at a surcharge. UNRWA's share of the profit, one fourth of the total, came to $246,000.*

* *Annual Report* (A/5214), 1962, Table 28. A subsequent venture, originated by UNHCR and of benefit to UNRWA, was sale of a long-playing record of popular music. A record of classical piano music followed. Among other outlets, arrangements were made with twenty airlines whereby records ordered in flight

UNRWA has since maintained the impetus of World Refugee Year. Films depict its operations. A newsletter begun in 1960 has continued; appearing bimonthly, it goes to interested individuals and to groups such as United Nations associations, voluntary agencies concerned with refugee problems, and organizations with interest in the Middle East. Since 1961 a liaison office in Geneva has facilitated contact with sources of income in Europe, while a similar office has been maintained from the beginning at the United Nations in New York to perform this function in the United States.

In his 1967 report[4] the Commissioner-General reviewed two suggestions by the Arab governments for assuring adequate income for UNRWA, one being support through the assessed budget of the United Nations. While a treaty, on the pattern of IRO, would be the appropriate instrument for financing UNRWA on an obligatory basis, even then governments would be loath to assume such a commitment without promise of a conclusive result. The second suggestion was one that the Special Political Committee has considered both before and since 1967. As early as 1960 and several times since, the Committee has voted to appoint a United Nations custodian of Arab property left behind in Israel, with the income to be used for the benefit of the refugees. However, the proposal has always failed to receive a two-third's majority in plenary session; and in any event this or any other method of using these assets would require the cooperation of Israel. As explained in Chapter I, obligation to compensate is acknowledged by Israel in principle but with payment conditional on a final peace settlement.

In a communication to the Special Political Committee in the fall of 1969, the Commissioner-General, seeking to forestall a looming financial crisis of major proportions, presented his own suggestions for the Committee's consideration.[5] One was to cope with the problem of deficits through a subvention incorporated in the UN's assessed budget. Another was to charge against the regular budget selected items of UNRWA expenditure, such as "common costs" at $7.4 million, or such costs (excluding supply and transport) as

were sent to designated addressees. UNRWA realized $16,000 from each record. UN Press Release (PA4/247), 3 August 1965. UNHCR's income from both records had by April 1966 come to $1,614,000. UNHCR (A/AC 96/INF. 56).

related to internal services and general administration at $3.8 million, or only such of the latter as to include salaries and emoluments of internationally recruited personnel at $2 million. A lump-sum subvention, the Commissioner-General pointed out, would be similar to the $6.9 million of technical assistance costs assumed by the UN's regular budget, while the Office of High Commissioner for Refugees afforded precedent for allocating administrative costs to the regular budget, with operations paid through voluntary contributions. None of these proposals was recommended or even debated by the Special Political Committee.

PATTERN OF EXPENDITURE

At its lowest, in 1952–53, UNRWA's annual expenditure was $26,800,000. In 1966—the last "normal" year prior to the 1967 hostilities—it was $37,500,000.[6] The difference reflects, in part, increased wages and rising prices and in part growth of the refugee population, which has meant higher expenditure for education and health (though not for rations in view of the ceiling imposed on the number of recipients). Shelter has become a much-reduced component of relief, while rehabilitation projects, costing $3,000,000 in 1952–53, have been dropped since 1960. Mainly the increase represents greater emphasis on education, which in 1966 accounted for $15,150,000, whereas the figure for 1952–53 was $1,500,000.[7]

UNRWA's finances in recent years have been subject to increasing stringency, as shown by the steady decline in its operational reserves. This account stabilized in 1957 at about $20,000,000, remained there through 1963, and in December 1969 had fallen to $10,375,000.[8] The difference reflects intervening deficits that have reduced reserves below the essential minimum for maintaining a pipeline of supplies and for providing in other regards the flexibility required by the Agency to meet its obligations.

In the fall of 1965, the Commissioner-General, anticipating a 1966 deficit of $4.2 million, warned the General Assembly that

remedial action either to increase income or to decrease costs can no longer be put off. . . . The issue is of such magnitude that the Commissioner-General and his staff cannot meet it on the administrative level. They have done what they can both to encourage additional income and to reduce costs in every possible way, short of materially curtailing services to the refugees. To go beyond this point requires action by Governments. . . .

If adequate funds cannot be provided, the Commissioner-General asks the General Assembly to direct him on how to deal with the situation which would result.[9]

Since 1963, the Commissioner-General said, the Agency had reduced its annual internal service and administrative costs by $750,000 and expected in 1966 to push this to $900,000. The international staff, he pointed out, had been reduced from 194 posts in 1963 to 117. Additional savings of $500,000 had been achieved through minor reductions in services to refugees: restrictions on blankets, used clothing, shelter assistance, and burial grants in hardship cases, as well as reductions in youth activities, university scholarships, and in clothing and tool kits for students in training centers.[10]

The General Assembly neglected to give the requested guidance, recommending merely that governments "make the most generous effort possible" to meet the Agency's needs. However, the Pledging Conference—the occasion for governments to announce contributions in support of the Agency for the ensuing year—left UNRWA with the prospect of less income in 1966 than the year before, mainly because the American government, in accord with a previously declared intent, reduced its contribution, contending that the burden should be more widely shared.

Yet UNRWA weathered 1966 without further curtailing its programs as a result of additionl contributions successfully solicited by the Commissioner-General in various Arab capitals and by the Deputy Commissioner-General, who made the rounds in Europe. Among the latter countries, a suggestion was made to governments accustomed to giving technical assistance that from funds earmarked for this purpose they might wish—over and above their normal contributions for relief—to finance UNRWA's training and scholarship programs at an annual cost of $3.4 million. The chief response to this approach was a Swedish contribution of $2 million. This, the Commissioner-General said, "was the turning point in averting a collapse of the Agency's services. . . ."[11] Even so, the operational reserve had diminished another million at year's end.

The next budgetary year was soon upon the Agency. At the end of May 1967, income was $4,000,000 short of meeting the budget. The Commissioner-General met twice with the Advisory Commission to consider the alternatives of progressively curtailing services to the refugees or of risking financial collapse when in a year or so UNRWA's last remaining reserves ran out, and a mid-year meeting was to consider the problem further.[12] Meanwhile the June hostilities put a new face on the situation, prompting by 31 August special contributions amounting to $6,400,000. Private donors, who had already contributed $600,000 that year, gave another $700,000. The rest came from governments: United States $2,000,000; France $1,000,000; Canada $1,000,000; United Kingdom $500,000; Denmark $217,000; Norway $210,000; Spain $167,000; Japan $100,000; Switzerland $58,000; Finland $50,000; Ireland $40,000, etc. Sweden, meanwhile, had repeated its contribution of $2,000,000 of the previous year for vocational and technical training but decided, in view of the emergency, to leave to the Agency's discretion the use of nearly all of it.[13] The World Food Program and UNICEF provided emergency assistance amounting to $6.3 million and $1 million respectively.[14] Meant for relief of persons who were displaced for the first time, these sums were not spent through UNRWA. However, the Agency was correspondingly relieved of the increased financial responsibility entailed under the General Assembly's humanitarian assistance resolution of 4 July 1967.*

At the end of 1967 UNRWA's reserves were higher than the year before. However, they dropped sharply in 1968 and were reduced to a bare minimum in 1969, depriving the Agency of further capacity to absorb deficits from funds that had originally gravitated to reserves from unused contributions marked for economic rehabilitation.† Alarm was sounded by the Commissioner-General in a statement circulated to all United Nations members in July 1969. The General Assembly, he said, would have to establish the Agency's finances on a firmer basis or order the elimination or reduction of certain of its services. "A choice between these courses now appears ineluctable, since the end of the present financial road has been

* See footnote above, p. 127.
† See above, p. 116.

reached." Having consulted his Advisory Commission, he reported that the Arab governments opposed any reduction in services "both on humanitarian grounds and also on their forecast of the serious consequences for stability in the area. Other members . . . also expressed the hope that reductions . . . could be avoided." Prudence, he said, demanded immediate steps to bring expenditure within expected income, but he considered "that the plight of the . . . refugees and the disturbed and tense situation" required that he postpone action until the General Assembly could once again consider the matter.[15]

Yet we saw that the Commissioner-General's suggestions for supplementing UNRWA's income through the UN budget were not acted upon, while the Pledging Conference in December 1969 was short by $4.8 million of meeting projected expenditure for 1970 (which he had estimated at $44,584,000, including only $683,000 in nonrecurrent expenditure for construction to be financed through earmarked contributions). Increased compensation of local staff to meet rising living costs, the Commissioner-General said, required nearly a million dollars, while enrollment in Agency schools had increased far beyond original expectations.[16]

Once again, as in previous years, the General Assembly failed to provide guidance for curtailing services; governments were merely admonished "as a matter of urgency to make the most generous efforts possible to meet the anticipated needs."[17] Meanwhile, the Commissioner-General in his communication of July 1969 had indicated reduction possibilities from which, if necessary, he would have to choose.[18]

BUDGETARY PROCEDURE

In common with other United Nations organs UNRWA is subject to annual audit. A Board of Auditors reports to the Advisory Committee on Administrative and Budgetary Questions, which transmits the information in summary to the United Nations membership. But little else about the Agency's fiscal procedures is uniform with other United Nations bodies, as a brief review of the Office of High Commissioner for Refugees and of the United Nation's Children's Fund makes apparent.

Inasmuch as UNHCR's administrative costs are financed through the regular United Nations budget—by about $3,500,000 in a recent year*—this portion of its expenditure is included in the annual budgetary estimates prepared by the Secretary-General. These are submitted to the Advisory Committee on Administrative and Budgetary Questions—a body of experts serving in an individual capacity—which scrutinizes the proposed expenditures and reports with recommendations to the Fifth Committee (Administrative and Budgetary) of the General Assembly. Final action is in plenary session.

UNHCR's operational budget (recently between $4 and $5 million) depends on voluntary contributions. It does not require General Assembly approval and goes neither to the Advisory Committee on Administrative and Budgetary Questions nor to the Fifth Committee. Subject exclusively to internal procedures, it is proposed by UNHCR's Secretariat and authorized by its Executive Committee, the latter consisting of representatives of thirty governments designated by the Social and Economic Council.

Since UNICEF relies on contributions to meet both administrative and operational costs—recently totaling about $44,500,000—no aspect of its budget concerns the General Assembly. Its Executive Board, consisting of representatives of thirty governments designated by the Economic and Social Council, is the controlling body.

UNRWA's budgetary procedures differ markedly from both UNICEF's and UNHCR's; they comprise still another pattern, the features of which are the exceptional responsibility falling to the Commissioner-General and the potential influence over policy available to individual contributors.

Initially, financial decisions were made by the Commissioner-General and the Advisory Commission in collaboration. We saw in Chapter II that together they submitted to the General-Assembly over-all, but not detailed, estimates of future expenditure. However, beginning with 1955 the Commissioner-General alone has submitted

* *Budget Estimates for the Financial year 1968* (A/6707), p. 53. UNHCR, in turn, makes a grant-in-aid to the United Nations consisting of ten percent of its operational budget—a recognition of the difficulty of distinguishing between administrative and operation costs.

the budget estimate for each ensuing year, with the Commission merely acknowledging in a letter to him that it has been apprised of his request. This sharp change coincided with the altered composition of the Advisory Commission, which was enlarged from the four governments originally designated in the founding resolution (Britain, France, Turkey, and the United States) to include the Arab host governments plus Belgium. The Commission thereupon ceased to provide a firm footing for planning UNRWA's finances.

Nor does the General Assembly fill the need. The Commissioner-General's annual report, which contains the budget, goes to the President of the General Assembly, who refers it to the Special Political Committee. Thus the budget by-passes both the Advisory Committee on Administrative and Budgetary Questions and the Fifth Committee,* while the Special Political Committee seldom employs the estimated expenditures as point of departure in discussions, but whose time, instead, is taken up with vituperative exchanges between the Arab and Israeli representatives over the past and future of Palestine. In earlier years the General Assembly formally authorized upper limits of expenditure in the broad categories of relief and rehabilitation, while more recently the annual resolution merely notes the Commissioner-General's report and its projected expenditures for the next fiscal year. Thus the General Assembly offers as little guidance to the Commissioner-General as does the Advisory Commission. Neither affords the political support that he needs and can rightly expect.

The first and most important step in funding UNRWA's budget is the Pledging Conference, which has the appearance of mere form, but which in fact makes evident the consequences for UNRWA of a budget that is never explicitly approved. Approval of a budget in

---

* The former has recommended uniformity in preparation of the administrative component of the budgets of the UN's voluntary programs and "a greater measure of central review and control" over that portion of them (A/7344, 20 November 1968, paras. 2 and 3). The Fifth Committee has endorsed the suggestion in principle, requesting the Advisory Committee to consult the agencies concerned (A/C.5/SR,1282, 18 December 1968, p. 2). In response UNRWA has emphasized the difficulty of distinguishing between its administrative and operational costs and also the suitability to its unique circumstances of its present accounting practices.

specific terms is at the same time authorization for a particular program. Though a large contributor naturally will have influence disproportionate to his single vote, a formally adopted budget stands between administrator and contributors.

The Pledging Conference presents to the contributor an opportunity to condition his support in terms of policy preferences. A situation in which donors contributed medium sums would minimize such intervention; UNRWA, however, depends in extraordinary degree on the United Kingdom and the United States. And the latter's contribution is considered not alone in the Department of State but also in Congress, where UNRWA is subject to inquiry in the foreign policy and appropriation committees.

In the 1963 Pledging Conference the United Kingdom and the United States announced contributions at the same level as in previous years, $5,400,000 and $24,700,000 respectively,* while each attached conditions to its pledge. The British representative said that his government was reducing its contribution to relief by five percent and by that amount was increasing its allocation to education and training. In his view, "close investigation would show that many ration cards could be withdrawn as no longer valid." He also said that, in allocating the following year's contribution between relief and education, his government would "need to take account of the progress which had been made in this matter."

The representative of the United States, noting satisfaction that the past year's expenditure of $25.5 million on relief had declined from the $26.3 million of the year before, stipulated that four percent of the United States 1964 contribution be shifted from relief to education and training.[19]

The following year's pledges of the United Kingdom and the United States remained at the same level, accompanied by the same emphasis. The British representative designated $2,430,000 for relief and $2,970,000 for health and education. Again expressing

* While mainly in currency (including the maximum utilization of United States–owned excess foreign currencies), a sizeable portion of the American contribution is in the form of commodities under Title II of P.L. 480—in recent years the equivalent of about $9,000,000. Furthermore, the United States has always stipulated that its contribution is not to exceed seventy percent of total contributions by governments.

dissatisfaction over rectification of the relief rolls, he announced that "next year, depending on the circumstances then prevailing, her Majesty's Government may have to consider making a reduction in the amount of money it allocates to the Agency for relief purposes, without making a corresponding increase, as it has done this time, in the amount allotted to health and education."

The American representative noted favorably a reduction in the amount budgeted for relief, expressed belief that still further economies could be realized by rectification of the rolls, and stressed the importance that the United States attached to education and vocational training:

Accordingly, in making our pledge we do so only on the understanding that the Agency will undertake the projected reduction in the relief budget as proposed in the Commissioner-General's annual report, but also on the understanding that funds allocated for education, health or other sections of the budget will not be transferred to the relief services budget. We believe, further, that any existing surplus should be conserved for future educational needs.

Finally, he announced that the United States, feeling that it was bearing an unduly high proportion of UNRWA's expenses, planned to reduce its contribution by one million dollars the following year.*

In 1965 the British representative announced a pledge of $5,-000,000, a reduction from the past of $400,000. The cut was to be restored if, at the end of the first half of UNRWA's 1966 fiscal year, there was evidence of effective cooperation between the host governments and UNRWA over rectification of the relief rolls. Meanwhile, the contribution announced by the American representative for use in 1966 was reduced by an even larger amount than the $1,000,000 forecast the year before.[20] An additional cut of

---

* *Ad Hoc Committee for the Announcement of Voluntary Contributions to UNRWA* (A/AC.120/PV.1), 17 February 1965. Of Canada's contribution ($1,200,000 in cash and in kind), $200,000 was earmarked for education. A twenty-five percent increase in the Dutch contribution (over-all $138,500) was "to stimulate the educational programmes of UNRWA; it . . . is intended for the . . . equipment of a gymnasium." Norway earmarked two-fifths of its $70,000 contribution for education and vocational training, while Sweden, one of the larger contributors, as usual heavily emphasized the same program objectives.

$800,000 had been initiated in the Foreign Affairs Committee of the House of Representatives.

Congressional critics have, in effect, charged UNRWA with submitting to the pressures of territorial authority. The Agency's indifferent success in purging the relief rolls has been a long-standing cause of criticism and there was sharp negative reaction before 1967 to refugees being conscripted in Gaza without removal from UNRWA's relief rolls. Much greater was the reaction in the fall of 1969 when refugee camps in Lebanon were taken over by Palestinian commandos. Textbooks used in UNRWA schools have also drawn fire. The Department of State, standing between Congress and UNRWA, often finds itself in the role of mediator.

CONCLUSION

UNRWA's need for political reinforcement is an invitation to American policy to wield its financial influence to that end. Yet to threaten deprivation of the refugees would further jeopardize American interests in the Arab world already seriously affected by the Palestine imbroglio. Ironically, a giant is immobilized by his own strength.

More orthodox budgetary procedures would effect a better match between program and income, affording the Commissioner-General and his aides the legislative guidance that is their due. Conceivably it could also have another result, one particularly gratifying to the United States. Serious debate over program might prompt disinterested governments to press the host governments and Israel to accord that measure of reciprocity commensurate with UNRWA's services and appropriate to its status. The United States is powerless to do this alone.

IX

Conclusion

WHILE ordinarily the United Nations serves as a forum for mediation, its role in some international disputes is that of a third party. Authorization of sanctions entails the taking of sides even to the point, as in the Korean case, of involving the United Nations as a belligerent.

Another kind of involvement, also third-party in nature, occurs in the exceptional circumstance in which legislative competence can be ascribed to the United Nations. Such a stance was assumed by the General Assembly over the disposition of the British Palestinian Mandate, and a similarly forward position was subsequently adopted by the Assembly toward the Arab refugees.* Humanitarian

---

* When in the fall of 1968 extension of UNRWA's mandate was again being considered, the Secretary-General personally intervened for the first time in the long succession of annual debates on the refugee question. Appearing before the Special Political Committee, he said that the international community "cannot abandon this very large group of people, for whose plight the United Nations must bear a considerable measure of responsibility, without dealing a harsh blow to international morality and to the conscience of humanity which the United Nations must always seek to reflect." In his view, not to continue UNRWA was "unthinkable." The elimination of its services, he said, "would make far more difficult the long-term settlement of the refugee problem which is being sought and must be achieved." Special Political Committee, 23rd Sess. (A/SPC/PV.612), 11 November 1968.

The following year the United States representative on the Committee, Joseph E. Johnson, observed that the "special attention which the United Nations has, over a twenty-one year period, devoted to the Arab refugee problem is understandable . . . in the light of the United Nations direct concern with the over-all problem that gave rise to the refugee situation. The direct responsibility

considerations alone would have prompted the utmost effort to relieve the plight of hundreds of thousands of Palestinians suddenly uprooted by the events of 1948, but the General Assembly chose to do more. Its resolution of December 1948 sought to solve the problem through repatriation or compensation and made the Conciliation Commission responsible for the formula's implementation. Again, as in the partition resolution, the General Assembly attempted more than it could manage, and it failed again for the same reason. In a situation where one man's meat is another man's poison—the refugees being the unavoidable counterpart of Israel's emergence as a viable Jewish state—there is little room for accommodation.

Yet, in August 1949 the Conciliation Commission by virtue of much prodding got concessions which held out the prospect that Israel would readmit a limited number of refugees and also that Jordan and Syria would resettle others. The concessions were highly tentative, but the Conciliation Commission, believing that promise of international economic assistance would further a settlement, seized the occasion to form the Economic Survey Mission, and the latter's recommendations in turn led to UNRWA's establishment.

Through UNRWA—the chief expression of the General Assembly's activist policy toward the refugee problem—the United Nations became involved in the performance of functions that orthodoxy assigns to territorial authority. While in the area of health UNRWA's relations with governments have been relatively smooth, in other areas the articulation of international with territorial authority has encountered major problems. In performing functions of economic rehabilitation, education, and welfare UNRWA has experienced many frustrations.

The attempt to cloak an essentially political problem in economic

---

of the United Nations for the Palestine refugees *per se* has found expression in a long series of General Assembly resolutions that began on 11 December 1948. While the United Nations might conceivably have undertaken similar commitments to other refugees at other times, the fact is it did not do so. It is essential that we not lose sight of this important distinction. . . . " Referring to possible curtailment of UNRWA's services for lack of funds, he feared "political consequences that would only serve to aggravate the inflamed situation in the Middle East." Special Political Committee, 24th Sess. (A/SPC/PV.673), 26 November 1969.

guise was bound to fail. Focusing on the refugees as such, UNRWA's projects for expanding the economic capacity of the countries of refuge were suspect as a contravention of the right of return. Economic well-being simply was not regarded by the refugees as the highest consideration. Practicality required, moreover, development in a national context larger than just the refugee community. In further extenuation of UNRWA's failure to contribute significantly to economic rehabilitation one must also recognize that nature is harsh in the Middle East. It can be offset only by technology and management of a high order, qualities which were sorely lacking in the Arab world during UNRWA's initial years. Endeavoring to compensate for these deficiencies, the Agency became operational to an extraordinary degree, but in so complex a matter as economic development it was not feasible for international organization to substitute its own processes for those of territorial authority. For these reasons, political and practical, UNRWA had ceased by 1956 to pursue large-scale development. On the other hand economic rehabilitation of individual families was politically acceptable and entailed only minimal involvement with territorial authority. However, the piecemeal approach was not only expensive but failed to make an appreciable dent in the ration rolls. After 1960 it, too, was dropped. Meanwhile, aid by other international bodies—free of UNRWA's handicaps—and by friendly governments had by 1967 promoted marked economic growth in the countries of refuge. UNRWA contributed indirectly to this growth, which was beneficial to the refugees. However, economic rehabilitation at best can contribute only secondarily to solution of the refugee problem.

Through education UNRWA's major emphasis shifted after 1960 to members of the oncoming generation. An international agency, thwarted in its goal of economic rehabilitation, became the administering authority for an increasingly large and complex educational enterprise consisting, on the one hand, of basic education at the elementary and preparatory levels, and, on the other, of a number of vocational, technical, and teacher-training centers. The methods and techniques taught by the UNRWA-Unesco centers have crossed cultural and national lines without precipitating major issues between international and territorial authority.

Basic education, however, poses for UNRWA and Unesco the extremely difficult question of curricular content in the areas of history and contemporary society. A people's need for security is both objective and subjective—objective in terms of the immediate circumstances of its existence, subjective in that its identity derives, in part, from the past. The quest for security is attended by anxiety, and depiction of past and present is subject not only to error but distortion. It is most improbable that an internationally supervised curriculum can correct such tendencies in the heat and passion of today's Middle East situation. Even from an abstract point of view —the Universal Declaration of Human Rights to the contrary notwithstanding—one doubts international organization's capacity to devise textbooks which are acceptable to a people whose past and present are being portrayed. Indeed UNRWA-Unesco experience with basic education shows that in matters touching on self-determination territorial authority is bound to prevail.*

UNRWA's relations with territorial authority have also been difficult in the area of relief. Separation from the ration rolls is typically regarded by the refugee as implying loss of Palestinian status, while rectification of the rolls encounters, as well, the normal evasions of authority practiced by welfare recipients. UNRWA has not and cannot institute the demographic and economic controls nor exercise the police power requisite to keeping a welfare program relatively free of deceptions. These functions—whether well or ill performed—inhere in territorial authority and cannot be exercised by international organization unless it were to assume territorial prerogatives.

Characteristic of UNRWA's mode of operation is the carrying out of programs for the direct benefit of recipients who remain subject to territorial authority; this means that the Agency is disadvantageously situated in relation to government. Much better situated

---

* The difficulty of the issue is reflected in the quandary of the American university when confronted with the demand of the Negro for a Black Studies curriculum.

is an international operational agency like the Office of High Commissioner for Refugees. The fact that its programs are carried out by governments or voluntary agencies rather than directly by UNHCR itself does not mean that the latter is less able than UNRWA to influence government policy and action. On the contrary, each of UNHCR's projects is the subject of specific agreement between the High Commissioner and the government concerned; thus the benefits to be conferred are contingent on government's adherence to a jointly agreed course of action. But such a strategy has not been available to UNRWA. When at the outset the General Assembly charged it with direct responsibility for the Palestinian refugees, UNRWA was deprived of the opportunity to negotiate the manner in which its programs would relate to territorial authority. All of the trumps were thereby passed to government hands, any subsequent pressuring of a government being inhibited by UNRWA's reluctance to threaten deprivation of the refugees. We have noted, however, that there are circumstances in which UNRWA can act solely at its own discretion without having to take government into account. Its bargaining power is unfettered in a situation where it disposes of special benefits involving an alteration of services to the advantage of a refugee family or individual.

However, that UNRWA has failed to dissipate the refugee problem is not to be attributed merely nor even mainly to the Agency's tactical disadvantage in relation to territorial authority. More fundamentally, the problem has persisted because its solution demands an approach from the standpoint of a Palestinian people and not merely in terms of the welfare of individual refugee families. UNRWA was founded on the basis of the latter approach. Yet UNRWA's ultimate significance may well be in terms of the former.

UNRWA has failed to further a solution of the Palestinian refugee problem in terms of the repatriation-compensation formula of 11 December 1948—to which resettlement in the countries of refuge must be appended as a further major, though unexpressed, element. On the one hand, Israel's need for security has militated against repatriation of the Palestinian refugees, while, on the other, their resettlement—even if accompanied by compensation—has not appealed to the refugees as an acceptable equivalent for loss of a homeland. Not only has UNRWA been caught in the stalemate; the question has been raised whether its prolonged existence may not have exacerbated the very problem to which it is addressed.*

Considering the violent rupture in the Arab Palestinian community that produced the refugees, one seriously doubts that UNRWA has been a factor in keeping alive the refugees' hostility toward Israel. The problem of the displaced Palestinians is not so ephemeral as to require a symbol for its perpetuation. One also questions whether UNRWA has been a hindrance to the absorption of the refugees in the countries of refuge. The camps—sheltering less than half the refugee population—have in no sense been places of internment but, on the contrary, have in themselves constituted a form of resettlement, with the inhabitants participating in the larger community where many find employment. Even if withdrawal of UNRWA's services were to force a greater rate of absorption of the Palestinians in the host countries, the final point remains that "absorption"—even assuming a high degree of economic rehabilitation—is not synonymous with resignation. We have noted before that the psychological and political aspects of exile tend to prevail over the economic.

However, this is not to deny the advantage accruing to the Arab cause by virtue of the Agency's involvement in the Palestine question. Indeed the willingness of the Arab host governments to cope with an international organization performing government functions in their territories is hardly explicable on financial grounds alone. All else being equal, they might well regard the cost of ministering to the refugees as a price worth paying for UNRWA's withdrawal. While UNRWA may feel that it receives rough treatment from the

---

* Ira Hirschmann (*Look*, 17 September 1968, p. 60 ff.) asserts that in supporting UNRWA the "American taxpayer, in the name of humanitarianism, has unwittingly written a blank check that is helping to develop a permanent Arab refugee body, intensify Arab-Israeli animosities and incite general war in the Middle East." UNRWA's "bureaucracy of 12,000 employees," he states, "is merely perpetuating itself . . . , and the suffering of the Arab refugees is perpetuated so that the Arab countries can continue to raise the refugee issue." Or again, "instead of helping to reduce the number of its charges, . . . [UNRWA] has cooperated with the Arab governments, who . . . [keep] the refugees virtually imprisoned in 'temporary' camps and . . . [use] them as a political weapon in their jousting with Israel."

governments, the latter do not find the Agency to be a comfortable bedfellow. Under compulsion of legal principles governing its status, UNRWA struggles to maintain the integrity of its programs against the pressures of the domestic and international politics of the region. It is subject to resentment and misrepresentation, and there have been extravagant charges against it in the Arab press. Even animus toward the refugees has been alleged, and the Agency has been depicted as a strategem for divorcing the Palestinian from his homeland. On balance, however, the host governments perceive that political advantage outweighs the discomfort of co-existing with UNRWA.*

UNRWA's approach to the problem of the displaced Palestinians has been predominantly one of welfare. Though many refugees still need relief, this approach is increasingly difficult to sustain. What the future holds in store for the Agency will be determined by three factors: the extent of its financial support, the character of its relations with the Arab host governments and Israel, and its adjustment to the emergence of the Palestinian movement.

Preponderant United States financial support of UNRWA is a circumstance with paradoxical consequence: the appearance of a controlling influence is illusory because of severe constraints on American policy imposed by the over-all situation. Already on the

* In a joint document circulated to the members of the General Assembly in the fall of 1965, the host governments, commenting on the Commissioner-General's annual report, detailed their opposition to any retraction of UNRWA's programs and reiterated as follows their position as regards the responsibility of the United Nations: "The Governments of the host countries consider the relief of the Palestine refugees to be an obligation devolving on the United Nations, which brought about the Palestine catastrophe and the refugee problem. Under the pressure of certain great Powers, it approved the partition of Palestine and the creation of Israel despite the warning of the Arab·States and their friends who opposed the partition resolution that grave consequences would inevitably ensue. It was in fact this resolution that led to the dispossession of the Palestine Arabs and their expulsion from their country by iniquitous aggressors who threatened them with genocide. It was the cause of their being despoiled of their money and property and has thrown the Near East into a state of perpetual turmoil and instability such as jeopardizes world peace and threatens to explode at any moment. It follows that the host-country representatives cannot condone any move to release the United Nations from this responsibility." A/SPC/106, 28 October 1965, p. 3.

defensive in the Arab world and struggling to maintain its remaining influence, the United States must consider the area-wide repercussions hostile to its interests that would ensue were it to threaten deprivation of the refugees. Therefore, American withdrawal of the support that has become UNRWA's mainstay is unlikely. But neither is there likelihood of the United States increasing its annual pledge, already upwards of seventy percent of UNRWA's budget. In response to the Agency's mounting financial crisis, the United States has urged fellow members of the United Nations to increase their contributions. However, unless UNRWA is provided with a new and promising rationale, such appeals largely will go unheeded, and for the first time the Agency will have to reduce radically the level of its services. Such a trend, once begun, would be impossible to reverse, and a large investment of money and twenty years of dedicated effort would become a fiasco.

The second major factor bearing on its future is UNRWA's relations with the governments within whose jurisdictions it operates. Poised between international and territorial authority, the Agency faces two ways. The General Assembly has been tolerant of the accommodations that UNRWA has had to make in the prosecution of tasks requiring governmental cooperation. However, reciprocation by government has fallen short of what can properly be demanded of it. Incumbent on the host governments is forebearance toward an agency accountable to international authority. The privileges and immunities of an international body corporate—one free of financial exactions, exercising independent control over its personnel, and possessing an initiative conducive to the integrity of its programs—are conditions of UNRWA's existence that it has struggled to secure and maintain. But there have been many setbacks, and it is a question of whether or not, in a situation of mounting hostility, UNRWA can preserve its footing against governments desperately insecure and resentful of a body that symbolizes so profound a dilemma as that of the Arab refugees.

In his dealings with the host governments and Israel—whether regarding the legal status of the Agency and its personnel or its programs of welfare and education—the Commissioner-General struggles almost alone. His Advisory Commission is used by the host governments to apply pressure to the Agency, which other Commission members can do little to counter. Neither the United States nor Great Britain sees the Advisory Commission as a forum for disputing their vexed relations with the Arab world; the refugees are not a propitious point of departure for such an airing. Thus the Advisory Commission is crippled as an instrument of counsel and support for the Commissioner-General.

The Americans and British are similarly inhibited in the Special Political Committee of the General Assembly, where problems of status and program posed by the Commissioner-General in his annual reports are lost in abusive exchanges between the parties to the Palestine question. Even admitting the hampering effect of the informal procedures with which UNRWA was endowed by its founding resolution, still one might suppose that governments of sober judgment without direct interests in the Middle East, solicitous of United Nations prestige, would find ways to strengthen the Commissioner-General's hand. Indeed, withdrawal of benefits would be an appropriate response to a government's serious disregard of UNRWA's international status or to failure by territorial authority to cooperate in UNRWA's task of ministering to the refugees.

Finally, the most influential factor bearing on UNRWA's future may well be the Palestinian movement. At the outset the refugees were a fragmented community. Even so basic a unit in traditional Arab society as the family suffered dispersion of its members and loss of economic capacity. Without organization of their own, indeed lacking the very attitudes and habits of a broadly based community, the refugees passed under the authority of the countries of refuge and within that jurisdictional framework UNRWA, while itself exempt from territorial authority, has been accustomed to ministering to their needs.

Twenty-three years after the initial exodus, the Palestinian refugees are no longer what they then were. They have become a self-conscious, assertive community. Adversity alone, though compounded by the devastating shock of the Six Day War, could not have brought this about. Education, too, has been a factor, the irony being that an agency designed to pacify the refugees through economic rehabilitation has through its schools contributed to their political solidarity. Yet it is not surprising that a conflict noneconomic in origin should have retained its purely political character, nor is it uncommon for policy to have unexpected results differing from original intent.

Whereas formerly UNRWA was ministering to a bewildered people, traditional in outlook, capable only of obstinacy, it now finds itself associated with a national movement. The consequences for the Agency are twofold. Increasingly hard pressed in its perpetual struggle with territorial authority, UNRWA may be unable to cope with relations rendered triangular by Palestinian self-assertion. The Agency holds territorial authority responsible for security and is dependent in many ways on its cooperation. Revolt against that same authority by the community to which UNRWA ministers is bound to present serious difficulties.

Palestinian demand for self-determination also raises the question of whether humanitarian regard for the needs of refugees has been changed into subsidy of a political movement. If so, the United Nations might wish to retreat from an activist policy in favor of a purely mediatory role. But this is not the only course open to it. A policy of third-party intervention could still be pursued.

As it did in the partition resolution of November 1947, the General Assembly could once again declare its support of a Palestinian Arab state. In such a context, the vain promise of repatriation could be abandoned. Furthermore, UNRWA would gain a new rationale. Instead of the invidious task of seeking through individual welfare to mollify a people for loss of a homeland, the Agency's acknowledged role would be to sustain emergence of the Palestinians as an independent national entity. Even prior to the new state, UNRWA's services and personnel could pass to control of the Palestinian community, which the Agency has prepared in many ways for assumption of civic responsibility. The United Nations could then relate to the Palestinians—for whose plight it cannot escape a measure of responsibility—as a source of financial and technical assistance. While the many repercussions of such a move by the General Assembly are not easily predictable, the net result might well be better rather than worse.

PROPOSALS OF THE CONCILIATION COMMISSION
Submitted to the Parties at Geneva
in September 1951

1. That an agreement be reached concerning war damages arising out of the hostilities of 1948, such an agreement to include, in the Commission's opinion, mutual cancellation of such claims by the Governments of Egypt, Jordan, Lebanon and Syria and the Government of Israel;

2. That the Government of Israel agree to the repatriation of a specified number of Arab refugees in categories which can be integrated into the economy of the State of Israel and who wish to return and live in peace with their neighbours;

3. That the Government of Israel accept the obligation to pay, as compensation for property abandoned by those refugees not repatriated, a global sum based upon the evaluation arrived at by the Commission's Refugee Office; that a payment plan, taking into consideration the Government of Israel's ability to pay, be set up by a special committee of economic and financial experts to be established by a United Nations trustee through whom payment of individual claims for compensation would be made;

4. That the Governments of Egypt, Jordan, Lebanon and Syria and the Government of Israel agree upon the mutual release of all blocked bank accounts and to make them payable in pounds sterling;

5. That the Government of Israel and the Governments of Egypt, Jordan, Lebanon and Syria agree to consider, under United Nations auspices, and in the light of the experience gained during the past three years, the revision or amendment of the Armistice Agreements between them, especially with regard to the following questions:

    (a) Territorial adjustments, including demilitarized zones;

    (b) The creation of an international water authority to deal with the problems of the use of the Jordan and Yarmuk Rivers and their tributaries, as well as the waters of Lake Tiberias;

    (c) The disposition of the Gaza strip;

    (d) The creation of a free port at Haifa;

(e) Border regulations between Israel and her neighbours with special attention to the need for free access to the Holy Places in the Jerusalem area, including Bethlehem;

(f) Health, narcotics and contraband control along the demarcation lines;

(g) Arrangements which will facilitate the economic development of the area: resumption of communications and economic relations between Israel and her neighbours. (A/1985, pp. 3-4.)

TEXT OF RESOLUTION 302 (IV)
ASSISTANCE TO PALESTINE REFUGEES
Adopted by the General Assembly of the United Nations
on 8 December 1949

THE GENERAL ASSEMBLY,

Recalling its resolutions 212 (III) of 19 November 1948 and 194 (III) of 11 December 1948, affirming in particular the provisions of paragraph 11 of the latter resolution,

Having examined with appreciation the first interim report of the United Nations Economic Survey Mission for the Middle East and the report of the Secretary-General on assistance to Palestine refugees,

1. *Expresses* its appreciation to the Governments which have generously responded to the appeal embodied in its resolution 212 (III), and to the appeal of the Secretary-General, to contribute in kind or in funds to the alleviation of the conditions of starvation and distress amongst the Palestine refugees;

2. *Expresses* also its gratitude to the International Committee of the Red Cross, to the League of Red Cross Societies and to the American Friends Service Committee for the contribution they have made to this humanitarian cause by discharging, in the face of great difficulties, the responsibility they voluntarily assumed for the distribution of relief supplies and the general care of the refugees; and welcomes the assurance they have given the Secretary-General that they will continue their cooperation with the United Nations until the end of March 1950 on a mutually acceptable basis;

3. *Commends* the United Nations International Children's Emergency Fund for the important contribution which it has made towards the United Nations programme of assistance; and commends those specialized agencies which have rendered assistance in their respective fields, in particular the World Health Organization, the United Nations Educational, Scientific and Cultural Organization and the International Refugee Organization;

4. *Expresses* its thanks to the numerous religious, charitable and humanitarian organizations which have materially assisted in bringing relief to Palestine refugees;

5. *Recognizes* that, without prejudice to the provisions of paragraph 11 of General Assembly resolution 194 (III) of 11 December 1948, continued assistance for the relief of the Palestine refugees is necessary to prevent conditions of starvation and distress among them and to further conditions of peace and stability, and that constructive measures should be undertaken at an early date with a view to the termination of international assistance for relief;

6. *Considers* that, subject to the provisions of paragraph 9 (d) of the present resolution, the equivalent of approximately $33.7 million will be required for direct relief and works programmes for the period 1 January to 31 December 1950 of which the equivalent of $20.2 million is required for direct relief and $13.5 million for works programmes; that the equivalent of approximately $21.2 million will be required for works programmes from 1 January to 30 June 1951, all inclusive of administrative expenses; and that direct relief should be terminated not later than 31 December 1950 unless otherwise determined by the General Assembly at its fifth regular session;

7. *Establishes* the United Nations Relief and Works Agency for Palestine Refugees in the Near East:

(a) To carry out in collaboration with local governments the direct relief and works programmes as recommended by the Economic Survey Mission;

(b) To consult with the interested Near Eastern Governments concerning measures to be taken by them preparatory to the time when international assistance for relief and works projects is no longer available;

8. *Establishes* an Advisory Commission consisting of representatives of France, Turkey, the United Kingdom of Great Britain and Northern Ireland, and the United States of America, with power to add not more than three additional members from contributing Governments, to advise and assist the Director of the United Nations Relief and Works Agency for Palestine Refugees in the Near East in the execution of the programme; the Director and the Advisory Commission shall consult with each Near Eastern Government concerned in the selection, planning and execution of projects;

9. *Requests* the Secretary-General to appoint the Director of the United Nations Relief and Works Agency for Palestine Refugees in the Near East in consultation with the Governments represented on the Advisory Commission;

(a) The Director shall be the chief executive officer of the United Nations Relief and Works Agency for Palestine Refugees in the Near East responsible to the General Assembly for the operation of the programme;

(b) The Director shall select and appoint his staff in accordance with general arrangements made in agreement with the Secretary-General, including such of the staff rules and regulations of the United Nations as the Director and the Secretary-General shall agree are applicable, and to the extent possible utilize the facilities and assistance of the Secretary-General;

(c) The Director shall, in consultation with the Secretary-General and the Advisory Committee on Administrative and Budgetary Questions, establish financial regulations for the United Nations Relief and Works Agency for Palestine Refugees in the Near East;

(d) Subject to the financial regulations established pursuant to clause (c) of the present paragraph, the Director, in consultation with the Advisory Commission, shall apportion available funds between direct relief and works projects in their discretion, in the event that the estimates in paragraph 6 require revision;

10. *Requests* the Director to convene the Advisory Commission at the earliest practicable date for the purpose of developing plans for the organization and administration of the programme, and of adopting rules of procedure;

11. *Continues* the United Nations Relief for Palestine Refugees as established under General Assembly resolution 212 (III) until 1 April 1950, or until such date thereafter as the transfer referred to in paragraph 12 is effected, and requests the Secretary-General in consultation with the operating agencies to continue the endeavour to reduce the numbers of rations by progressive stages in the light of the findings and recommendations of the Economic Survey Mission;

12. *Instructs* the Secretary-General to transfer to the United Nations Relief and Works Agency for Palestine Refugees in the Near East the assets and liabilities of the United Nations Relief for Palestine Refugees by 1 April, 1950, or at such date as may be agreed by him and the

Director of the United Nations Relief and Works Agency for Palestine Refugees in the Near East;

13. *Urges* all Members of the United Nations and non-members to make voluntary contributions in funds or in kind to ensure that the amount of supplies and funds required is obtained for each period of the programme as set out in paragraph 6; contributions in funds may be made in currencies other than the United States dollar in so far as the programme can be carried out in such currencies;

14. *Authorizes* the Secretary-General, in consultation with the Advisory Committee on Administrative and Budgetary Questions, to advance funds deemed to be available for this purpose and not exceeding $5 million from the Working Capital Fund to finance operations pursuant to the present resolution, such sum to be repaid not later than 31 December 1950 from the voluntary governmental contributions requested under paragraph 13 above;

15. *Authorizes* the Secretary-General, in consultation with the Advisory Committee on Administrative and Budgetary Questions, to negotiate with the International Refugee Organization for an interest-free loan in an amount not to exceed the equivalent of $2.8 million to finance the programme subject to mutually satisfactory conditions for repayment;

16. *Authorizes* the Secretary-General to continue the Special Fund established under General Assembly resolution 212 (III) and to make withdrawals therefrom for the operation of the United Nations Relief for Palestine Refugees and, upon the request of the Director, for the operations of the United Nations Relief and Works Agency for Palestine Refugees in the Near East;

17. *Calls* upon the Governments concerned to accord to the United Nations Relief and Works Agency for Palestine Refugees in the Near East the privileges, immunities, exemptions and facilities which have been granted to the United Nations Relief for Palestine Refugees, together with all other privileges, immunities, exemptions and facilities necessary for the fulfilment of its functions;

18. *Urges* the United Nations International Children's Emergency Fund, the International Refugee Organization, the World Health Organization, the United Nations Educational, Scientific and Cultural Organization, the Food and Agriculture Organization and other appropriate agencies and private groups and organizations, in consultation with the

Director of the United Nations Relief and works Agency for Palestine Refugees in the Near East, to furnish assistance within the framework of the programme;

19. *Requests* the Director of the United Nations Relief and Works Agency for Palestine Refugees in the Near East:

(a) To appoint a representative to attend the meeting of the Technical Assistance Board as observer so that the technical assistance activities of the United Nations Relief and Works Agency for Palestine Refugees in the Near East may be co-ordinated with the technical assistance programmes of the United Nations and specialized agencies referred to in Economic and Social Council resolution 222 (IX) A of 15 August 1949;

(b) To place at the disposal of the Technical Assistance Board full information concerning any technical assistance work which may be done by the United Nations Relief and Works Agency for Palestine Refugees in the Near East, in order that it may be included in the reports submitted by the Technical Assistance Board to the Technical Assistance Committee of the Economic and Social Council:

20. *Directs* the United Nations Relief and Works Agency for Palestine Refugees in the Near East to consult with the United Nations Conciliation Commission for Palestine in the best interests of their respective tasks, with particular reference to paragraph 11 of General Assembly resolution 194 (III) of 11 December 1948;

21. *Requests* the Director to submit to the General Assembly of the United Nations an annual report on the work of the United Nations Relief and Works Agency for Palestine Refugees in the Near East, including an audit of funds, and invites him to submit to the Secretary-General such other reports as the United Nations Relief and Works Agency for Palestine Refugees in the Near East may wish to bring to the attention of Members of the United Nations, or its appropriate organs;

22. *Instructs* the United Nations Conciliation Commission for Palestine to transmit the final report of the Economic Survey Mission, with such comments as it may wish to make, to the Secretary-General for transmission to the Members of the United Nations and to the United Nations Relief and Works Agency for Palestine Refugees in the Near East.

CONVENTION ON THE PRIVILEGES AND IMMUNITIES OF THE UNITED NATIONS

Adopted by the General Assembly of the United Nations
on 13 February 1946

WHEREAS Article 104 of the Charter of the United Nations provides that the Organization shall enjoy in the territory of each of its Members such legal capacity as may be necessary for the exercise of its functions and the fulfilment of its purposes and

WHEREAS Article 105 of the Charter of the United Nations provides that the Organization shall enjoy in the territory of each of its Members such privileges and immunities as are necessary for the fulfilment of its purposes and that representatives of the Members of the United Nations and officials of the Organization shall similarly enjoy such privileges and immunities as are necessary for the independent exercise of their functions in connection with the Organization.

CONSEQUENTLY the General Assembly by a Resolution adopted on the 13 February 1946, approved the following Convention and proposed it for accession by each Member of the United Nations.

ARTICLE I
JURIDICAL PERSONALITY

SECTION 1. The United Nations shall possess juridical personality. It shall have the capacity:
(a) to contract;
(b) to acquire and dispose of immovable and movable property;
(c) to institute legal proceedings.

ARTICLE II
PROPERTY, FUNDS AND ASSETS

SECTION 2. The United Nations, its property and assets wherever located and by whomsoever held, shall enjoy immunity from every form of legal process except insofar as in any particular case it has expressly waived its immunity. It is, however, understood that no waiver of immunity shall extend to any measure of execution.

SECTION 3. The premises of the United Nations shall be inviolable. The property and assets of the United Nations, wherever located and by whomsoever held, shall be immune from search, requisition, confiscation, expropriation and any other form of interference, whether by executive, administrative, judicial or legislative action.

SECTION 4. The archives of the United Nations, and in general all documents belonging to it or held by it, shall be inviolable wherever located.

SECTION 5. Without being restricted by financial controls, regulations or moratoria of any kind,

(a) the United Nations may hold funds, gold or currency of any kind and operate accounts in any currency;

(b) the United Nations shall be free to transfer its funds, gold or currency from one country to another or within any country and to convert any currency held by it into any other currency.

SECTION 6. In exercising its rights under Section 5 above, the United Nations shall pay due regard to any representations made by the Government of any Member insofar as it is considered that effect can be given to such representations without detriment to the interests of the United Nations.

SECTION 7. The United Nations, its assets, income and other property shall be:

(a) exempt from all direct taxes; it is understood, however, that the United Nations will not claim exemption from taxes which are, in fact, no more than charges for public utility services;

(b) exempt from customs duties and prohibitions and restrictions on imports and exports in respect of articles imported or exported by the United Nations for its official use. It is understood, however, that articles imported under such exemption will not be sold in the country into which they were imported except under conditions agreed with the Government of that country;

(c) exempt from customs duties and prohibitions and restrictions on imports and exports in respect of its publications.

SECTION 8. While the United Nations will not, as a general rule, claim exemption from excise duties and from taxes on the sale of movable and immovable property which form part of the price to be paid, nevertheless when the United Nations is making important purchases for official use of property on which such duties and taxes have been charged or are chargeable, Members will, whenever possible, make appropriate administrative arrangements for the remission or return of the amount of duty or tax.

ARTICLE III
FACILITIES IN RESPECT OF COMMUNICATIONS

SECTION 9. The United Nations shall enjoy in the territory of each Member for its official communications treatment not less favourable than that accorded by the Government of that Member to any other Government including its diplomatic mission in the matter of priorities, rates and taxes on mails, cables, telegrams, radiograms, telephotos, telephone and other communications; and press rates for information to the press and radio. No censorship shall be applied to the official correspondence and other official communications of the United Nations.

SECTION 10. The United Nations shall have the right to use codes and to despatch and receive its correspondence by courier or in bags, which shall have the same immunities and privileges as diplomatic couriers and bags.

. . . .

ARTICLE V
OFFICIALS

SECTION 17. The Secretary-General will specify the categories of officials to which the provisions of this Article and Article VII shall apply. He shall submit these categories to the General Assembly. Thereafter these categories shall be communicated to the Governments of all Members. The names of the officials included in these categories shall from time to time be made known to the Governments of Members.

SECTION 18. Officials of the United Nations shall:

(a) be immune from legal process in respect of words spoken or written and all acts performed by them in their official capacity;

(b) be exempt from taxation on the salaries and emoluments paid to them by the United Nations;

(c) be immune from national service obligations;

(d) be immune, together with their spouses and relatives dependent on them, from immigration restrictions and alien registration;

(e) be accorded the same privileges in respect of exchange facilities as are accorded to the officials of comparable ranks forming part of diplomatic missions to the Government concerned;

(f) be given, together with their spouses and relatives dependent on them, the same repatriation facilities in time of international crisis as diplomatic envoys;

(g) have the right to import free of duty their furniture and effects at the time of first taking up their post in the country in question.

SECTION 19. In addition to the immunities and privileges specified in Section 18, the Secretary-General and all Assistant Secretaries-General shall be accorded in respect of themselves, their spouses and minor children, the privileges and immunities, exemptions and facilities accorded to diplomatic envoys, in accordance with international law.

SECTION 20. Privileges and immunities are granted to officials in the interests of the United Nations and not for the personal benefit of the individuals themselves. The Secretary-General shall have the right and the duty to waive the immunity of any official in any case where, in his opinion, the immunity would impede the course of justice and can be waived without prejudice to the interests of the United Nations. In the case of the Secretary-General, the Security Council shall have the right to waive immunity.

SECTION 21. The United Nations shall co-operate at all times with the appropriate authorities of Members to facilitate the proper administration of justice, secure the observance of police regulations and prevent the occurrence of any abuse in connection with the privileges, immunities and facilities mentioned in this Article.

. . . .

ARTICLE VII

UNITED NATIONS LAISSEZ-PASSER

SECTION 24. The United Nations may issue United Nations laissez-passer to its officials. These laissez-passer shall be recognized and accepted as valid travel documents by the authorities of Members, taking into account the provisions of Section 25.

SECTION 25. Applications for visas (where required) from the holders of United Nations laissez-passer, when accompanied by a certificate that

they are travelling on the business of the United Nations, shall be dealt
with as speedily as possible. In addition, such persons shall be granted
facilities for speedy travel.

SECTION 26. Similar facilities to those specified in Section 25 shall be
accorded to experts and other persons who, though not the holders of
United Nations laissez-passer, have a certificate that they are travelling
on the business of the United Nations.

SECTION 27. The Secretary-General, Assistant Secretaries-General and
Directors travelling on United Nations laissez-passer on the business of
the United Nations shall be granted the same facilities as are accorded to diplomatic envoys.

SECTION 28. The provisions of this article may be applied to the comparable officials of specialized agencies if the agreements for relationship made under Article 63 of the Charter so provide.

ARTICLE VIII
SETTLEMENT OF DISPUTES

SECTION 29. The United Nations shall make provisions for appropriate
modes of settlement of:

(a) disputes arising out of contracts or other disputes of a private
law character to which the United Nations is a party;

(b) disputes involving any official of the United Nations who by
reason of his official position enjoys immunity, if immunity has not
been waived by the Secretary-General.

SECTION 30. All differences arising out of the interpretation or application of the present convention shall be referred to the International
Court of Justice, unless in any case it is agreed by the parties to have
recourse to another mode of settlement. If a difference arises between
the United Nations on the one hand and a Member on the other hand,
a request shall be made for an advisory opinion on any legal question
involved in accordance with Article 96 of the Charter and Article 65 of
the Statute of the Court. The opinion given by the Court shall be accepted as decisive by the parties.

Notes

CHAPTER I

1. United Nations, General Assembly, 2nd Sess., *Report of UN Special Committee on Palestine,* Suppl. No. 11, Vol. I, p. 54.

2. These are the estimates of Don Peretz, a leading student of the Arab refugee problem. *Israel and the Palestine Arabs* (Washington, D.C.: The Middle East Institute, 1958), p. 95.

3. *Progress Report of the UN Mediator,* 3rd Sess., Suppl. No. 11 (A/648), 16 September 1948, p. 52.

4. Ibid., p. 14.

5. Ibid., p. 14 for Bernadotte's proposal and pp. 27–28 for Sharett's reply. The present text follows the more usual spelling of the Foreign Minister's name.

6. Ibid., p. 18.

7. Unless otherwise indicated, this account of the repatriation issue is based on the *Historical Survey of Efforts of the UN Conciliation Commission for Palestine to secure the implementation of paragraph 11 of GA resolution 194 (III): The Question of Reintegration by Repatriation or Resettlement* (A/AC. 25/W.82/Rev. 1), 2 October 1961. Prepared by the UN Secretariat, it is taken from the periodic reports of the Conciliation Commission.

7a. American Assembly, *The United States and the Middle East* (Englewood Cliffs: Prentice Hall, 1964).

8. New York *Times,* 22 December 1969.

9. The following account of the compensation issue, unless otherwise indicated, is based on an historical survey parallel to the document cited above in note No. 7, also prepared by the UN Secretariat (A/AC.25/W.81Rev. 2), 2 October 1961.

10. *Report of the Secretary-General on Assistance to Palestine Refugees,* 4th Sess. (A/1060), 4 November 1949, Annex III.

11. A/648, op. cit., pp. 52, 53, 57.

12. Ibid., p. 49.

13. A summary of assistance from the Specialized Agencies during the first year is contained in the Secretary-General's report (A/1060), op. cit., Annex III.

14. United Nations, General Assembly, 3rd Sess., *Progress Report of the Acting Mediator,* Suppl. 11a (supplementary to A/648), no date, pp. 1, 2, 3.

15. Resolution 212 (III), 19 November 1948.

16. A/1060, op. cit., p. 20.

17. Ibid., paras. 47–53.

18. A/1452, op. cit., p. 28.

19. *Annual Report of the Commissioner-General*, 1962 (A/5213), para. 7.

20. Peter Dodd and Halim Barakat, *River without Bridges: A Study of the Exodus of the 1967 Palestinian Arab Refugees* (Beirut: The Institute for Palestine Studies, 1969), pp. 48, 50, 51, 53.

21. United Nations, General Assembly, *Final Report of the UN Economic Survey Mission*, 28 December, 1949, Part I, p. 30. The Interim Report of 8 November 1949 is contained as an annex to this document.

22. Ibid., p. 2.

23. Ibid., p. 6.

24. Ibid., p. 12.

25. *Interim Report of Economic Survey Mission*, op. cit., p. 17.

26. Ibid.

27. Ibid., p. 18.

28. U.S. Congress, House, Committee on Foreign Affairs, *Hearings on Palestine Refugees*, 81st Cong., 2nd Sess. S. J. Res. 153, February 16, 17, 1950 (Washington: USGPO, 1950), p. 9.

29. *Interim Report of Economic Survey Mission*, op. cit., p. 22.

30. Ibid., pp. 17, 22.

31. *Annual Report*, 1951 (A/1905), para. 16.

32. Annual Report, 1967 (A/6713), Annex I, Table 1.

33. *Census of Population, 1967: West Bank of the Jordan, Gaza Strip and Northern Sinai, Golan Heights* (Jerusalem: Central Bureau of Statistics, 1967).

34. *Annual Report*, 1968 (A/7213), paras. 1, 8, 9, 15, 16.

35. Ibid., para. 8.

36. *Annual Report*, 1969 (A/7614), para. 10.

37. *Report of Special Representative of the Secretary General* (A/6797), 15 September 1967, pp. 52–55; and A/6713, op. cit., paras. 34–36.

CHAPTER II

1. George Woodbridge, *UNRRA* (New York: Columbia University Press, 1950), Vol. I, pp. 240–241, 242, 244.

2. Ibid., Chapters III, Part Two; IV; and V, Part One.

3. Ibid., I, pp. 52–60; II, p. 551; III, pp. 21–32 (Article III). For UNRRA's significant role as a third party between contributing and receiving states, see II, pp. 550–551.

4. Louise W. Holborn, *The International Refugee Organization* (London: Oxford University Press, 1956), pp. 40, 41.

5. Ibid., p. 590.

6. Ibid., Appendix I.

7. Ibid., p. 61.

8. Ibid., Articles 10 and 12 of the treaty.

9. Ibid., p. 87.

10. Ibid., pp. 102, 122, 125.

11. D. S. Cheever and H. F. Haviland, *Organizing for Peace* (New York: Houghton Mifflin Co., 1954), p. 657.

12. Resolution 428 (V), 14 December 1950.

13. Resolution 1038 (XI), 7 December 1956.

14. Resolutions 832 (IX), 21 October 1954; and 1958 (XVIII), 12 December 1963.

15. A/1950/Add. 1, 28 November 1951; A/2171/Add. 1, 13 October 1952; and A/2717/Add. 1, 1954.

16. Resolutions 1167 (XII), 26 November 1957; 1286 (XIII), 5 December 1958; and 1388 (XIV), 20 November 1959.

17. New York *Times*, 1 November 1967, p. 20.

18. *Background Paper on UNHCR* (MHCR/48/66/Rev. 2), June 1966, p. 8.

CHAPTER III

1. *Annual Report*, 1959 (A/4213), paras. 45 and 47.

2. *Annual Report*, 1967 (A/6713), Annex II, para. 4.

3. Identical agreements were subsequently signed with Lebanon 6 September 1948 and with Jordan 21 September 1948. Upon termination of the Mediator's Mission, Syria, Lebanon and Jordan by exchange of letters extended the agreements to UNRPR and the cooperating voluntary agencies ST/Leg/2, pp. 104–106. Egypt's first agreement, signed 31 December 1948, was with the Director of UNRPR and a representative of the American Friends Service Committee. *Ibid.*, pp. 106–109.

4. *UN Treaty Series*, Vol. 121, No. 1630 (the Egyptian Agreement); Vol. 120, No. 394 (the Jordanian Agreement).

5. *Annual Reports*, 1954 (A/2717), Annex G, para. 12; and 1957, A/3686, p. 48.

6. *UN Treaty Series*, Vol. 202, No. 2728.

7. Respectively, Ibid., Vol. 280, No. 4063; and *Annual Report*, 1967 (A/6713), Annex III.

8. *Annual Report*, 1959 (A/4213), Annex H. Para. 8.

9. Exchange of notes with Lebanese government 26 November 1954, *UN Treaty Series*, Vol. 202, No. 2728; and *Annual Reports* for 1952 (A/2171), p. 43; 1959 (A/4213), Annex H., para. 32; and 1967 (A/6713), Annex II, para 12.

10. *Annual Reports*, 1954 (A/2717), Annex G, paras. 4 and 11; and 1956 (A/3212), Annex G, para. 5.

11. *Annual Reports*, 1953 (A/2470), para. 249; and 1954 (A/2717), Annex G, para. 3; 1958 (A/3931), Annex H, para. 4; 1960 (A/4478), para. 99; 1967 (A/6713), Annex II, paras. 11, 19; and 1968, (A/7213), Annex H, paras. 22–24.

12. *Annual Reports*, 1953 (A/2470), para. 232; and 1954 (A/2717), Annex G, para. 14.

13. *Annual Reports*, 1959 (A/4213), Annex H, para. 32; and 1967 (A/6713), Annex II, para. 12.

14. *Annual Report*, 1967 (A/6713), Annex II, paras. 12, 14.

15. Ibid.

16. *Annual Report*, 1968 (A/7213), Annex II, paras. 12–15. See also *Annual Report*, 1969 (A/7614), paras. 152 and 153.

17. *Annual Reports,* 1959 (A/4213), Annex H, para. 28; 1967 (A/6713), Annex II, para. 17; 1968 (A/7213), Annex II, paras. 19, 20; and 1969 (A/7614), paras. 156, 157.

18. *Annual Reports,* 1953 (A/2470), paras. 237–247; and 1959 (A/4213), Annex H, para. 20.

19. *Annual Report,* 1959 (A/4213), Annex H, para. 24.

CHAPTER IV

1. *UN Treaty Series,* Vol. 202, No. 2729. Also *Annual Report,* 1957 (A/3686), Annex H, para. 19.

2. A/SPC/9, 11 February 1957. Also see footnote above, p. 69.

3. Ibid.

4. Annual report, 1969 (A/7614), para. 148.

5. *Annual Reports,* 1957 (A/3686), Annex H, para. 22; and 1969 (A/7614), para. 149. Also A/SPC/PV.665, 17 November 1969; and *Annual Report,* 1970 (A/8013), para. 16.

6. *Annual Reports,* 1957 (A/3686), Annex H, para. 13; 1959 (A/4213), Annex H, para. 25; 1954 (A/2717), Annex G, para. 16; and 1959 (A/4213), Annex H, para. 13.

7. *Annual Report,* 1959 (A/4213), Annex H, para. 25.

8. Ibid., para. 20.

9. New York *Times,* 14 June 1966.

10. *Annual Report,* 1966 (A/6313), para. 26.

11. Ahluwalia, Kuljit, *The Legal Status, Privileges and Immunities of the Specialized Agencies* (The Hague, Martinus Nijhoff, 1964), pp. 108–109.

12. *Annual Report,* 1969 (A/7614), paras. 7, 8.

13. Ibid., para. 9.

14. *Annual Reports,* 1953 (A/2470), para. 244; 1954 (A/2717), Annex G, para. 11; and 1956 (A/3212), para. 79. See also 1959 (A/4213), Annex H, para. 20.

15. *Annual Report,* 1969 (A/7614), para. 140.

16. For general background on international organization's autonomy in relations with its staff see C. Wilfred Jenks, *The Proper Law of International Organizations* (Dobbs Ferry, N.Y.: Oceana Publications, 1962), Part Two, "The International Administrative Law Governing the Internal Legal Relations of International Organizations," pp. 25–128; Kenneth S. Carlston, "International Administrative Law: A Venture in Legal Theory," *Journal of Public Law,* Vol. VIII (1959), pp. 329–380; and M. B. Akehurst, *The Law Governing Employment in International Organizations* (London: Cambridge University Press, 1967). For a brief but informative account of the United Nations Administrative Tribunal see the article by that name, Wolfgang Friedman and Arghyrios A. Fatouros, *International Organization,* Vol. XI, No. 1, 1957, pp. 13–29. For treatment at greater length see Byung Chul Koh, *The United Nations Administrative Tribunal* (Baton Rouge: Louisiana State University Press, 1966).

17. *Report of UNRWA/Unesco Department of Education on the 1968–69*

School Year, mimeographed. Beirut: UNRWA, pp. 7–9; and *Annual Report,* 1970 (A/8013), para. 97.

18. *Staff Rules Applicable to Area Staff Members,* mimeographed. Beirut: UNRWA, 106.4.

19. Ibid., 11.1 and 11.2.

20. *Judgments of the United Nations Administrative Tribunal* (New York: United Nations, 1958). For Hilpern vs. UNRWA, see Judgments 57, 63, and 65. For Radicopoulos vs. UNRWA, see Judgment 70. The quotations are at pp. 303 and 425, respectively.

CHAPTER V

1. *Annual Report,* 1952 (A/2171), para. 32.

2. Resolution 393 (V), 2 December 1950.

3. Special report of the Director and Advisory Commission of UNRWA, 1951 (A/1905/Add. 1), pp. 1, 2, 3 and Annex A. Also General Assembly resolution 513 (VI), 26 January 1952.

4. *Annual Report,* 1954 (A/2717), Annex C, paras. 64–69 and appended Tables.

5. The basic agreement with Jordan, signed 30 December 1953, is in *UN Treaty Series,* Vol. 165, p. 317 ff; that with Egypt, signed 14 October 1953, Ibid., Vol. 190, p. 14 ff.

6. *Annual Reports,* 1955 (A/2978), Annex D. para. 5; and 1956 (A/3212), Annex D, paras. 7 and 8.

7. *Annual Report,* 1955 (A/2978), Annex C, paras. 33–35.

8. *Annual Report,* 1956 (A/3212), Annex D, para. 9.

9. *Annual Report,* 1956 (A/3212), para. 73.

10. Resolution 1018 (XI), 28 February 1957, para. 5.

11. *Annual Report,* 1953 (A/2470), para. 48.

12. *Annual Report,* 1954 (A/2717), Annex C, para. 62.

13. *Annual Report,* 1958 (A/3931), p. 23.

14. *Annual Reports,* 1966 (A/6313), para. 95; and 1967 (A/6713), paras. 139 and 151. Also "Fourteenth Annual Report of the Development Bank of Jordan," mimeographed (Beirut: UNRWA), 31 March 1965.

15. *Annual Report,* 1959 (A/4213), Annex D, para. 6.

16. *Annual Report,* 1964 (A/5813), para. 12.

CHAPTER VI

1. *Annual Report,* 1964 (A/5813), para. 9.

2. *Annual Report,* 1969 (A/7614), Table 5, and paras. 50–54.

3. Ibid., para. 63.

4. Ibid., para. 65.

5. Ibid., Table B, p. 52.

6. *Annual Report,* 1962 (A/5213), para. 7.

7. A/2978/Add. 1, 15 October 1955. The Report included an account of

2,700 refugee families in Egypt, largely provided for by the government there, and of 11,000 Bedouins in Jordan, Egypt, and Lebanon not on UNRWA's rolls.

8. *Annual Report,* 1961 (A/4861), para. 41.

9. *Annual Report,* 1965 (A/6013), para. 16.

10. *Annual Report,* 1963 (A/5513), para. 15.

11. Ibid., para. 16.

12. *Annual Report,* 1957 (A/3686), para. 11.

13. *Special Report of the Director,* 1955 (A/2978/Add. 1), paras. 73 and 74.

14. *Annual Report,* 1965 (A/6013), para. 24. All subsequent references to the Commissioner-General's proposal are taken from the same report, specifically paras. 19 (5), 22, 23, 24, and 27.

15. *Annual Report,* 1966 (A/6313), para. 42.

16. *Annual Report,* 1968 (A/7213), para. 13.

17. *Annual Report,* 1969 (A/7614), Table B; and "Annual Report of the Director of Health 1968," mimeographed (Beirut: UNRWA), Tables 1 and 2. These reports are the sources of the description of the health program that follows.

18. "Annual Report of the Director of Health 1966, mimeographed (Beirut: UNRWA).

19. Ibid.

20. Annual report, 1952 (A/2171), p. 26.

CHAPTER VII

1. Description of the UNRWA-Unesco system as of 1968–69 is based on "Report of the UNRWA-Unesco Department of Education on the 1968–69 school Year, mimeographed (Beirut: UNRWA); and on the *Annual Report,* 1969 (A/7614). Estimate of numbers of refugee children in school is taken from *Progress Report on School Year 1966–67,* mimeographed. Beirut: UNRWA, para. 21. The comparative percentages for the host countries were supplied to the author by UNRWA.

2. "The In-Service Training Programme for UNRWA/UNESCO Teachers," *New Educational Media in Action-Case Studies for Planners,* vol. 2, Unesco/IIEP, 1967.

3. *Annual Report,* 1951 (A/1905), paras. 135, 204.

4. Resolution 7.81 adopted 30 November 1956 in plenary meeting of the 9th session of the Unesco General Conference.

5. "Memorandum on Allegations of Political Indoctrination in UNRWA-Unesco Schools," UNRWA to Israeli Ministry of Foreign Affairs, 17 July 1967. Unesco, *Summary Record of Executive Board* (77 EX/34), 6 October 1967, Annex II.

6. Ibid., Annex III.

7. Ibid., p. 4; and Resolution 6.8, adopted by the Executive Board, 3 November 1967, at its 77th session.

8. The Commissioner-General to the Director-General, 24 May 1968. Unesco, *Summary Record of Executive Board,* (78 EX/16 Add., 31 May 1968, p. 9); and "Report of the UNRWA-Unesco Department of Education for the 1968–69 School Year," mimeographed (Beirut: UNRWA), para. 5.

9. Ibid., p. 2. Italics in original.

10. Syrian Ministry of Education to Unesco, 1 May 1968 Unesco, *Summary Record of Executive Board* (78 EX/16 Add., 31 May 1968, pp. 2–7).

11. Resolution 7.4, adopted 20 June 1968 at the 78th session of the Executive Board.

12. The Commission's interim and final reports are Annexes I and II respectively of Unesco (82 EX/8), 4 April 1969.

13. Unesco (84 EX/5), 29 April 1970, Annex I.

14. Permanent Delegate of Israel to the Director-General, 18 April 1969. Unesco, *Summary Record of Executive Board* (82 EX/8 Add., 24 April 1969); and Israeli Foreign Office to the Director-General, 20 August 1969. Unesco, *Summary Record of Advisory Board* (83 EX/8, 19 September 1969).

15. Unesco, *Summary Record of Advisory Board* (83 EX/8 Add.), 7 October 1969, para. 4.

16. Letter to Director-General, 29 January 1970 (84 EX/5), p. 2.

17. Letter to Director-General, 16 February 1970, Ibid., p. 6.

18. Ibid., p. 8, and information supplied to the author by UNRWA.

19. Ibid.

CHAPTER VIII

1. Unless otherwise indicated, the account of UNRWA's income is based on the *Annual Report* for 1969 (A/7614), Tables 19 and 20.

2. Ibid., Table 22.

3. *Annual Report,* 1962 (A/5214), Table 28, showing World Refugee contributions, 1 July 1959 to 31 December 1961.

4. *Annual Report,* 1967 (A/6713), para. 9.

5. A/SPC/34, 21 November 1969, pp. 4–5.

6. See Table 19 of *Annual Report,* 1969 (A/7614).

7. *Annual Report,* 1953 (A/2470), para. 40. The figure for education cannot be precisely determined because of intervening changes in accounting practices.

8. *Annual Report,* 1969 (A/7614), Table 19.

9. *Annual Report,* 1965 (A/6013), paras. 13 and 15.

10. Ibid., paras. 9 and 10.

11. *Annual Report,* 1966 (A/6313), para. 18.

12. *Annual Report,* 1967 (A/6713), para. 5.

13. Ibid., Table 20.

14. Commissioner-General to Special Political Committee, 21 November 1969 (A/SPC/134), p. 6.

15. A/7577, 31 July 1969, p. 6.

16. Ad Hoc Committee for Announcement of Voluntary Contributions to 1969, (A/SPC/133), para. 3.

17. General Assembly resolution 2535 (XXIV), 18 December 1969.

18. A/7577, Op. cit., Annex IV.

19. Ad Hoc Committee for Announcement of Voluntary Contributions to UNRWA (A/AC.116/PV.2), 9 December 1963.

20. Ibid. (A/AC.122/PV.2), 20 December 1965.

Index

Abandoned property: blocked bank accounts, 22; landed property, 22–25; evaluation of latter and personal property, 24–25

Advisory Commission: structure, early functioning, and subsequent decline, 55–57

Advisory Committee on Administrative and Budgetary Questions, 174, 175

American Friends Service Committee, 30; account of conditions in Gaza, 30n, and of attitudes among refugees, 32n

American Middle East Rehabilitation Inc., 168

Arab League: July 1948 appeal to Secretary-General, 26; agreement to reimburse UNRWA for Gaza recruits, 97

Arbitration of commercial disputes, 73

Article 22: basis of UNRWA's founding, 43, 49, 51; point of departure for legislative enactments, 51

Balfour declaration, 14 and *n*

Barakat. *See* Dodd

Ben Gurion: on solution of the refugee problem, 15

Bernadotte, Folke: appointment as mediator, 5; assassination, 5; recommendations for solution of refugee problem, 11–14 *passim;* actions providing relief, 26–28; agreement with Syria on immunities, 68

Bunche, Ralph: appointment as acting-mediator, 5; warns of urgent need for relief, 28

Camps: as permanent settlements, 124–125 and *n*; number of camps and of refugees so housed, 128–129 and *n;* a typical hut, 129; environmental sanitation therein, 144

Census, Israeli, of occupied territories, 40

Claims for reimbursement from Lebanon, Syria, and Jordan, 74, 76–79 *passim*

Claims for reparations: against Jordan and Egypt, 90n; against Israel, 91n

Clapp, Gordon R.: head of Economic Survey Mission, 33; testimony before House committee, 35n

Commission of Outside Experts: review of textbooks and recommendations, 161–163

Local staff (*cont.*)
    UNRWA and government over re-
    cruitment, 103–105; terms of em-
    ployment, 107–108. *See* Official acts
    and statements; International ad-
    ministrative law

McGhee, George: testimony favoring
    US contribution to UNRWA, 37
Mediator: appointment of Count Bern-
    adotte, 4. *See* Bernadotte, Folke
"Merchant" trafficking in ration cards:
    nature of practice, 139; suppression
    thereof, 142

National service: exemption of inter-
    national civil servants, 94–95; in
    Lebanon and Jordan, 95; in Syria,
    95–96; in Gaza, 96 and *n*
Near East Emergency Donations Inc.
    (NEED), 169

Official acts and statements, immunity
    pertaining thereto: difficulty in dis-
    tinguishing from private acts, 97–
    98; in relation to crime, 98–100; in
    relation to politics, 100–103
Operational agency, definition of, 49*n*

Palestine Arab Refugees Institute, 135–
    136
Palestine Liberation Organization, 96
Paragraph 11 of General Assembly
    resolution of 11 December 1948:
    adopted on Bernadotte's recommen-
    dation, 13; text quoted, 13–14; com-
    pared to Balfour declaration, 14; its
    persistence to present, 20; men-
    tioned, 16, 19, 21, 22, 116, 117, 134
Partition resolution of 29 November
    1947: terms of partition, 3–4; distri-
    bution of Arab and Jewish popula-
    tion, 10

Persona non grata: in relation to inter-
    national civil servants, 85; incidents
    involving Egypt and Syria respec-
    tively, 85–86
Pledging Conference, 172, 176–177
Privileges and Immunities: Convention
    on, 65–66; Bernadotte agreement
    with Syria, 68; special agreement
    with Jordan, 69; with Egypt, 69;
    with Lebanon, 70; with Israel, 70;
    immunity from suit, 72; from cus-
    toms dues, 73–74; from embargoes,
    74; from transportation restrictions,
    74; from tax on interest, 76; from
    stamp taxes, 76; from public utility
    surcharges, 76; definition of "direct
    taxes," 76*n;* exemption from excise
    taxes, 76–77; from garnishee of
    wages, 79; exemption of employees
    from income tax, 79–81; from alien
    registration, 86*n*. *See* Diplomatic
    privileges and immunities; Local
    staff; Traffic violations; Inviolability;
    National service; Official acts and
    statements
Public works: failure to achieve pur-
    pose, 113–114

Radicopoulos case, 110–111
Rations: numbers and ceilings thereon,
    127; content, 127*n*; various cate-
    gories of ration cards, 131; difficulty
    in applying criterion of need, 137–
    138; imposing a deprivation con-
    trasted with conferring a benefit, 138
Recruitment of teachers, 152–153
Rectification of relief rolls: initial dis-
    tortions, 38–39; resistance thereto,
    134–135; situation in Lebanon, 135;
    in Syria, 135–136; in Gaza, 136; in
    Jordan, 136–137, 138–39, 141–142;
    proposal to make government re-